W9-CBN-567

Managing in Four Worlds

From Competition to Co-creation

RONNIE LESSEM AND
SUDHANSHU PALSULE

For our respective families and friends in the four worlds who have helped us create the centre

Copyright © Ronnie Lessem and Sudhanshu Palsule, 1997

The right of Ronnie Lessem and Sudhanshu Palsule to be identified as author of this work has been asserted in accordance with the Copyright, Designs and Patents Act 1988.

First published 1997
Reprinted 2000

Blackwell Publishers Ltd
108 Cowley Road
Oxford OX4 1JF
UK

Blackwell Publishers Inc.
350 Main Street
Malden, Massachusetts 02148
USA

British Library Cataloguing in Publication Data

A CIP catalogue record for this book is available from the British Library.

Library of Congress Cataloging-in-Publication Data
Lessem, Ronnie.
  Managing in four worlds / Ronnie Lessem and Sudhanshu Palsule.
    p. cm. – (Developmental management)
  Includes bibliographical references and index.
  ISBN 0–631–19933–0
  1. Industrial management – Cross-cultural studies. 2. Corporate culture – Cross-cultural studies 3. Organizational effectiveness – Cross-cultural studies. I. Palsule, Sudhanshu. II. Title. III. Series.
  HD30.17.L477 1997
  658–dc21   96-40874
                                                           CIP

Typeset in 10 on 12 pt Ehrhardt
By Best-set Typesetter Ltd, Hong Kong
Printed in Great Britain by T.J. International, Padstow, Cornwall

This book is printed on acid-free paper

Contents

Preface

We had just finished the morning session of a Management MBA workshop. As we stood there, waiting for the last of our manager 'students' to leave the room before doing the customary, quick debrief on the session, one of them walked hesitantly towards us. Groping to find words, he finally blurted out with uncharacteristic emotion: 'I understand what you have been trying to tell us for so long! For the first time, I can clearly see my journey through the four worlds.'

What we have seen again and again is that magical moment when somebody realizes that the four worlds of North, South, East and West are not just 'out there' in a geographical sense but that they are simultaneously a part of the person and the organization. More importantly, the natural continuum between the four worlds forms a dynamic process in a person's and an organization's developmental journey. As part of a natural evolutionary cycle, every person and every organization must necessarily transit and develop through four worlds.

There are many examples. Companies like Anglian Water have initiated a company-wide developmental plan called 'The Transformation Journey', based on the four-world model. As a company, Anglian is located in the South and West quadrants of the model by default: Southern, due to its long history of being in the community-service business and Western, because of its predominant cultural background in Britain. Anglian is at a crucial stage in its history, having been privatized in 1989 and now poised to become a global learning organization. Its biggest challenge is to nourish and develop its Eastern and Northern dimensions. In that sense, Anglians' learning must come not so much from the Americans or the British themselves, but from the Scandinavians and the Japanese. Using this perspective, there is now within its corporate university, the newly formed College of International Learning which is seeking to create precisely such a matrix of international learning. By a twist of meaningful coincidence, much of Anglian's international business is emerging from South and South-East Asia. There could be no better opportunity to learn about the

East than from the East. As Anglian water moves Northwards and Eastwards, it comes that much closer to becoming a genuinely global company.

Finally, there is that emerging rainbow nation, South Africa, with which one of us has been intimately involved since its rebirth. Several thousands of managers are working with the four-world model there with a view to reorienting their businesses towards the global businessphere.

The Path

The book is divided into five sections, each one simultaneously autonomous and linked to the other four.

Section A: Tapping into Worldly Philosophies

The first section, focused on economic and social philosophy, provides a comprehensive tour into the four respective philosophies of *pragmatism, rationalism, holism* and *humanism*. The *raison d'être* for this section is the authors' conviction that the global businessphere is grounded in an invisible foundation of philosophy which it must continually tap into for sustenance. Starting at home in the West, chapter 1 on 'Free Enterprise' provides the pragmatic underpinning to society and business through the philosophical concepts and ideas of people like Francis Bacon, Samuel Smiles, Adam Smith and Reg Revans. Chapter 2 is about the 'Ethical Organization' from the rational North, underpinned by the works of the Norwegian Thorstein Veblen, and the Danish educationist and national hero, Nicolai Grundtvig, who, as we will discover, are embodyments of a Northern rational and egalitarian ethic, that characterizes Northern companies. Chapter 3, called the 'Creative Spirit', takes the reader to the holistic East which is based on the philosophies of Taoism, Vedanta and Buddhism and the business edge of Japan Inc. and the emergent Asian business edge. Finally, chapter 4, 'Community Spirit', is aided and abetted by the '*Orisa*', the energy forces of the Yoruba peoples of Nigeria, creating a philosophical context for Southern, particularly African business.

Section B: Drawing Upon the World's Environments

Whereas section A provides the reader with a more diffuse background of the four respective philosophical foundations of the four worlds, section B supplies the cutting-edge focus by drawing upon modern physics in chapter 5 and contemporary ecology in chapter 6, modern psychology in chapter 7 and anthropology in chapter 8. By drawing upon contemporary insights made by these disciplines, we are taking management into a new realm, breaking free from the Newtonian-Darwinian models that have dominated organizations and management for so long. Each of these four chapters is about the four environments of business: *physical, ecological, psychological* and *cultural*. These chapters altogether, stretch beyond the traditionally economic environment of business, duly spanning the worlds environments.

Section C: Global Knowledge Creation

Section C is about knowledge. It begins with chapter 9 on 'Knowledge Creation' which is a detailed account on the four worlds of knowledge and how they can be leveraged by any organization. Our research has shown us time and again that if organizations want to succeed and develop, they must become 'creators of knowledge'. Moreover, they must encourage and guide their people into forms of knowledge creation that are not endemic to the predominant culture in the company and the larger culture of the society. Chapter 10 takes the reader into the new world of the 'knowledge-creating organization' and the world of our Japanese colleagues, Nonaka and Takeuchi. Chapter 11 is about another new world, that of the 'symbolic analyst' whom we believe will be in the 1990s and the coming decades of the next century what Porter's strategist was until now. This chapter deals with the concepts of static and dynamic strategy and of managing in a 'far-from-equilibrium' organization.

Section D: Making the Worlds Work for You

Section D contains two chapters, covering individual and organizational work.

It is a curious contradiction of our modern societies that while close to a billion people are out of work in the world, in our organizations, millions of people are 'worked' instead of working. The so-called job crisis in the world is in actuality a symptom of something deeper, what Matthew Fox calls a crisis in our relationship to work and the challenge put to our species today to reinvent it'. He goes on to call it a 'truly radical and creative moment . . . when we are asked to redefine work'. In chapter 12 we take the reader into the four worlds of individual work: *job, role, calling* and *vocation*. Chapter 13 deals with the four worlds of organizational work: *structure, system, process* and *value*, the four dimensions of any organization. With this chapter, the book comes to an important juncture in which *value* becomes the ultimate bedrock for business.

Section E: Doing Business Worldwide

Finally, section E provides the reader with four case-studies that reflect and optimize the philosophical, environmental, knowledge- and work-related aspects of the respective worlds they emerge from. Rather than going in for *Fortune* 500 names, we have chosen four companies that are somewhat unique. Chapter 14 is about Psion Computers, the largest supplier of palm-top computers in the world and the first (Western) world of David Potter, a Britain; chapter 15 is about Oticon, the most innovative hearing-care companies in the world, one that Tom Peters has raved about, and the second (Northern) world of Lars Kolind from Denmark; chapter 16 is about Ahuja Designs, one of the world's most eclectic home-design companies and the third (Eastern) world of Shyam Ahuja, from India; chapter 17 is about Cashbuild, a business icon within the rainbow nation and the fourth (Southern) world of South African, Albert Koopman. Each of these four chapters reflects the respective philosophical underpinning and carries the stamp of the uniqueness of culture in which the respective company is grounded.

Audience

As authors, we want this book to be read by all those amongst you who have a global perspective on organizational life. In writing it, we had in mind the practising manager and the academic; the research student as well as the corporate leader; the consultant as well as the change agent. *Managing in Four Worlds* is not only about recreating your organization, it is about simultaneously helping to recreate your society so that it can enable your organization to grow and sustain it. At first glance, some of you might wonder about the inclusion of philosophy, science and culture in a book about management. The truth is, to make profound changes in yourself and in your organization, you must be able to fundamentally transform the way you think. The transformation of mind-sets is the only solution for organizations and societies that are labouring under obsolete mental baggage. These apparently unrelated disciplines provide a context for change and the tools you will need for creating precisely such a mind-shift. That applies to you whether you are a corporate leader or occupy a non-managerial role; in the knowledge-creating organization, change and transformation is effected and actioned by anyone who wants to play a role – the future is literally 'up for grabs'.

For us, writing this book has been part of an ongoing journey that began with '*Global Business*' (Prentice Hall, 1987). The journey has been, to say the least, eventful and every new turn in the road has been a source of learning and knowledge. The four-worlds project continues and there is so much more to learn – about people, our cultures, why we manage our organizations in the way we do and how and why we have to change. On this path, we have met many others who are involved in a similar search and we have learnt much from them. There is clearly a definite shift from an 'old paradigm' organizational structure and management to a new one. It involves a new morality, a new awareness and sensibility of the needs and aspirations of people and societies, environmental concerns, a growing sensitivity to issues of race, gender and culture, insights into the potentials of the human brain, discoveries and research in science and technology, particularly in the sphere of computers and information. We believe that *Managing in Four Worlds* is an essential part of this global movement. The subject matter it covers is new and above all is all-encompassing of the global businessphere. It is naturally much open to criticism on the grounds of empirical validity and universalism and we can rely on your feedback and support to take us further.

Acknowledgements

A project such as this can never sustain itself without the support, advice and encouragement of many people who have acted as sponsors, helpers, advisors or just been there for a dialogue when we needed them.

We would like, first and foremost, to thank those who have sponsored the four-worlds model with the conviction that this was the right thing to do. They include Alan Smith, Peter Matthews and the other directors at Anglian Water; Prof. Nick Binedell at the Witwatersrand Business School and Keith Holland at the City University Business School. Many thanks to Tim Goodfellow and Paul Stringer at Blackwell for taking on the publication of this project.

We also thank Debbie Dyson, Terry Cook, Steve Gatley, Peter Christie and Barbara Nussbaum for participating in this common journey. We would like to express our gratitude to David Potter, Lars Kolind, Shyam Ahuja, Vikram and Meera Ahuja, and Albert Koopman for embodying the four worlds in their work and businesses.

Our thanks also to those hundreds of faculty and students on the City University MMBA based in the UK, Europe and the Middle East for participating in the development of the model and becoming its first recipients. Likewise, heartfelt thanks to the many hundreds of students at The International College in Denmark who brought their respective worlds into one tiny place and demonstrated that cross-cultural learning is the only possibility for the future of the world. Also, to those thousands of employees on Anglian Water's 'Transformation Journey' who have put their faith in and progressively encompassed our four worlds.

This list would not be complete without thanking our respective partners, Joey Lessem and Saumya Balsari for their patience, understanding and support in this project. Finally, our hearts reach out to the millions of Southern Africans who have entered wholeheartedly into the global businessphere, and the billions of people on the planet who each day, bring the four worlds into our lives.

Ronnie Lessem
Sudhanshu Palsule

Prologue:
The Next American Nation

Entering the Management Laboratory

Whenever writing a book about management in general, or about business strategy in particular, the inevitable point of departure is the USA. When IBMers Sam Manning and Henry Blythe, two of the most imaginative managers on our Management MBA programme, asked me (Ronnie Lessem) to do a presentation in London for their American client, Hancock Insurance, I welcomed the opportunity.

Ever since the sixties, when I had spent two years at Harvard, I have had this nagging feeling that America and I had something to give each other. On the one hand, I have always regarded the United States as the management laboratory of the world. As a business academic and consultant, therefore, I am constantly reaching out to that Western part of the globe for new ideas. On the other hand, every time I return to my alma mater I am shocked by the parochialism. It is as if the diversity of management ideas that I relish so much get all too quickly melted down into bland uniformity. That makes me all the more determined to uncover the original variety. Perhaps that was at the back of my mind when I told Sam and Henry that I wanted to focus on the cultural diversity that was so strong a part of America's heritage. Although I knew that Hancock had its roots in New England, I had also gathered that its life insurance business extended all over America, thereby covering Hispanics and Afro-Americans, Anglo-, Irish-, German-, Italian-, and Chinese- and Korean- Americans.

Yet as the presentation grew nearer I got cold feet. Would Hancock's tied agents really be that interested in managing cultural diversity? Probably not. So I decided to shift my emphasis towards considering the future of the global insurance business. After all, I had majored for my MBA at Harvard in long-range planning. So I focused my talk on ways in which these entrepreneurial agents might develop insurance products that scaled Maslow's hierachy of needs. For all too many, such products were oriented towards satisfying physiological and security needs; all too few were focused on self-actualization.

The response from the Hancock audience was very mixed. Perhaps it was too much to expect these salesmen and entrepreneurs, over an English breakfast, to resonate with the farther reaches of business strategy. Yet, as I was about to take my leave I was stopped by Senator William V. Irons. The senator happened to be not only an insurance agent but also the chairman of the Rhode Island Labor Committee. He thought I had something valuable to say, and wanted to keep in contact. That made me feel a little better, so I decided to stay on for the rest of the morning's proceedings. Hancock was presenting its agents with the company's annual sales performance awards. As I was particularly interested in corporate culture, I became engrossed. In fact, not only were awards being presented, but the three major prize winners had been filmed, each video telling their personal story, a kind of cameo of the American dream, covered with Hancock wrapping. Yet there was more to it than that.

The American Melting Pot

The first film depicted, with suitably dramatic undertones, an agent who had lost everything he owned because of a fraudulent business partner, but who had recently come back from the dead. It was all very moving. The man, and his devoted wife, had made it back to the land of prosperous living against all odds. He had struggled, he had persisted, he had taken many a calculated risk, and in the end he had triumphed over adversity. As such, he was a true American, a symbol of the Western spirit of enterprise.

Interestingly enough the senior Hancock executives, presenting the awards, were very different in character from such a man. They appeared to be altogether more circumspect, more cautious, more analytical, more reserved, and more rationally minded. The contrast between them and the next two award winners could not have been greater. For these two were Afro-Americans from the deep South. The films we saw of them portrayed two communally oriented characters, whose social conscience was only matched by their individual enterprise. Moreover, both were religious, part of largely black congregations which were heavily involved in gospel singing, and with the other engaging rhythms of the South. As someone born and bred in Africa, I not only responded warmly to their communal spirits, but was also reminded of the powerful influence of southern Europe, as well as of Africa and of Latin America, on the United States.

This Southern influence was further accentuated by our guest speaker, who had been flown in from America, as Hancock's big surprise. He turned out to be no less a personality than ex-Governor Cuomo, an Italian American from New York. I was taken aback, immediately, by his Southern passion. He came across as a man of the people who felt betrayed by the American politicians currently in power. His was an impassioned plea for the other America, that increasing number of unemployed and underprivileged Americans who were being left out in the cold. It was as if the gap between the North and the South, so much a feature of our global economy, was most poignantly reflected within the USA. For Cuomo, at least, the spirit of enterprise from the West was unable to bridge the gap between the North and the South.

Then, all of a sudden it hit me. Where, oh where, was the East? America appears as a country where there is Southern passion, Western performance and Northern prudence, but no Eastern presence. There are certainly many Chinese and Indians who have become naturalized Americans, but in the process they have submerged their own identities. No wonder America and Japan fought a trade war. The prospective creative tension between West and East, now that the destructive tension between capitalism and communism had gone, was making itself felt. The problem was, of course, that this tension could only be productively dealt with, along with the North–South divide, by something other than the customary melting pot. How might this come to be?

The First Anglo-American Era

By happy coincidence, a few weeks after the Hancock escapade, I was speaking to Don Beck, a fellow Blackwell author. Don is a Texan colleague based at the National Values Center in Denton. He played a significant part, as a sports psychologist, in securing South Africa's victory in the 1995 Rugby World Cup. While we were conversing in the airport lounge in London about culture and business, Don mentioned a book that he had recently read, entitled *The Next American Nation*. When I was in Toronto the following week I made a point of getting hold of a copy. It was as if Michael Lind, the author, had taken up from where Hancock Insurance had left off.

For Lind, a prominent political commentator on the American scene, the United States was about to hopefully enter the fourth stage of its development. The first stage was the so-called 'Anglo-American' one, which we identify in this book as 'western' or pragmatic. Almost without exception, when the framers of the Constitution and their successors in the first half of the nineteenth century spoke of the American people, they meant white Americans of English descent, or immigrants from the British Isles or the Germanic countries who had lost their cultures and assimilated to the Anglo-American norm. Lind quotes Emerson, who wrote; 'That which lures a solitary American in the woods with the wish to see England, is the moral peculiarity of the Saxon race – its commanding sense of right and wrong.'

The predominant ethic in Anglo-America, in fact, was an evangelical Protestant one. According to a Cincinnati-based Presbyterian evangelist Charles Boynton, 'Puritanism, Protestantism and True Americanism are only different terms to designate the same set of principles.' For Lind, then, the sixteenth- and seventeenth-century idea of England's exceptional destiny as the homeland of Protestant reformation and political liberty transferred to the English colonies in North America, and then to the United States; it became the basis for what is today 'the American creed'. The Civil War then, which in fact destroyed Anglo-America, was not simply a war between Anglo-Americans; rather, it can be described as a conflict between the Anglo-American South and a new, Euro-American Society emerging in the North. The Northern society was ethnically different from that in the South because of the German and Irish immigrants.

The Second Euro-American Era

As late as 1900 in fact, 60 per cent of Americans were primarily of British descent. By 1920 that was down to 40 per cent. By 1980 only 20 per cent identified themselves as being primarily British; the largest group was of German-Americans. The importance of the German and Irish migrations for the present-day population can be seen in the fact that, in 1990, Americans who identified themselves by ancestry were predominantly of German (23 per cent) and Irish (16 per cent) extraction, with self-described Anglo-Americans coming in third (13 per cent). In fact the birth and growth of rationally based, 'managerial' capitalism, as opposed to the more personally based variety, was strongly attributable to the European North.

The railroad industry, in fact, was the laboratory for what became the American version of modern managerial capitalism. Railroad corporations pioneered the adoption of modern large-scale business management. From this railroad era to the great depression, according to Lind, American capitalism, dominated by a few major banking and corporate groups, was much more like modern German capitalism than like the post-New Deal American variety. Powerful investment bankers, sitting on the boards of major corporations, used their influence to consolidate and rationalize American industry. Victorian Oxbridge and the German research university replaced the earlier model of the genteel Christian gentleman's college. Anglo-America had seemingly become a Saxon Protestant federal republic.

Anglo-America then – pragmatic and Western – was a rickety foundation that collapsed, as a result of stresses induced by an expansion, into the horror of civil war. Euro-America – rational and Northern – rising above the ashes of the Civil War, achieved first economic and then geopolitical primacy in the world in only a few generations. The structure of its race relations, Lind maintains, however, had been built on he interlocking framework of disenfranchisement of blacks and Asians, a segregated labour market, and restriction on the immigration and naturalization of non-whites. White supremacy was so interwoven with the American public and private institutions that it could not be removed without unravelling the entire fabric.

The Third Multicultural Era

In the 1950s, 68 per cent of the legal immigrants originated from Europe and Canada. By contrast, between 1971 and 1991, the overwhelming majority of immigrants came from Mexico, Latin America and the Caribbean (48 per cent), and Asia (35 per cent), Europe and Canada contributing just 14 per cent. By the 1980s, as a place of origin for immigrants, Britian ranked twelfth after Mexico, the Philippines, Korea, Cuba, India and China. Such a multicultural America, for Lind, represented the third stage of the nation's development; its legal and political underpinnings were assembled in the late 1960s and early 1970s. Multiculturalists believe that the melting-pot conception of American identify has been, or should be, repudiated in favour of a new understanding of American society as a 'mosaic' of five races or 'racelike' communities – whites, blacks, Hispanics (or Latinos), Asians and Pacific Islanders, and native Americans. These races are not mere ingredients to be blended in a future unity, Lind argues, but permanently distinct communities. It is at this third stage that Michael Lind, in fact, because of his lack of appreciation for 'Eastern' harmony, begins to lead us astray.

To date, he argues, the Third Republic has failed to gain legitimacy in the eyes of most Americans. Why then should this be?

'To find yourself in Multicultural America you need find only your ghetto, and adopt its politics, its style of dress, and its approved beliefs about the world and humanity. Having done so, you can then demand that society at large recognize your individuality, that is to say, your abject conformity.

'What is this self that must be accepted? It is not the achieved self, the constructed self, of classical ethics – Greek biblical, Confucian – rather it is the raw self before improvement (or disfigurement), before education, the basic biological self, constituted by genetic ancestry, sex and temperament. The ideal of authenticity, then, is profoundly reductionist – to be oneself is to be determined by biology.'

What Lind fails to realize is that the very rawness of the multicultural self, whether as a Mexican- or as a Korean-American, is prescribed by a melting-pot culture, where a deeply set Mexican or Korean individuality is negated. Such a deep-set diversity-in-unity is in fact cited by Horace Kallen, an Austrian-American writing in the 1920s, whom Lind quotes. Kallen uses the metaphor of an orchestra.

'As in an orchestra every type of instrument has its specific timbre and tonality, founded in its substance and form, as every type has its appropriate theme and melody in the whole symphony, so it society, each ethnic group may be the natural instrument, its temper and culture may be its theme and melody and the harmony and dissonances and discords of them may make the symphony of civilization.'

Ironically Lind, reflecting a 'Western' blindspot, completely misconstrues the holistic and developmental nature of Kallen's 'Eastern' orientation.

The Fourth Era of Liberal Nationalism

Michael Lind envisages, for twenty-first-century America, neither a cultural mosiac nor a unity-in-variety, but rather a reinvigorated national community: 'What Americans borrow from other cultures, then, tends to be something that is already compatible with the deep grammar of Americanness.' If to be an American is to be a self-made man, then for Lind there has never been anyone more American than the slave born in 1817 as Frederick Bailey who escaped in 1938 and took the name of the hero of a romance by Sir Walter Scott: Frederick Douglass. In other words, you can be successfully American, and black, as long as you pretend you are white!

Around this Anglo-American/black-American core, the nation has grown from the influx first of European immigrants, and now of immigrants from Latin America, Asia and the Middle East. In the final analysis, Lind emphasizes that the collective unconscious of the American mind has been shaped most profoundly by seventeenth-century English Protestantism. Whereas Northern rationalism and Southern humanism have their place, ultimately Western pragmatism rules, and Eastern holism – notwithstanding the influence from Japan – fades into the background.

Departing from the Management Laboratory

Starting out in America, then, this book subsequently journeys across to the UK and to Scandinavia, to India and to South Africa, so as to encompass the whole of what we have termed the 'global businessphere', duly completing its journey in the Middle East. This leaves companies like Hancock Insurance to imagine for themselves what kind of truly global strategies they might evolve, thereby creating, out of dissonance, resonance between West and East, North and South.

Bibliography

Beck, D. and Cowan, C. (1996) *Spiral Dynamics: Mastering Values, Leadership, and Change*. Blackwell Publishers.

Lind, M. (1995) *The Next American Nation*. Free Press.

Introduction

'Hear me, four quarters of the world – a relative I am. Give me the strength to walk the soft earth, a relative to all that is.'

Black Elk, 1932

A Personal History

The scene is still vivid in our minds. We had been discussing the issue for hours. Late into a cold January night in England, we wrestled with the notion of what constituted an organization. What place did cultural philosophies have in the management of organizations? Why did organizations all over the world gravitate towards a common denominator culture instead of celebrating their diversity? How could organizations reach into the grounds of their cultures and out of that source create a new globality?

We brought our own differences of perception in. As Easterner and Southerner we met up in the familiar surroundings of the North and the West. Underlying the cultural differences, we shared a passionate concern for how organizations could provide human beings with a transformative tool and an agenda for inventing the future of humankind. We were long convinced that business was not just about creating profit for shareholders but was also about creating sustainable societies in which individuals could develop their potentials to the fullest; that organizations were not just about capital and people but that they had soul and spirit; and that there was more than one cultural way of perceiving the world and managing our organizations.

We were drawing upon many sources. One was Carl Jung, the Swiss-German psychologist who had written that a human personality consisted of the four dimensions of *sensing*, *thinking*, *intuiting* and *feeling* (figure 0.1).

Jung had also referred to the so-called 'individuation' process as the full development of personality, which emerged from the unconscious and manifested itself in the conscious. We were also drawing upon Bernard Lievegoed, the Dutch psychologist and organizational thinker, who referred to the development of an organism (and organization) as being constituted of four structural

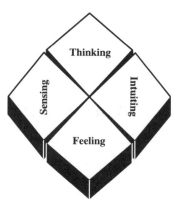

Figure 0.1

crises; (1) the *growth* stage; (2) the *differentiation* stage; (3) the *hierarchization* stage; and (4) the *integration* stage (figure 0.2).

Lievegoed had built a powerful model of human and organizational development as passing through the four stages of youth, adulthood, renewal and maturity. Thirdly, one of us had worked extensively with Kevin Kingsland's spectral model and had adapted it to organizations. Kingsland had spent many years in the East and had developed a model based on the ancient Indian knowledge of energy centres. It provided a creative technique for mapping out the stages of development in a human being. However, we were still unclear about how a model like this applied to an organization as a whole. Instinctively, we knew that the model must hold whether we were referring to an individual or to an organization. But, in relation to terminology, we were still caught up in the Western mode of perceiving reality in terms of fragmentations. The individual and the organization were essentially separate.

The only way to tackle this problem, we realized, was to dig out our unique cultural sources: one from the East, the other from the South. The Easternness brought out a distinct notion of reality being a coincidence of opposites that complemented one another. Leading-edge developments in science were saying precisely the same thing: reality in the new physics was no longer about atoms and masses, but about energy and spirit within and around these entities. The East informed us that any being, whether an individual or an organization consisted of two opposing, yet complementary fields: the material and the spiritual. Matter and spirit, but what lay in between? Eastern philosophy repeatedly stressed that the 'observer is the observed', thereby pointing out that the world and the organizations we create are a reflection of the patterns of our thought. Moreover, thought left to itself is divisive and we carry that divisiveness into organizations. We were looking for a higher *order* which would contain our tendency to divide as a tool but not be dominated by it.

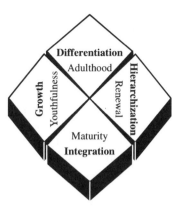

Figure 0.2

The South was different. A powerful sense of the past and a profound feeling for community. The Southernness instinctively told us that an organization was a story involving people and events. But what links did the South have with the day-to-day business of managing organizations? What did the South have that the others did not? A sense of rootedness, of belonging to the soil? How did that translate into a management agenda? In the African tradition of the Shona people of Zimbabwe there is a practice called 'Nhorowondo', which involves tracing everything back to its roots, that is uncovering its evolutionary history. That was something we would need to do with our managers, organizations and cultures. The questioning went on into the night.

Then of course, there were the West and the North. Pragmatic and rational, where did they meet the East and the South? All these sources and questions were referring to another reality, something that hadn't yet been tapped into in our organizations, ourselves and in the societies we lived in. As the night wore on, the pattern began to emerge. Firstly, we realized that the organization did not just belong geographically in the West or the North or in the East or South. This was only one half of the reality. The rest of the story was exactly the other way around: the four worlds emerged out of the organization. And out of ourselves, as well as through the stages of our life's way. And suddenly it was there: the model of the four worlds was an isomorph! It replicated itself at every level: in our places of work, within our business enterprises, in our very beings and in our societies. So, Jung's model of sensing, thinking, intuiting and feeling revealed not only the four cultural forms of the West, North, East and South respectively, but the four-fold nature of our brains and, simultaneously, of our organizations. Whereas the left brain controls logical processes, and the right brain is more metaphorical in orientation, the cerebral cortex is concept oriented while the limbic brain is emotionally centred.

It now began to emerge: each of the four cultural philosophies were isomorphic copies of the four respective modes of Jung and four distinct organizational personalities. The same four aspects were prevalent both in our personalities and in the kind of societies we build in the four worlds. These four worlds are also present in the world's natural ecosystems. Firstly, ecosystems are marked by the drive towards survival through accumulation of resources. Secondly, there is the shift towards stabilization through conservation of resources. Thirdly, there is a regeneration of resources through cyclical processes and finally, in the fourth world, there is the state of homeostasis, where there is preservation of resources. We wondered if these four worlds were an organizational archetype, existing in an unconscious state. In other words, we have embryonic structures and systems, processes and values ripe for development, if the conditions are right.

So the four worlds simultaneously exist on all levels both, 'out there' and 'in here'. On the one hand, the quaternity of forces are distinct and separate. Yet each of these worlds contains the other three enfolded in it. You may be an Anglo-Saxon Westerner, but you have latently within you, the spirit of the East, the reason of the North and the rhythm of the South. We are not merely talking, here, literally of cultural empathy or understanding. What we are saying is that the four cultural forms are like the quaternity that exist in each one of us as four forms of knowledge. What we need to do is to first become aware of their existence and develop the skills and the art of tapping into those modes. It was with this realization that this book was born.

Forming Allies

This all happened three years ago. As the fundamental idea began to shape itself, we found allies along the way. First on the list was Howard Gardner's and David Lazear's work on 'Multiple intelligences'. From their research at Harvard, they had concluded that each individual possessed multiple ways of learning and knowing about the world. What is most familiar to us in the 'West' – that is the 'verbal/linguistic' and the 'logical/mathematical' intelligence – are just two of the many multiple intelligences. We took Gardener's model a step further by mapping the intelligences on to a four-worlds matrix.

We then came across the Japanese management thinker Ikijiro Nonaka's work on the knowledge-creating organization. It was clear to us that Nonaka's four steps of 'socialization', 'externalization', 'combination' and 'internalization', were not just about the cycle of knowledge creation as he pointed out, but about traversing the cycle through the four worlds. If what Nonaka was saying about knowledge creation was true (and we were convinced it was), it meant that a knowledge-creating organization must necessarily position itself at the centre of the four worlds.

Reinventing the Organization

As we have said, the four quarters of the globe are more than just geographical entities: they exist not only around us, but also within us. Each of the four worlds has a unique quality that is generic to it. When they are taken together, they provide us with a new ecology for the transformation of organizations and individuals, businesses and products. In an emergent socio-economic reality in which the main factors of production are shifting away from land, labour and capital towards self, knowledge and culture, the four-world archetype provides us – individually and collectively – with the learning technology to evolve.

What is clear is that unless we reinvent our organizations, they are simply not going to be able to make the changes required to both compete and co-operate in the twenty-first century. What is not clear, however, is the technology that we need to use to make the transformation. From total quality management to business reengineering, there is a proliferation of new management concepts. Some are merely convenient euphemisms for downsizing, others are targeted at self-development while yet more are about corporate vision and the transformation of values. What is fundamentally lacking, however, is a coherent and consistent model that links the various approaches into a cohesive whole, at the level of the individual, the team, the organization, the society and the planetary ecosystem. The transformation of one must necessarily involve that of the others, without which all aproaches become piecemeal. What we need is the management equivalent of a 'Grand Unification Theory' within which the individual employee, the enterprise, the society, the culture and the ecosystem find their rightful places. We believe that the four-world archetype does precisely that.

What does such a unifying model constitute? Firstly, as we have just said, it must apply *consistently* on all levels. Isolating the individual's competencies and needs from those of the organization might be a convenient notion, but self-defeating in the long run. Secondly, it must be *global*. If one thing is clear about the emergent paradigm it is that we can no longer continue wearing our parochial lenses. The world is a networked, tightly woven entity and the sooner we take that on board within our organizations, the better. Thirdly, the model must create a *link* between modern science and technology, and ancient traditional cultural foundations. Both are needed to fulfil all the needs of the individual and the organization.

Awakening the Four Worlds

The four worlds, then, represent a universal archetype of organization. This archetype recurs and replicates itself at all levels, from the psychological structure of a human being, to the physical and economic structure of a corporation, to the natural structure of the ecosystem. Like Jung's cultural archetype, the archetype of the four worlds lies in the realms of our 'collective unconscious'. Jung saw the conversion of what was unconscious into what became conscious, as a process he termed 'individuation'. This according to him was the unique task of being human, ultimately forming our personality. Be it of an organization or an individual, personality emerges out of the depths of the unconscious, which includes, in potentia, the four worlds.

So, the four worlds are the generic principle through which life organizes itself. Whether it is an organism or an organization, the process of individuation must include four aspects: *identify*, *entity*, *non-entity* and *community*.

West: The First World of Identity

'To be or not to be'

William Shakespeare, *Hamlet*

An organization derives its identity from its separateness from the environment. The physical and economic structure seeks to survive and grow through an accumulation-through-exploitation of resources. In the case of organisms and ecosystems, it is through accumulating minerals and fat tissue; in the human individual, it is through acquiring personality traits; and in the case of the business enterprise, it is through accumulating physical, financial and human capital. The resources ensure that the entity is able to survive and grow in physical size. The emphasis here is on building and maintaining an area of dominance within and without the enterprise, and seeking to continually expand that area. Within the organization, this first world management style involves operating with *physical and financial structures*, akin to the *immune defence mechanism* of the body that guards against toxic elements and viruses.

North: The Second World of Entity

'Cogito ergo sum: I think therefore I am'

René Descartes, *Discourse on Method*

With his or her identity in place, an ambitious entrepreneur like David Potter seeks to establish a fully fledged organizational entity that is Psion (see chapter 15). As an entity, the enterprise is not so much concerned with its survival and growth, but with its maintenance and consolidation. This is done through a configuration of its internal mechanisms whereby it becomes a communication system serving to conserve resources. This is illustrated, at Oticon, through the lateral networks that remove any blocks to resource distribution. In the case of organisms and ecosystems, this is achieved through interconnected metabolic networks and spatial matrices whereby resources get distributed over the entire system. In the case of a business enterprise like Oticon then, this stage is represented through the emergence of cross-functional networks straddling the physical, financial and human elements of the company. Information technology, therefore, serves as an important enabling vehicle for the establishment of the business as a functional entity. This second world, 'Northern' management style involves operating with *information systems*, akin to the *neural networks* of the human body.

East: The Third World of Non-entity

'Aham Brahmasmi: I am the Universe'

The Upanishads

The third, 'Eastern' world is a contradiction in terms, when viewed from the perspective of the first and the second ones. The Western world is all about defining identity through formation of structures and the articulation of boundaries, and the Northern one about becoming a concrete entity. In contrast, the Eastern world is about dissolving one's finite and local identity in order to discover one's infinite and global 'non-entity' or universality. This requires a completely different orientation in which the object is no longer the search for security but, curiously enough, the working through of insecurity. In the organizational archetype, this serves the important purpose of generating continually new challenges to the single-mindedness of the first world and to the channelled nature of the second. In organisms and ecosystems, this is made possible through the catalytic and hypercatalytic loops that inextricably link the system to its environment. The organism simultaneously depends on the environment for its sustenance and also changes it. Development occurs when the catalytic processes between the organism and the environment reach a critical mass and the old form becomes redundant. In the case of the business enterprise, it is the stage of 'letting-go' of traditional categories in which resources have been allocated. Development of new knowledge and products takes place when the organization becomes a 'non-entity'. In the case of Toyota, for example, their products have no recognizable and overall brand image. This (in our terms) 'third' world, 'Eastern' management style involves operating with *developmental processes* akin to the *regenerative healing* system that continually destroys old cells and tissues and creates new ones.

South: The Fourth World of Community

'I am because you are'

Lovemore Mbigi, *Ubuntu*

Finally, the organization exists as part of a larger family or a community to which it is bound by forces of evolution. The 'purpose' of the organization is, therefore, to continually operate in a way in which the links to the past are upheld. This is accomplished through a communal value-sharing process whereby a dynamic balance is maintained between the entity and the environment. In the case of the organism and the ecosystem, this is done through a shared evolutionary heritage that creates a natural ecological balance between the organism and its larger community. Resources are constantly being shared in the 'circle of life'. In a business enterprise, the stage of becoming a community, as we shall be seeing in the case of South Africa's Cashbuild, is when it develops a human-centredness, by purposefully identifying the evolutionary story that establishes its links to society. This fourth world, 'Southern' management style involves working with the *emotional grounds* of the organization akin to the *hormonal system* of the body.

The four-world quaternity, therefore, looks as shown in figure 0.3.

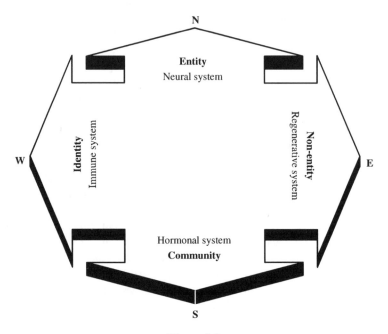

Figure 0.3

The Centre of the Four Worlds:
Static and Dynamic Quality

From the above description, we can make one particularly important observation: the four-world archetype is a confluence of two opposing and yet complementary forces, one of stability and the other of instability. The force of instability is created along the West–East axis while that of stability arises North–South. The West is constantly unstable because it has to either keep searching for its identity or to expand it. The East is unstable for different reasons: it has to continually strive to dissolve its identity, or to subsume it within a higher order. On the other hand, having become an entity, the North strives either to maintain itself or to accommodate ever greater complexity; the South strives to preserve its links with the community or to root itself more deeply in the communal grounds. In each wordly case, moreover, as the striving becomes more respectively expansive, requisite, transcendent or grounded so one world begins to meet up with another.

What we have not yet sufficiently recognized in business or organizational life is that stability and instability, both of which are dissonant forces in themselves, must go hand-in-hand in any resonant process of strategy formulation. According to Robert Pirsig, who pioneered an era of 'quality' in the West, the bedrock of quality is formed by the interaction of the two forces of 'static and dynamic quality'. Pirsig said neither the static nor the dynamic order can survive without the other. He calls dynamic quality, that is our East–West axis, the 'quality of freedom' which creates and transforms business enterprises. But life cannot exist on dynamic quality alone. It has no staying power. To cling to dynamic quality apart from any static patterns is to 'cling to chaos'. Static patterns provide a necessary stabilizing force to protect dynamic quality from degeneration, and thereby serve to preserve our corporations. However, static quality patterns are dead when they become exclusive, when they demand 'blind obedience and suppress dynamic change'.

At the centre of the two opposing and complementary strategic forces is the area of 'resonance' that is at once *harmonic* and *cosmic*. The cosmic is the centrifugal force thriving on the contradicting energy between the stable and unstable elements and moving outwards, expanding into new spaces and transforming business through inspired action. Each of the four characters in our case studies, individually, that is David Potter of Psion Computers in Britain, Lars Kolind of Oticon in Denmark, Shyam Ahuja in India, and Albert Koopman of Cashbuild in South Africa, exhibit such cosmic intelligence. The harmonic is the more static, centripetal force working symbiotically through the complementary aspect of the opposite forces, moving into inner spaces and integrating business and society through harmony. Each of the four characters, in turn, has been inadvertently or consciously drawing upon the underlying cultures in which the businesses are based.

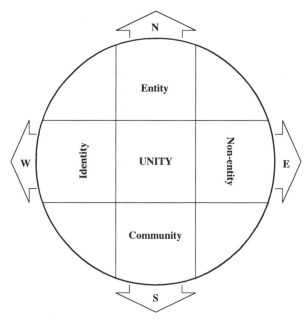

Figure 0.4

The resonance at the centre of the four worlds is between the cosmic and the harmonic. The cosmic force takes the business out into the world whereas the harmonic brings the world into the business. One protects the other: while the harmonic prevents the cosmic from degenerating, the cosmic prevents the harmonic from ossifying. The principle of evolution, be it of life itself or of the business enterprise, is based on the resonance between the cosmic and the harmonic at the centre of the four worlds. Evolution can never be a continuous forward advance. According to Pirsig, 'evolution is a process of ratchet-like steps in which there is dynamic movement up some new incline'. If the result looks successful, the static quality latches on to the gain that has been made. When there is a dynamic advance, it is always followed by a static latch. If a dynamic increment of the cosmic finds that there is no 'latching-on' by the harmonic, the cosmic falls back to a previously latched position. Whereas the cosmic force makes the organization more versatile, the harmonic force increases the power of the organization so that it does not fall to hostile forces. Taken together, they represent the archetypal yin and yang of organizations which together create *unity* (figure 0.4).

Conclusion

Like many indigenous peoples of the world, the native people of America perceive the four directions of the earth in terms of their generic, natural strengths. One of the symbols that expresses most completely the native American vision of the relationship between human beings and the world of nature sorrounding them is a cross inscribed in a circle. The belief is that the power of the world always works in circles. A tree flowers because it exists at the centre of the circle of the four quarters. The East gives peace and light, the South gives warmth, the West gives rain and the North with its cold and mighty wind gives strength and endurance. According to native American tradition, at the centre of the circle, uniting with the four directions of the cross, is the human being. And, according to us, so is the organization. The awareness of bearing within this sacred centre is what distinguishes the one who has become human from the less than human. In Jung's terminology, this is the ultimate unravelling of the cultural unconscious. In Black Elk's words: 'Peace . . . comes within the souls of men when they realize their relationship, their oneness with the universe, . . . and when they realize that . . . this centre (of the universe) is really everywhere, it is within each of us.'

This book invites you to journey to the unifying centre of the universe and consequently of the four worlds within our places of work and within our managerial souls. We live in a social context where our place of work has all but replaced the more traditional institutions of church, extended families and communities. As such, it is the singularly vital interface between the inner world of our 'selves' and the outer world of the societies in which we live and the earth that we inhabit. Through our work, and through a transforming of the organization we work in, we have the potential of transforming both, our inner selves and the outer world of our societies. In creating truly global organizations through the four worlds, we 'globalize' our selves and create genuinely global societies.

Bibliography

Jung, C.G. (1968) *Analytical Psychology: Its Theory and Practice. The Tavistock Lectures.* New York: Random House, Vintage Books.

Lievegoed, B. (1979) *Phases: Crisis and Development in the Individual.* London: Steiner Press.

Gardener, H. (1983) *Frames of Mind: The Theory of Multiple Intelligences.* New York: Harper & Row.

Nonaka, I. and Takeuchi, H. (1995) *The Knowledge Creating Company*. Oxford: Oxford University Press.

Pirsig, R. (1974) *Zen and the Art of Motorcycle Maintenance*. London: The Bodley Head Ltd.

Brown, J.E. (1953) *The Sacred Pipe*. Oklahoma: Norman Oklahoma.

PHILOSOPHY

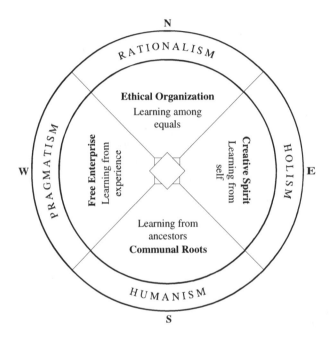

You can't do without philosophy, since everything has its hidden meaning which we must know

Maxim Gorky, The Zykovs, 1914

To be a philosopher is not merely to have subtle thoughts . . . but so to love wisdom as to live according to its dictates, a life of simplicity, independence, magnanimity, and trust

Henry D. Thoreau, *Walden* (1854)

The human merry-go-round sees many changes: the illusion that cost India the efforts of thousands of years to unmask is the same illusion that the West has laboured just as hard to maintain and strengthen

Hermann Hesse

The Earth belongs to the dead, the living and the unborn

African saying

Your Cultural Philosophies

When embarking on any journey, you need a map. However, the usefulness of a map depends on whether you have a sound idea of where you currently are. Your future direction is predicated on a knowledge of your present orientation; without it, the map is obsolete.

To travel to the four worlds, we must know our 'here and now'. This is determined by the kind of 'mental models' and philosophies that we unconsciously use. We construct our organizations and manage them on the basis of these models. They are a source of generic strength and yet, at the same time, they are obstacles to other models and ways of thinking. Because they are so deeply ingrained in us through our cultures and ways of behaviour, we often don't realize the extent to which we make use of them. We contend that there are four culturally generic philosophies in the world: those of *pragmatism*, *rationalism*, *holism* and *humanism*. We also contend that the organizations we manage are based on one or more of these philosophies.

At the end of this section, you will have developed the following:

- The tools to identify the Philosophy (perhaps, more than one) in which your organization is anchored
- The information necessary to chart the strengths and weaknesses of belonging to one or more of the four Cultural Philosophies
- The skills to recognize the destination: the centre of the four worlds, which includes elements of all of them
- The knowledge to begin an initial plan of starting a journey for yourself and your organization into the other worlds and eventually to the *cosmic/harmonic* centre of the four worlds.

1

Free Enterprise

Introduction: The Pragmatic Space

The pragmatically based approach to business and management is centreed upon the individual person, and upon the autonomous enterprise. Pragmatism, as a philosophical mainstem, rooted in individual *self-consciousness*, is often linked to both empiricism and also to individualism. Such a pragmatic approach to business is particularly strong in the Anglo-Saxon world. In this chapter, we shall be looking at the roots of such empiricist and pragmatic philosophy. Our guides in this venture will be Francis Bacon, Adam Smith and Samuel Smiles. From that potent source has sprung the *free market*, economically, the competitively inclined *enterprise*, commercially, and the independent minded *entrepreneur*, psychologically. The combined fruits are *profitable* commercial and personal *growth*, commercial growth being outer directed, personal growth inner directed.

The present day apostle of pragmatism, experimentation and individualism in management is of course Tom Peters in America. However, the American pragmatic approach, within the organization, has been imbued with other philosophical streams, particularly the rationalist one against which Peters so stongly reacts. For a purer form of managerial pragmatism we shall turn to England, and ultimately to its greatest management thinker Reg Revans. As we shall see, it was Revans who was able to bring together the notions of free enterprise, self-help and individual learning. Indeed, as we shall soon see, it is Revans' concept of 'action learning' which serves to link up the 'old' pragmatic world view of enterprise, leadership and commercial growth, with the 'new' experiential perspective on learning, empowerment and personal growth.

Within a historical perspective, the entrepreneur, rooted in Victorian traditions of *self-help*, is now being transformed into a modern manager, engaging in individual *self-development*. In that context the self-assertive entrepreneur is being supplanted by the self-actualizing manager. Similarly, the independent firm, having been based in classical free enterprise, is now beginning to emerge as a *learning company*. In this chapter we shall be outlining the empirically based images and ideas – the roots and mainstem, as it were – of pragmatism.

The Philosophy of Pragmatism

Unlike the rational world view, pragmatism sticks as close as possible to life. From life it borrows its complexity, its elasticity, its delicate shading. It does not worry beforehand about form. *Whereas thinking implies a separation from things thought, experience is a stream of life which bathes the individual at every moment in a well of practicality*. When the outcome in hand, therefore, is that of inspiration, the neglect of form allows a greater freedom on the part of the creative spirit. That spirit is enhanced when allied to a deep sense of social service: 'A kind of internal inspiration seems then to guide the work, like the instinct that guides the root towards the richer layer of earth'. Reg Revans, as we shall see later, is a typical case in point.

Pragmatism can be traced back for our purposes to the inductively based scientific investigations of Queen Elizabeth I's Lord Chancellor, Francis Bacon, in the seventeenth century. Its immediate economic derivatives are those of Adam Smith's eighteenth-century free enterprise and Samuel Smiles' nineteenth-century self-help. Finally, a twentieth-century social philosopher and management thinker has fused together enterprise and learning, self-help and self-development. The originator of this 'action learning' is England's Cambridge-based physicist and highly original management thinker, Reg Revans.

Francis Bacon – the advancement of learning

A life devoted to one great idea

The exponent of a new philosophy in the latter part of the sixteenth century, Bacon was born into a new world that, in the same way as the EU today, was becoming part of a new European and global order. England, then, had detached herself from feudal Europe and was becoming a nation state with a national church. Power was being transferred from the church to the laity, perhaps in the same way as power today is shifting from unionized labour towards professionally based knowledge workers. In the so-called 'device' of 1592, Bacon analysed the problem which confronted his age. The learning of the day bore little relation to the productive processes of industry. That proclamation has a familiar ring to it, some 400 years later!

The story of Francis Bacon, in effect, is that of a life devoted to one great idea. The idea gripped him as a boy, grew with the varied experience of his life, and occupied him on his deathbed. The idea is now commonplace, partly realized, partly tarnished, still often misunderstood. But in his day it was a novelty. It was simply, according to Bacon's biographer Benjamin Farrington, that knowledge ought to bear fruit in works, and that science ought to be applicable to industry. 'May God the Creator,' Bacon urged, 'protect and guide this work both in its ascent to glory and in its descent to the service of man.' The ascent to glory is the inductive process leading to the highest axioms. The descent to the service of man is the deductive process by which science is applied to works. These, for Farrington, are the two chief moments of Bacon's scientific process. The ascent we may describe as learning, and the descent as innovation.

Only learned men therefore, Bacon in fact maintained, find business as agreeable to health of mind as exercise is to health of body.

Man, Bacon insisted, must find out the facts about the universe. He must maintain the great continuity and transmission of learning through universities dedicated not to the dry husks of ancient learning alone but to research upon the natural world of the present. Then and only then would the invisible world drawn from man's mind become a genuine reality. Lamentably 'Elizabethan craftsmen or seafarers sometimes made discoveries', Bacon noted, 'but the experiments of calloused hands were often scorned by gentlemen'. For Bacon, Artisan and scribe, action and learning, need to be inextricably intertwined. This was certainly not so for his predecessors.

Touching the popular mind

Truth then, for the medieval schoolmen, rested upon the belief that reality lay in the world of ideas largely independent of our sense perceptions. Francis Bacon presented quite another 'engine', as he termed it, for the attainment of truth. This engine of inductive logic he opposed to the old way of thinking. In essence his argument was as follows. People must refrain from deducing general principles for which they have no real evidence in nature. Instead, they must dismiss much of what they think we know and begin anew patiently to collect facts from nature. They must never stray far from reality until it is possible through close observation to deduce more general laws. 'The real problem for Bacon', according to his American biographer, the scientist and philosopher Loren Eisler, 'was to break with the dead hand of the traditional past, to free latent intellectual talent, to arrest and touch with hope the popular mind'. Though he sought to combine the discoveries of the practical craftsman with the insights of the philosopher, Bacon saw more clearly than any of the other Renaissance writers the development of the experimental method itself. Science, for him, was inherently democratic.

Bacon therefore eliminated reliance upon the rare elusive genius as a safe road into the future. It involved too much risk and chance to rely upon such men alone. Bacon, instead, placed his hope for Utopia in the education of plain Tom Jones and Dick Thickhead, as did Jan Carlzon 400 years later. Bacon had an enormous trust in the capacities of the human mind, even though no one had defined better than he its idols and distortions.

Perhaps Bacon imposed too much hope on the common man. He, the Lord Chancellor, was willing to build his empire of hope from common clay. It is not, Bacon explained, the pleasure of curiosity, nor ambition or fame, that are the true ends of learning. Rather it is a restitution in man of the sovereignty and power which he had in the first state of creation.

Combining reason and will

Francis Bacon regarded learning as having of two parts. First there is existing knowledge, organized and disseminated through books and other forms of communication. Second, there is the discovery of new knowledge through experience and, indeed, through experiment. In the first event or occurrence after the fall of man, Bacon argues, we see an image of the two estates, the contemplative and the active state. They are presented in the two persons of Abel and Cain, and in the two simplest and most primitive trades of life, that of the shepherd and that of the husbandman. 'The knowledge, with respecteth the faculties of mind, is of two kinds: the one representing *understanding and reason*, and the other his *will, appetite and action*; whereof the former produceth position or degree, the latter action and execution.' While, for example, we might turn to Michael Porter's *Competitive Strategy* for position and degree, we would look to John Harvey Jones to '*Make it Happen*', through appetite and will. The two, hitherto, were disconnected.

The Great Instauration – creating a learning society

To remedy this situation Bacon suggested in the 'device' of 1594 that royal assistance is required. A library of books ancient and modern in all tongues should be collected. There should be botanical gardens and a zoo in the grandest scale, fully accessible to observation. A museum should contain and classify inanimate natural objects and the products of man's ingenuity and skill. A laboratory should be equipped with all materials required for experimental research. Bacon calls such societal learning or re-learning, *instauration*, that is a restoration or renewal. He takes 31 ancient fables of the Greeks and draws out of them his own political and scientific views. The title page tells us that the book is *The Great Instauration* of Francis of Verulam, Lord Chancellor of England.

Bacon tried to make of man an actively anticipatory, rather than a reminiscent or 'present' creature. To anticipate, however, the human being must be made conscious of his own culture. Education must assume a role unguessed in his time and imperfectly realized in ours. It must neither denigrate nor worship the past. It must learn from it. Bacon is not content to subsist in the natural world as it exists, nor to drift aimlessly in history. The focal point for all his thinking is action, not system building: 'The organizing principle of all his vast erudition was the aim of extending, not man's power of argument, but his power of action. But the special character of his enterprise was his insistence that a reform in practice depended on a reform in thought. Progress in power and progress in knowledge are two aspects of the same thing. Works were the test of truth rather than having value above it'. Bacon then, like your typically 'Western' manager, was a pragmatist. Aristotle's logic was an aid to thinking; its goal was logical consistency. Bacon's logic was a guide to action; its test was whether it worked. The same applied to Adam Smith's free market economics.

The policy of the free market
Adam Smith – promoting free enterprise

Competition promotes liberty

Adam Smith was a Scottish Professor of Moral Philosophy in the late eighteenth century. The naturalist school of philosophy to which both Bacon and Smith belonged, had an unbroken tradition from the later Greek Stoics onwards. It received an enormous stimulus in the Renaissance and Reformation, and showed itself in a modified form in Hobbes and Locke. It then came to full flower in the latter part of the seventeenth century. In spite of their sharp distinctions the Stoics, Francis Bacon and Adam Smith – according to the British economic historian Eric Roll – can be regarded as representative of a single stream of naturalist thought.

Its essence is a reliance on what is natural as against what is contrived. For Smith, *only complete competition was consistent with natural liberty*. Only such competition could ensure that everybody obtained the full rewards of his efforts, and added his full contribution to the common good. Human conduct, according to Adam Smith, was naturally activated by six motives. These were self love, sympathy, the desire to be free, a sense of propriety, a habit of labour, and the propensity to truck, barter and exchange one thing for another. Given these springs of conduct, each man was naturally the best judge of his own interest and should therefore be left to pursue his task in his own way.

If left to himself he would not only attain his own best advantage, but he would also further the common good. Each individual was left by an invisible hand to promote the interest of society. The medievalists had called for good works; the reformers for faith. The classicists demanded neither; their concern being this worldly rather than other worldly. Instead Smith drove home the demand for laissez faire, a system of natural liberty, as the best means of bringing about the wealth of nations. In such a system individuals could pursue their own self-interest, but, regardless of their intentions, a providential order would tend to turn the pursuit of self-interest into an instrument serving the interest of society.

Smith's labour theory of value

Let us now pursue the argument, in Smith's own words from *The Wealth of Nations*. 'The annual labour fund of every nation must be regulated by two different circumstances. First it is regulated by the skill, dexterity and judgment with which its labour is generally applied; and secondly by the proportion of those who are engaged in useful labour, and those who are not.' However, the division of that labour, Smith argues, is not the effect of a conscious plan. Rather, 'it is the necessary, though very slow and gradual consequence of a certain propensity in human nature. This has in view the propensity to truck, barter and exchange one thing for another.'

In almost every other race of animals, Smith continues, when it is grown up to maturity, it is entirely independent, and in its natural state has occasion for the assistance of no other living creature. But man has constant occasion for the help of his fellow creatures, and it is in vain for him to expect it from their benevolence only. 'He will be more likely to prevail if he can interest their self love in his favour, and show them that it is for their own advantage to do for him what he requires of them. It is not for the benevolence of the butcher, the brewer or the baker that we expect our dinner but from their regard to their own interest.' Among men, Smith maintains, the most dissimilar geniuses are of use to each other. 'Every man thus lives by exchanging, or becomes in some measure a merchant, and the society itself grows to be what is properly a commercial society.' The spirit of self-help underlying Smith's *The Wealth of Nations* was spelt out one hundred years later by his English compatriot, Samuel Smiles.

The practice of Samuel Smiles – promoting self-help

Mutual improvement societies

For Samuel Smiles, free enterprise, as an institutionally based firm, was fuelled by self-help, in its personal form. *Self Help* was published in 1859, the same year as Darwin's *Origin of Species* and Mills' *Essay on Liberty*. Smiles built the book on a series of talks he had given to young artisans who had formed in Leeds an evening school for mutual improvement. It was a time when little was expected of government but much was expected of individuals. The cults of self-help and self-improvement were well spread, representing the value of achievement over that of birth. There were in 1860 over 200,000 members of mechanics institutes and mutual improvement societies, lyceums and libraries. Adult education took place at most of them. There were three million members, moreover, of Friendly and Provident societies.

What Smiles applauded was not so much success itself as the moral character that lies behind it. In tune with the religious professions of the age he celebrated patience, courage, endeavour, and the perseverance with which worthy objectives were pursued. He praised individualism, unlike his Scottish predecessor, Adam Smith, not soley as a means to worldly gain, but also as the path to independence and to self-fulfilment.

Help from within

For Samuel Smiles the spirit of self-help is the root of all genuine growth in the individual. Moreover, exhibited in the lives of many, it constitutes the true source of national vigour and strength. Help from without, he said in *Self Help*, is inevitably enfeebling in its effect, but help from within invariably invigorates: 'Indeed the worth and strength of a State depends far less upon the form of its institutions than upon the character of its men. For the nation is only an aggregate of individual conditions. Therefore civilization itself is but a question of the personal improvement of the men, women and children of whom society is composed.'

National progress, he added, is the sum of individual industry, energy and uprightness. It follows that 'the highest patriotism and philanthropy consist, not so much in altering laws and modifying institutions, as in helping and stimulating men to elevate and improve themselves by their own free and independent individual action.' It may be of comparatively little consequence how a man is governed from without. Everything depends, for Smiles, on how he governs himself from within, including the careful utilization of his energies. The solid foundations of liberty must rest upon individual character.

Education through life

The spirit of self-help then, according to Smiles, as exhibited in the energetic action of individuals, has in all times been a marked feature in the English character. Schools, academies and colleges give but the merest beginnings of a culture. Far more influential is the life education daily given in people's homes, in the streets, behind counters, in workshops, at the loom and the plough, in counting houses and factories, and in the busy haunts of men. *A men perfects himself by work more than by reading*. It is life rather than literature, action rather than study, and character rather than biography, which tends perpetually to renovate mankind.

The career of industry, he therefore indicates, which the nation has pursued, has also proved its best education. No bread eaten by man is so sweet as that earned by his own labour, whether bodily or mental. The duty of work is written on the muscles of the limbs, the mechanism of the hand, the nerves and lobes of the brain. In the school of labour, then, is taught the best practical wisdom.

Servant of the marketplace – contracting out

Samuel Smiles, in the nineteenth century then, under the guise of self-help, managed to combine enterprise and learning. Modern capitalism in the twentieth century, on the other hand, loses the connection between self-assertiveness (enterprise) and self-development (learning). It is this loss of connection which, as we shall see, has recently led classically free market economics astray.

The British economist, Andrew Shonfield, made this observation in *Modern Capitalism* during the mid-1960s: 'It is noticeable that some of the nations which made the most complete and successful adaptation to the political problems of the earlier era of capitalism seem to be stuck with especially inefficient political machinery when they apply themselves to new problems.' This is outstandingly true, Shonfield argues, of the Anglo-Saxon countries. Britain and the US, both holding to common-law tradition, were brilliantly inventive in using their legal systems to create an environment in which a great reserve of previously suppressed business initiative was liberated. They concentrated the main weight of their effort on the protection and enlargement of private property, just as Ronald Reagan and Margaret Thatcher did in the 1980s.

The arrangements governing society were turned into a series of contracts between owners of various things, including owners of their own labour, about the terms of which such property was to be used. The system was harsh, but its product, Shonfield maintains, was a degree of personal liberty rarely, if ever, realized before.

Traders above all

The British, for Shonfield as for Napoleon before him, have seen themselves as traders above all. Such a pragmatic individual is thought of as being no more than a servant of the market, responding, just like a merchant, to a series of transient opportunities. 'The notion of a supplier with a long-term production policy, with a product that is distinctive and special, is not something readily absorbed into the thinking of British capitalism,' wrote Shonfield.

In Britain then – unlike, for example, in France, Holland or in Sweden – the state is not visualized as the carrier of an overriding national interest. It is, rather, seen as one among several entities who compete with one another on behalf of their individual, and differing interests. As a result personal liberty is probably more secure than in a more interventionist setting. Yet the state's inhibitions also make it less inclined to pursue, as in Germany and in Scandinavia, positive social goals. Witness the stand Britain has been taking, until the advent of New Labour against the EU's social policies!

Classical economics, then, as preached by Adam Smith, is the picture of a perfect market, unimpeded by the influence of any public authority, with a vast multiplicity of buyers and sellers, none of them strong enough to impose a desired direction on events. 'The market place, the small independent trader, and the non-interventionist public authority were indissolubly associated with political freedom,' observed Shonfield. The resulting economic emphasis has led to what we might term a 'pragmatic imbalance'. We now turn to Reg Revans to seek a more balanced interpretation of the 'free enterprise'.

Action Learning

Re-searching within

Reg Revans has spent the past 50 years trying to raise managers', and nations', consciousness of their unique origins and destiny. In the process he has run management development programmes in Belgium and Britain, in America and Australia, in India and in Egypt. Revans has continually maintained that the salvation of individual countries, and their enterprises, is not to be found by observers scouring the world – particularly, today, the American or Japanese worlds – in the hope of turning up some miracle there. Their salvation, their 'Kingdom of God', *is to be found within their own shores* and within the wills of their own people. Moreover, at the level of the individual firm, he argues, it is not unreasonable to suggest that an essential part of any research and development policy is the study of the human effort. For it is out of this that the saleable products of the enterprise are largely created.

Identifying with learning

In this respect Revans decries that social innovation, the rationally based division of labour, for which Adam Smith bears so much responsibility. The main contribution that people have to make to a collective task, he says, is their own time. If they feel that the management which determines both what their tasks are to be, and the ways in which they should do them, is remote – and perhaps neither very competent nor particularly sympathetic – they are bound to regard their employment as an insult to their self-respect.

In *The Advancement of Learning*, we find Bacon's ideas on the learning process: 'The fundamental questions of adaptation today lie in the field of human learning. *Human beings learn only when they want to learn, and only when they*

identify with the persons for whom, or from whom, they want to do so.' What might
be called the smoothness of the horizontal flow of work and the willingness of
people to do the work are inextricably mixed. Hence, the division of industrial
problems into relations between processes and between people, for Revans, is an
illusion. There is one field of difficulty alone. Human relations in the factory
depend upon the extent to which people perceive their work to be economically
and effectively arranged. Where this is not so, discontent will arise. The
over-organized factory impairs freedom of thought and decision. The under-
organized one fritters away the hours of life that all of us, who deplore wasting
time, can live only once. That is pragmatism for you!

Forming learningful groups

It is the task of management, Revans maintains, to distribute authority in such
a way as to give all employees the level of problems they can settle on their own
or by consulting other people. It is in the big organization, then, that the centre
of decision and the periphery of action face the greatest risk of mutual
misunderstanding.

Learning must demand not only information about the latest shift of policy.
It must demand power to get the knowledge needed to see one's part in what is
going on. In particular one needs to know the effect of one's behaviour upon
those with whom one works.

Revans, in effect, has taken a leaf out of Adam Smith's book, in so far as he has
focused on the importance of learningful exchange in the creation of wealth. At
the same time, and in direct contrast to his illustrious predecessor, he has
accentuated the value of combining forces. For Revans, this is best achieved
within small 'action learning' groups rather than in large-scale business
consortia.

Reg Revans, three hundred years after Adam Smith, has witnessed a revolution not only in the physical sciences but also, and more importantly for our
purposes, in social studies. Real progress is found to consist, Revans argues
through Arnold Toynbee's *Study of History*, in a process defined as *etherealiza-
tion*. This involves overcoming of material obstacles, which serves to release the
energies of society. People now respond to challenges which are internal rather
than external, spiritual rather than material. In this respect, Revans' view is not
dissimilar to Francis Bacon's. However, it draws on recent work in experiential
psychology, which has emerged out of the pragmatic–empirical tradition.

Managing experientially

One of the outstanding needs in the education of managers, according to
Revans, is a frame of reference for describing, communicating and evaluating

the subjective consciousness of personal action. The language of the management academy, he says, is a code of depersonalized abstractions, such as economic theory and network analysis, taught by experts.

There are, he says, or simply can be, no professionals to instruct us on what to do nor even upon how to do it, for the method of the lesson is also its content. Knowledge is the consequence of action, and *to know is the same as to do.* Thus self-knowledge, the key to mastery in an uncertain world, is the same as self-development. Revans locates the manager, then, as the individual he or she is and must always remain, at the centre of the activity that engages him or her.

According to Bacon: 'A real decision, firstly, is always that of a particular person, with his own ends not to be neglected. He has his own fears to amplify his problems, his own hopes a mirage to amplify his resources, and his own prejudices, often called experience, to colour the data in which he works. A choice of goals, secondly, so much bound up with decision theory, is yet distinct from it. The ends for which one strives, deliberately or subconsciously, as an individual or with others, are but partly determined by the calculations of economic strategy. For behind them jostle the egocentric drives of the individual. Thirdly, there is the relevance of information, that product of which the raw material is data and the manufacturing process the personal sensitivities of the individual. Fourthly, the theory of systems describes the web in which the wordline of a particular manager is entangled. The assessment of probability is, fifthly, that farrago of mathematical statistics and simple guesswork by which we attempt to assess our forgotten experience, our present wishfulness and our future hope. And, sixthly, the learning process integrates everything that one has so far become, and one's hope for future improvement.'

In combining subjective awareness with objective method, therefore, a manager cannot change the system of which he or she is in command – at least in any new sense – unless the individual is him or herself changed in the process. The logical structures of both, for Revans, are in correspondence. *The change in the system we call action; that in the self we call learning.* Learning, he says, to act effectively is also learning how to learn effectively. Revans, in fact, is revisiting and reconstituting the philosophies of both Bacon and also Locke, in managerial mode.

According to Locke's theory, man comes into the world with his mind a blank tablet (tabula rasa), void of ideas as of knowledge. It is the senses which first 'convey into the mind several distinct perceptions of things'. As described in Eisley's biography of Bacon, this source of ideas Locke designated as 'sensation'. The second source is 'the perception of the operations of our mind within us, as it is employed about the ideas it has got. Such operations furnish the understanding with another set of ideas, which could not be had from things without'. This second, and only other, source of ideas, Locke designated as 'reflection'. Knowledge, in other words, is the product of experience in both an outer (sensation) and an inner (reflection) sense. Therein lie the seeds of pragmatically based learning, which, for Revans, must exceed the rate of change.

Enhancing productivity through learning

When the rate of change is high, Revans argues, if it is to be met with equanimity, then the learning must be rapid. Those who cannot keep up with what is new will lose control of their surroundings, while those who take innovation in their stride will profit by being able to turn it to their advantage. *In epochs of convulsion the advantage lies with those who are able to learn.* Those who have consciously learnt how to learn, have in particular learned to recognize the difference between two things. Firstly, there is the acquisition of knowledge already known to other persons, which Revans calls 'programmed'. It has already been (or could be) written down. Secondly, there is the exploration of the managers' own manifest ignorance, so as to clearly identify what questions they need to ask if they are to master the unknown that lies ahead. Revans denotes the overall *capacity to learn* as L, the former ability to acquire *programmed knowledge* as P, and the latter power to identify such *discriminating questions* as Q. $L = f(P, Q)$. Such a learning formula, with its two kinds of knowledge, harks back to both Bacon and Locke.

Becoming an action learner

In the final analysis, Revans' action learning renews Francis Bacon's instauration, in contemporary scientific guise. On the other hand, it reconstitutes Adam Smith's wealth of nations, duly informed by today's experientially based psychology. 'It is a virtue of action learning, that like truth itself, it is a seamless garment; with its help, all parties alike, manager and workman, should tackle their common foe, the external problem,' wrote Revans. In that sense, outer directed competition between man and his wily competitors is replaced by the inner directed struggle between man and the thorny problems he faces.

In this way Revans' road to managerial, as opposed to personality-based, capitalism is not paved with a rationally based, Ford-style division of labour. Rather it involves a scientifically based approach to problem solving. Similarly his path to co-operative endeavour is paved not with institutionally based strategic alliances but with reciprocal exchange in small groups.

More specifically, then, in Revans' modern-day extension of both Bacon's great seventeenth century instauration and Smiles' Victorian practice of self-help:

- The *reinterpretation of knowledge is in effect a social process*, carried on among two or more learners in purposefully structured small groups. They, by the apparent incongruity of their exchanges, frequently cause each other to examine afresh many ideas.
- Within the context of such a social process *managers learn with and from each other* by mutual support, advice and criticism during their attacks on real

problems. They alternate between active project management and reflective review, in small groups, of themselves and their activities.

- Within such action learning sets, finally, *there are no Chiefs and Indians*, only 'comrades in adversity' and a set facilitator. Each manager may, therefore, in seeking to enrich and enlarge his or her own subjective self through 'spiritual barter', reciprocally help to enrich and enlarge the subjective selves of his fellows.

Revans, standing on the shoulders of his predecessors Bacon, Smith and Smiles, has interwoven the advancement of learning, among managers with mutual support among 'comrades in adversity'.

It is also worth noting that Revans focused most of his attention, in Britain at least, on nurses and coalminers, duly reinforcing his identification with the man and woman in the street. Finally, Revans was also honouring the individualistic, pragmatic tradition, albeit reinforced by mutual interest, whereby people stood together, but each on their own two feet.

Conclusion

Action-centred leadership

An individualistic culture, like the Anglo–Saxon one, is bound to focus upon leadership as a primary subject of management concern. In fact, during the 1980s there was a renewed focus on personality-based leadership in the managerial literature, as opposed to impersonally based management.

Interestingly enough, moreover, in America the focus has been upon the inspirational aspects of leadership whereas in Britain, action-centred leadership has taken root. Pragmatism has made its duly 'sense/thought'-oriented mark over humanism's 'intuition/feeling'-orientation. This focus on leadership, finally, remains outer directed towards free enterprise, whereas the signs of our times are increasingly inner directed towards the advancement of learning.

Manager self-development

Francis Bacon, a chancellor of England, originated scientific method in the time of Queen Elizabeth I; Reg Revans, a Cambridge physicist, applied scientific method to management in the time of Elizabeth II. While Bacon studied the classics as he attended to his country's affairs, Revans studied the bible while attending to the Coal Board's productivity problems. Like the best of pragmatists, they not only learnt from their own lives but enabled others to learn from theirs.

Pragmatic imbalance

In effect, as we have seen, the pragmatic world view – with its dual conditions of enterprise and learning – has only been partially adopted in recent times. The enterprising expression of individual liberty, reflected in the Adam Smith's promotion of the 'free market', has eclipsed the learning approach promoted by Francis Bacon. While pragmatism of the outer directed variety enhances market awareness, individualism of the inner directed kind reinforces self-awareness.

It is one's perception of a problem, Revans maintains, one's evaluation of what is to be gained by solving it, and one's estimate of the processes at hand to resolve it that together provide the springs for human action. Moreover, the present speed of technological change means the problems to be solved differ from one day to the next. It follows that everybody in the organization, from those who frame the policies to those who manipulate the details of technique, must be endowed to the greatest possible extent with a method of learning.

We now turn from the pragmatic philosophy of the free enterprise to the rational philosophy of the ethical organization.

Bibliography

Steiner, R. (1972) *World Economy*. London: Steiner Press.
Faulkner Jones, L. (1932) *The English Spirit*. London: Steiner Press.
De Madariaga, S. (1966) *Portrait of Europe*. Hollis and Carter.
Durant, W. (1962) *Outlines of Philosophy*. Earnest Benn.
Farrington, B. (1973) *Francis Bacon*. London: Macmillan.
Bacon, Francis (1961 edn.) *The Advancement of Learning*. Dent.
Eisley, L. (1962) *Francis Bacon and the Modern Dilemma*. Nebraska University Press.
Roll, E. (1953) *A History of Economic Thought*. Faber.
Spiegel, Henry (1971) *The Growth of Economic Thought*. Duke University Press.
Smith, Adam (1975) *The Wealth of Nations*. Everyman.
Smiles, Samuel (1986) *Self Help*. Penguin.
Shonfield, A. (1965) *Modern Capitalism*. Oxford University Press.
Toynbee, A. (1934–61) *Study of History*. (In 12 volumes.)
Revans, R.W. (1979) *Action Learning*.
Revans, R.W. (1982) *The Origins and Growth of Action Learning*.
Revans, R.W. (1982) *The ABC of Action Learning*. Chartwell Brett.

2

Ethical Organization

Introduction: The Rational Ethic

From the free enterprise that marks the pragmatic oganization of the West, we now turn our attention to its counterpart in the North. The Northern organization is characterized by the second world of 'entity', as opposed to the Western world of 'identity'. Rationalism is that system of philosophical belief which asserts that human reason is competent to attain objective truth unaided. It furthers the notion that knowledge can be deduced from a priori concepts and as such is different from emotion or intuition. The rational mode seeks out external coherence in systems, and a sense of uniformity and order.

A rational approach to business is particularly strong in Scandinavia, although rationalism as a mode of knowldege spreads itself from the Indian sub-continent in the East across the North to the West. Northern rationalism depends on two premises:

1 that any phenomenon – world, society or organization – can be perceived and managed as a system obeying rational laws and procedures; and
2 although individual deviation from the norm is possible, the system as a whole is a collective one which means that the parameters of, say, profit are set by the system and not by the individual (i.e. the formula supersedes individually gathered data).

As a result, the Northern business environment is inherently different from the Western one, although, on an outward level, there is very little difference. Unlike in the West, in the North it is not the free market which supersedes all other economic considerations, but the *welfare system* which regulates, within the free market economy, the tension between individual profitabilty and collective benefits. What is at stake in the Northern world is not so much the growth of individual, but the development of the system.

Present-day rationalism in Scandinavia has come a long way from its beginnings in the Descartian conception of the world (and consequently of the organization) as a well-functioning machine. Over the centuries, it has moved away from its machine-like characteristics to include the human dimension. As we shall see later in this chapter, at the forefront of organizational management in Scandinavia is the notion of the *ethical organization*. This is a direct consequence of the evolution of rationality over the centuries into a highly sophisticated formulation of 'ethical rationalism'. However, to get to the stage of modern-day ethics in the North, we start at the beginning with the work of the Norwegian economist Thorsten Veblen.

The Rational Economics of Thorstein Veblen

From a historical perspective, the first document articulating a rational picture of reality was the work of the Frenchman René Descartes. Descartes wanted to build a grand system of mathematics that would explain all phenomena in the universe. According to Descartes, the universe was a gigantic machine, composed of highly intricate parts joined to one another to form an undivided whole. The machine obeyed fixed laws and ticked away like a perfect clock. This Cartesian view of reality was a highly systematic one, a matrix of interconnections that revealed an underlying, mechanical pattern. At the age of 23, Descartes experienced a vision that changed his life. As he wrote, '. . . I would like to give the public . . . a completely new science which would resolve all questions of quantity, continuous or discontinuous.' Descartes' vision was about the certainty of reason. Soon, Descartes' conception of a mechanical universe became a *cause célèbre* in Northern European thinking about science and, along with Newton's work, formed a powerful agenda for the coming of the scientific and technological revolution.

Countries like France developed the political aspects of rationality through notions of the collective good and the rule of the masses. But unlike the violent uprisings in France and in other parts of Europe, the Danish egalitarian movement of the 1800s was unique in its non-violent character and the consensus it had among ruler and ruled alike. Feudal owners voluntarily relinquished control over land. Some of these fuedal owners were in fact the champions of the process that led to the reforms. A 200-year-old tradition of absolute monarchy was ended by none other than the king himself.

Owing to an archetypal cultural trait of seeking for the collective good of the community, the genuinely social dimensions of rationalism manifested themselves in the Scandinavian countries of Denmark, Sweden and Norway rather than in France. Through the welfare system, the highly effectve co-operatives and a public dislike for dehumanizing technology, Scandinavia was able to do what France could not. It could channel its rational archetype into the development of an *ethical rationalism*, one that has become a powerful model for organizational behaviour and management.

Thorstein Veblen was known as the *enfant terrible* of economic thought. Born in America of Norwegian parentage, Veblen's economics was a curious mixture of some Western empiricism and a whole lot of the Scandinavian cultural archetype. Born a hundred years after Adam Smith, Veblen's economics had none of the Anglo-Saxon bias towards individual growth and profit. 'What is the nature of economic man, and how does it happen that he so builds his community that it will have a leisure class?' were the questions that Veblen began his erratic career with. What made these questions more potent was the economic climate of the time, particularly in America where Adam Smith's work, crystallized in *The Wealth of Nations*, had laid the foundations of a pragmatic, capitalist culture. The classical economists of the day saw the world in terms of individuals who sought to better serve their own self-interest. By and large, humans were seen as pragmatic beings who competed for available resources. It was perfectly natural, therefore, that in the competetion some rose to the top while some stayed at the bottom, and those who were fortunate or sagacious enough to prosper quite naturally took advantage of their fortune to minimize their work. All simple and reasonable.

Whether it was his Nordic roots or just a personal aversion to accept a division in society between the haves and the have-nots, Veblen questioned the view that the force that bound society together was self-interest. Veblen also questioned the preference of leisure over work. The irksomeness of work, which the classical economists thought to be inherent in the nature of the human being, Veblen saw as a degradation of the human spirit. The cause of this degradation, he thought, was an old predator instinct which had got the upper hand of man's more collective instinct. But far from being regarded as wasters or spoilers, the leisure class were looked up to as the strong and able. Veblen felt that the leisure class had changed its occupation and refined its methods, but its aim was still the same – predatory seizure of goods without work. Booty or women had been replaced by money but the predators were following the same old pattern. 'In order to stand well in the eyes of the community,' explained Veblen, 'it is necessary to come up to a certain, somewhat indefinite conventional standard of wealth; just as in the earlier predatory stage it is necessary for the barbarian man to come up to his tribe's standard of physical endurance, cunning and skill at arms.'

Veblen published *The Theory of Business Enterprise* in 1904. It made more controversial reading for Americans than his previous one, *The Theory of the Leisure Class*. Adam Smith's seminal work in pragmatic economics had established the capitalist as the driving figure in the economic world, the 'central generator of economic progress'. Veblen turned this neat and tidy capitalist world upside down. In his version, the profiteering businessman was not the driving force of the economy, but the saboteur of the system. Unlike Marx, who saw the problem as a clash of human interests, Veblen went back into the Descartian metaphor of modern science: the machine itself. From his 'rational' perspective, Veblen saw nothing wrong with the machine *per se*, or the fact that societies were being constructed on the lines of a machine, timed to regularity, standardization, accuracy and precision. Moreover, Veblan perceived the economic process itself as being mechanical in character. Economics was all about production and production by its very nature engendered a social machine that depended on goods produced. In true Cartesian fashion, Veblan perceived society as a gigantic and specialized human clock. Since adjustments and coordination are always necessary to maintain a machine, it made the role of the engineer important in Veblan's eyes. But the machine was not concerned with profits; it only produced goods. As a result, the businessman had no function – unless he turned engineer. But being a member of the leisure class, the businessman only wanted to accumulate and so he achieved his ends by conspiring against the social machine. His function was not to aid in the manufacture of goods, but to impede the production process and the flow of goods, thereby leading to a fluctuation of values which he would capitalize on. The need to accumulate vaster profits only meant one thing: a conscious misdirecting of the efforts of the social system to provide basic needs for the collective good.

Veblen's next book was *The Engineers and the Price System*, followed by *Absentee Ownership and Business Enterprise*. In both, the theme was the development of a new society based on the collective good brought about by production of goods and services that would benefit all. Resurrecting the old rational motif of the machine, Veblen stressed that the machine was inherently classless. It healed the divide of the rich and the poor, and replaced it with another divide – the engineer versus the profiteer. Eventually, the engineers would dispense with the 'lieutanants of absentee ownership' and run the economy so that it would benefit all.

Veblen's criticism of the profiteering businessmen may seem extreme and out of place. However, it must be remembered that his criticism was part of a context in which some of the rail and steel barons of America were doing precisely what Veblen alleged. But, like others after him, Veblen underestimated the self-corrective nature of pragmatism and individual enterprise. All said and done, Veblen brought another dimension of Northern reasoning to American pragmatism, but his ideas remained foreign until the end.

The Teachings of Nikolai Grundtvig:
The Spirit of the People

Nikolai Grundtvig was born in Denmark in 1783 and became renowned in his life time as Scandinavia's cultural hero. He was bard, philosopher, priest and theologian, historian, politician and educationist. But it was as a Norse mythologist that Grundtvig found his greatest source of inspiration that he translated into a living philosophy. Today, the heritage of Grundtvig belongs to every group in Denmark: economic, religious, educational and commercial. Grundtvig's main contribution to the Nordic countries and Denmark in particular was the revitalization of Norse mythology with a view to oppose the elitism of Latin and that of the educated. His main thrust was always on free, living and popular education based not on books, but primarily on the living, spoken word in the native language. Later on, as a politician, he spoke out on behalf of the common man in general and the peasantry in particular. He left his mark on the economic restructuring of Danish agriculture at the end of nineteenth century and on the whole co-operative movement. 'Man is nothing in himself,' wrote Grundtvig, 'but encircled by and dependent on not just a visible world but on an invisible reality that ranges much wider.'

'The popular' was the central concept for Grundtvig, leading to two other concepts of 'spirit of the people' and 'Danishness'. Behind these terms lay the conviction that a nation is more than just a randomly composed group of people who live in the same place and are bound together by political, economic and social ties. Within the nation lies a mysterious and invisible power, the spirit of the people, which is the underlying unifying force. The spirit of the people expresses itself through the native language, the living language and the living word. Far removed from Veblen's use of the machine as a collective metaphor, the spirit of the people nevertheless pointed the way to another side of rationalism, which is ethics. Even today, this Danishness remains a highly effective shield against any external force that may disrupt its homogeneity. For unlike the individualistic West which invites diversity, the collective culture of the North abhors it. Its emphasis is not on personal growth but on collective security. A curious law called '*Jantelovn*', named after a Norwegian named Jante, spells out the ten Nordic commandments as follows:

1   You shall not believe that you are somebody.
2   You shall not believe that you are worth as much as **we** are.
3   You shall not believe you are more clever than **us**.
4   You shall not fool yourself by thinking that you are better than **us**.
5   You shall not believe that you know more than **us**.
6   You shall not believe that you are more than **us**.
7   You shall not believe that **you** are exceptional at anything.
8   You shall not laugh at **us**.
9   You shall not believe that anybody fancies **you**.
10 You shall not believe that you can teach **us** anything.

Although at worst, the *Jantelovn* can, and has, led to aspects of a common denominator society, it has mostly resulted in preserving the spirit of the people and that is its greatest success. In general, there are three tenets to Grundtvigian thought that are as follows:

1 **The Living Word**   The antithesis to knowledge acquired from theory and books. The living word is not taught but discovered in dialogue among equals.
2 **Learning for Life**   This was a criticism of the prevailing educational system that prepared the student for examinations but not for life. Education was essentially an ongoing process that continued for all of one's life.
3 **People's Enlightenment**   This was based on the conviction that each person was part of an collective, ethical system. The goal of any society, according to Grundtvig was – through far-sighted policies – to create the conditions that would facilitate people's enlightenment.

Grundtvig's opposition to any kind of domination was different from the French idea of liberal democracy that was adapted so readily in the more pragmatic cultures. Grundtvig, ever the ethical rationalist, insisted upon a mutual recognition that each instituition, each power centre could both teach and learn in a *dialogue* predicated on mutual respect. In fact, his emphasis on dialogue became legendary and has become the core component of the concept of the '*ethical organization*'. Oticon, one of Denmark's most succesful companies, and the subject of a case-study in chapter 15, is a curious synthesis of modern electronic technology and the living word. In an office where each employee is given a mobile desk, an electronic paper scanner, a personal computer and a mobile phone, sending in-house messages by means of memos or electronic mail are virtually forbidden. Communication involves walking to the person you wish to talk to and saying it in person. According to Grundtvig, it is dialogue that in the long run creates a society with widened social perspectives. The legendary Danish Folk High Schools that award neither diploma nor degree, but are fully supported by the government as vital, life-long Adult Learning Centres, are another instance of education through dialogue. The basis of Northern ethical rationalism is that learning occurs in dialogue between equals. In a truly egalitarian sense, peasant and professional still come together to these Folk High Schools to learn from one another in ethical dialogue.

Grundtvig's legacy has left behind the following ethical values that continue to permeate every aspect of Danish society and organization. They are:

1 Democracy and Egalitarianism
2 A Balanced Society
3 The Collective Spirit
4 Welfare and Social Responsibility.

It is precisely these four characteristics that have become the Danish and Scandinavian imprints of the ethical organization. From high standards of schooling to equal salaries and benefits for men and women, Denmark's ethical rationalism is obvious in all walks of life.

The Ethical Organization: Straddling the West and the East

The Northern manager is a genuinely ethical rationalist. Unlike his or her more individualistic Western counterpart, whose dictum is 'do well', the Northerner is motivated by a deep sense of 'doing right' and that of a collective good. A long history of successful co-operative movements and a welfare system that continues to work successfully has nurtured an ethical context for organizations. There are two aspects to the Northern organizational model. Firstly, the notion of forming co-operative alliances between different organizations is starkly prevalent in Denmark, Sweden and Norway. So, although the free market is very much a part of Danish economic and political reality, competetion does not apply to organizations in the same sense that it does in the Anglo-Saxon model of the UK and the USA. Rather, co-operative competition is what works best to preserve the spirit of the people and their organizations. Secondly, organizations see ethical responsibility as more important than responsibility to shareholders and the other parameters that define a classical Western company. It is therefore not surprising that the Northern world is now the global leader in the development of an articulated vision of an ethical organization.

The figure at the leading edge of developments in this area is Peter Pruzan of the Copenhagen Business School. Originally an American, but a Danish citizen by choice for the past 25 years, Pruzan is a systems scientist and an economist by profession. With Western roots in the USA and a passion for Eastern spirituality, Pruzan's home in the North serves as an apt interface in the creative tension between the two worlds. The tension between a 'demand for freedom' and a demand for wholeness' are one of the nine fields of ethical tension that Pruzan talks about. Writing in *The Corporate Soul*, Pruzan talks about the 'phoenix of ethics', an emergent ethical revolution which will bring social responsibility on to the centre stage of organizational management. 'In a world which is confused by its own dynamics, where institutions such as family, church, nation have come to be regarded by many as unreliable sources of stability, dignity and shared values, appeals are being made to "organizations" – to corporations, unions, institutions, local governments – to accept their responsibilities and to promote ethical behaviour.' Pruzan writes about the renaissance of social responsibility and ethics as a 'necessary supplement' to the classical quaternity of organizational management, namely economics, power, law and science. The emphasis is now increasingly turning away from shareholders to stakeholders; the employees, customers, suppliers, owners and local society who are beginning to demand that organizations begin thinking about their ethical responsibility and orient themselves towards a 'broader, value-based approach to management'.

Stakeholder Dialogue

Northern ethical rationality is a confluence of the ends and the means of doing business and managing organizations. While the ends mark out the genuine service organization, the means include both, a systematic, rational articulation of ethics and a deeply human-centred drive towards dialogue and consensus. As Pruzan writes in *Conflict and Consensus*, 'Verifying the social claims of business is not therefore simply a matter of checking up on what companies have been up to. It also opens up the possibility for intelligent dialogue about what types of social responsibility are possible in different structures and how best they can be achieved, evaluated and communicated.' 'Socially responsible business,' according to Pruzan, 'enables organizations to reflect upon their behavior, . . . to substantiate their claims, and to engage with diverse groups of people . . .' Pruzan introduces the term 'Open Systems Decision Making', which is defined as 'a practice that reflects the values, views, and contexts of the entire spectrum of contexts in which the organization co-exists with people, other living creatures and the natural environment.'

It was in the late 1980s that the notion of 'stakeholder dialogue' emerged in Denmark. This meant that values against which an organization should be evaluated were selected not by the organization, but by key stakeholder groups. This approach was systematically adopted by Peter Pruzan in his 'Ethical Accounting System' (EAS). Today more than 50 private and public Danish organizations have developed ethical accounting processes. This method was first used by the SBN bank of Denmark in 1989. Increasing numbers of companies are beginning to show an interest in the EAS, like the Body Shop or America's Ben and Jerry's, both of which have adopted this technique, with an exclusive focus on stakeholder views in their Social Performance Reports.

According to Pruzan, 'The interest in organizational ethics reflects both a search for new approaches to strategic planning as well as for shared values, which can provide a framework for constructively treating the complexity, specialization and pluralism which characterize the post-industrial society.' He maintains that traditional approaches to decision making provided by economics, science, technology, law and even formal democracy are not able to meet many of the challenges the organization faces today. 'A result is fragmented perspectives at the top management level, ad hoc and inconsistent decisions, inefficient use of resources, and conflicts both within the organization and between the organization and the outside world.'

Reaching far back into Danish cultral roots, Pruzan says, 'Development of ethical competence is the development of a common language and shared values, and an orientation towards wholeness–in short, a dialogue-based culture which promotes consensus.' The basic principle of ethics is that a decision is ethical if it rationally can be agreed upon by all those parties who will be affected by it. This leads to a reformulation of the Golden Northern Rule: 'Do only unto others what you and the others have agreed upon'. As the 1993 SBN Bank statement on ethical accounting mentions, 'Recent hard times have perhaps caused us – briefly are unconsciously – to tone down the basic values of the bank. It is therefore now that the concept of Value-Based Management must prove its worth.'

Ethics, according to Pruzan has two distinctive characteristics: in the first place, it is rational, and thereby open to dialogue; secondly, it is formalistic, the focus switching from the substantive content of moral rules to the form of interaction between subcultures of different rules. He lists five characteristics that form a prelude to the Ethical According System:

1 Prices are not enough
2 Science does not provide the truth, the whole truth and nothing but the truth
3 The search for technological effectiveness leads to inefficiency
4 What is legal may not be legitimate
5 The moral majority may be unethical.

The Ethical Accounting System (EAS)

The EAS focuses on values which are shared by the organization and its stakeholders: owners, employees, customers, suppliers, local society, environment, etc. These values are identified in conversations between representatives for the various parties and are operationalized by them in a series of postulates which can be measured on a scale from 'I totally agree' to 'I totally disagree'. The annual evaluation is performed by stakeholders, not by accountants hired by the company. This evaluation is summarized and presented in the EAS balance sheet, together with the organization's evaluation of its own endeavours to promote the values shared by the company and its stakeholders. 'One of the strengths of the EAS is that it enables us to quickly register changes in attitude among our customers, employees, shareholders and the local community,' reports Pruzan in *Conflict and Consensus*.

The EAS is distinguished from the conventional accounting system in three ways:

1 It not only employs monetary units of measure, but a spectrum of quantitative and qualitative values

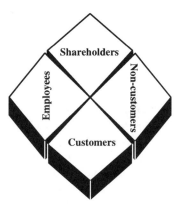

Figure 2.1

2   Instead of being simply a abstract communication, oriented towards the owners, it is value-based and oriented towards the various stakeholders

3   It is designed and produced by the stakeholders themselves.

The EAS of SBN Bank begins with the following passage written by Peter Pruzan and his colleague Ole Thyssen: 'Many people think of ethics as personal matters that really cannot be discussed. Others regard ethics as a checklist that can be used to determine right and wrong. We have a different perspective. The idea behind the concept (EAS) is that ethics are socially constructive and that they can and should be discussed. A discussion of ethics does not elicit any unambiguous answers, but rather initiates a process in which the parties involved, each with their own values, must determine what they can agree is right and wrong.' The SBN accounting statement is divided into four tightly woven worlds: customers, employees, shareholders and non-customers (figure 2.1).

For Pruzan, an organization is essentially an 'autopoetic social system' or a self-organizing system. An autopoetic system does not consist of elements but the elements get their distinctive characteristics in the autopoetic process itself. A company creates its own reality as a system of communications among its employees and other stakeholders. Unlike what the mechanical paradigm dictates, it is not built up of separate parts and cannot be separated and put together again. Therefore, it cannot be reduced to constituents. However detailed the description of the parts may be, it still cannot provide a full description of the organization as a whole. The more explicate level of the organization is all the separate people and artefacts, without whom there would be no organization. On a deeper, implicate level, the organization consists of the underlying communication field that co-ordinates the people and artefacts. 'Through its communication process, the enterprise defines itself and distinguishes itself from its environment,' explains Pruzan. An autopoetic social system depends on a shared language of an ethical culture. This again is a quality of the system, not of its members. The goals and strategies of an organization are then 'qualities which are inherent in the self-organization of the company as a whole'.

Outlining the Northern position that balances the Western and Eastern worlds, Pruzan writes: 'We stand on the threshold of a new society, beyond both the Eastern and the Western models. The value which has received the highest priority in the East, consideration of the whole, must be reconciled with the major value espoused by the West, consideration of the individual . . . (an ethical) enterprise can escape from its self-imposed isolation and actively integrate itself in the new society.'

Bibliography

Heilbroner, Robert (1961) *The Worldly Philosophers*. New York: Simon and Schuster.

Thodberg, C. and Thyssen, A. (eds) (1993) *N.F.S. Grundtvig – Tradition and Renewal*. The Danish Institute.

Borish, Steven (1993) *The Land of the Living*. Denmark: Blue Dolphin.

Pruzan, P. (1995) 'The Ethical Accounting System', *World Business Academy Perspectives*.

Pruzan, P. and Thyssen, O. (1990) 'Conflict and Consensus: Ethics as a Shared Value Horizon for Strategic Planning', *Human Systems Management*, Vol. 9, No. 3, pp. 135–51.

Zadek, S., Pruzan, P. and Evans, R. (1997) *Building Corporate Accountability: the emerging practice of social and ethical accounting, auditing and reporting*. London: Earthscan.

3

The Creative Spirit

Introduction

We now leave the relatively familiar worlds of the West and the North and journey to the East. As we said before, this is the archetypal world of the 'non-entity' organization. As we shall see in this chapter, there is a fundamental complementarity between the West and the East; the archetypes of 'identity' and 'non-entity' have the same complementarity as the archetypal interplay of matter and spirit, of presence and absence or of day and night. While the West continually seeks to affirm, the East seeks to dissolve; while the Western archetype is about outwardly directed movement, the Eastern one is inwardly directed. While Western knowledge is masculine in character, because of its complete dependency on abstraction and logical consistency, Eastern knowledge is fundamentally feminine because of its intrinsic lack of division and categories. It is in the dialectical interplay between the two (as between the North and South) that the centre of the four worlds lies.

The Emergence of Spirit

The electronic age has done more to revolutionize the business world than anything in history. Modems, electronic nets, fax machines and state-of-the-art technology have ushered in an age of electronic globality. Like fine blood capillaries, the information network has woven the world into a unitary whole, and the business organization into an amorphous global network. Managing an enterprise that silently reaches out of the confines of closed space, single time-zones, job routines, concepts of nations and cultures and the simple rules of manufacturing and selling, has reached staggering dimensions of complexity. But despite the growing amorphousness of the modern world and an emergent globality based on scientific insights, technological development and a borderless market economy, we still remain parochial in our fragmentary mind-sets.

In this climate of overwhelming turbulence, managers are beginning to discover that fragmentary thinking and the old mental models of managing organizations are not only unfeasible, they are downright dangerous. Developments in science and technology show us that information is not triggered by a material impact; in Gregory Bateson's famous formulation, it is triggered by an event of consciousness and not an impact of matter. The view that follows from this is that our world and, more importantly, our electronic business reality, is not made of stuff, but of patterns. Like the pathways of the human mind that extend outside the brain, the pathways created by electronic technology extend the business organization outside its mechanical context, into non-material processes.

The emergence of abstract thought as a critical point of evolution was intimately bound up in the emergence of the alphabet for the Phoenicians and the Greeks. Today, the emergence of spirit, made aware by electronics and computers, and a new emergent globality, is bound up in the emergence of the hypertext. Old ways of perceiving business and organizations are fast becoming obsolete in a world that has gone beyond the premise of matter as the ultimate building block into extended neural pathways. Interestingly, as we in the Western and the Northern quadrants of the world move into electronic and quantum-mechanical hyper-space, we find ourselves returning to the world of *spirit* and the notion of *holism* which is so central to the cultures of the East and the South.

The Eastern Archetype

The cultural archetype of the East spreads across the Indian sub-continent, a spectral curve over China into Japan, Korea, Taiwan and the other East Asian cultures. While there are relative differences that occur in varying degrees over the curve, the fundamental archetype remains the same.

The dominant characteristic of this Eastern archetype is its tendency to grasp reality in its 'suchness' or 'isness' – which implies, in its totality. This is in complete contrast to the Western and Northern mind which favours a descriptive or abstractive meaning over what in the East is called the 'true nature of things'. And so while the Western and the Northern mind abhors paradoxes, contradictions and emptiness, and attempt to flatten out apparent discontinuities in the search for unity, to the East they represent reality as it is. This tendency – not to 'abstract' (move away from) – grows sharper as we move more Eastwards until by the time we reach Japan there is a very clear absence of abstract thinking. Charles Moore quotes Hideki Yukawa, the Nobel laureate

Japanese physicist as saying: 'The Japanese mentality is, in most cases, unfit for abstract thinking. This is the origin of the Japanese excellence in technical art . . .'

In general, although in the East there have traditionally existed systematic philosophies and logical systems of the '*Nyaya*' logicians and grammarians in India and of the Mohist logicians in China, these rationalistically oriented movements in alternative Asian cultures are analogous to the counter-culture movements in mainstream Western tradition. The fact is that these do not occupy the centre stage in the Eastern philosophical and spiritual theatre which has the tendency to prefer the totality of things and processes. In other words, 'multiple perspectives' gain precedence over 'agreements' and 'formula'.

Scientific and Aesthetic Construction

To use a distinction made well-known by David Hall, the Eastern archetype fundamentally promotes an 'aesthetic' rather than a 'scientific' sense of coherence. To illustrate the use of the term 'aesthetic' here, we can contrast two organizations of people. For one of these organizations, if the overall conduct of its people is decided by an appeal to a pre-assigned pattern that categorizes all relationships within the organization, and if everyone conforms to the pattern faithfully, it is a scientific construction. On the other hand, if the people interact freely and without any obligation to any pre-assigned principle, and if the organization then emerges out of the uniqueness of its employees as particulars, it is an aesthetic composition. Quite clearly, while the scientific construction belongs to the Western and the Northern world, the home ground of the aesthetic construction is the East and the South.

This means that, in the absence of a rational system which 'organizes' experience, the Eastern archetype has typically sought analogical similarities rather than identities among particulars. Since for all the major Eastern traditions, order is not reducible beyond a discernible harmony between the unique particulars, there is a significant resistance to abstract notions that are dependent upon the assumption of a universalizing principle. This, by way of contrast, is precisely the characteristic that unifies the Western and Northern traditions. If you remember, both in the world of 'agreement' and that of 'formula', the underpinning principle was that universals were the best indicators of absolute truth. This meant that there was one way of doing things, whether taking decisions, managing organizations or developing new products. Eastern organizations thrive on multiple realities and have multiple perspectives on managing them. What applies today need not apply tomorrow as all reality – you and the organization included – is flux. Therefore, what makes things clear in the distinctly Eastern mode of thinking is often an effectively focused image, not a theory or even a concept; an inexpressible and inimitable experience, not an argument; an evocative metaphor, not a logically demonstrated truth. Let us first look at the scientific contruction of the West and the North and then compare it with the aesthetic one.

Scientific construction

- The starting point for a scientific construction is always a *pre-assigned* pattern of relatedness, a 'blueprint' in which unity is given sanction over plurality. All functions in the organization are *categorized* and assigned on the basis of this blueprint. A company becomes a scientific construction when it has been based on, and is managed in the context of, the assumption that the totality of the company is the sum of its parts, and that it is possible to accurately *predict* the totality, once having ascertained the parts.
- Secondly, the concrete particularity of any product is registered only to the extent that it satisfies this pre-assigned pattern. Since the pattern is assumed to be fixed and unchanging, it is possible to maintain the uniqueness of any product within this pattern. It is further possible to maintain *control* over such unique particulars through a *hierarchical* decision-making structure, so that product-feasibility and quality is always maintained and controlled.
- Scientific construction necessarily involves a process of formal *abstraction*, which means moving from the particular to the universal. *Standardization* is a direct consequence of the abstractive quality of such a construction. This helps maintain strict controls on quality.
- Scientific construction constitutes an act of 'closure', that is the satisfaction of predetermined *specifications*, and is hence describable in *quantitative* terms. The company is perceived as either a static entity or a dynamic place with a strong identity. Subjectivity is perceived as being cumbersome and qualitative characteristics are seen as being needlessly controversial, sometimes producing paradoxical results, which undermine the very basis of the scientific organization.
- Creativity is achieved through *conformity* to successful product-lines and not through novelty. In fact, novelty is sacrificed under the assumption that the high level of control and standardization that steps up production and makes the process more financially viable, more than compensates for lack of novelty.
- The rightness of actions within the organization and of management decisions are gauged by the degree of conformity to the pre-assigned pattern. Other external inputs of information that are based on qualitative feedback from customers and stakeholders are often seen as secondary. As long as the pre-assigned pattern is reinforced and the *forecasting* proven to be more or less *accurate*, the objective of the company is assumed to have been satisfactorily met.
- It is the functions that the employees carry out which decide their

relationship to the scientific organization and to each other within the organization. This automatically renders the form of the scientific organization more important than the people who are part of it. Loyalty to the shareholder gains precedence over loyalty to the larger community.

- The employee–company relationship is clearly defined and articulated in very clear rational terms, based on the functional competence of the individual and not the 'true self' of the person. As a consequence, the scientific organization favours the expert-for-the-job syndrome, with clearly demarcated tasks.
- At its best, a scientific organization is attuned to a dynamic *role* culture, which is heavily structured hierarchical and where management style is necessarily channelled through an elaborate formal, legalistic and even bureaucratic machinery. At its worst, it is an *automatist* culture in which management style is channelled through a manipulative political structure.
- Finally, the characteristics that mark a scientific construction are: (1) efficiency, (2) consistency, (3) predictability, (4) reducibility to smaller units.

Aesthetic construction

- The aesthetic construction begins with the *uniqueness* of the one particular as it collaborates with other particulars in an emergent complex pattern of *relatedness*. Plurality is perceived to be primary to unity and disjunction is seen as being prior to conjunction. Functions evolve out of the *unfolding* of the pattern. A company can be said to have an aesthetic construction if it is based upon, and managed within, the context that the totality of the company is an *organic whole* containing all the various related particulars enfolded in it.
- It takes the concrete particularity of the product and a specific detail as its focus, whose unique perspective then reveals an order in which this detail is in *harmony* with many others. Since the pattern of the company evolves out of the relationship between unique particulars, managing an aesthetic company involves loosening up on the control systems, and instead maintaining a *flexible* environment in which the relationships can best arise.
- Aesthetic construction necessarily involves moving away from any universal characteristic to the concrete detail. This follows from above. There is a sacrifice on standardization, but greater flexibility is encouraged in the areas of design and processing.
- In contrast to the closure of a scientific construction, the aesthetic construction constitutes an act of 'disclosure' – the achieved *co-ordination* of concrete details in novel patterns that reflect their uniqueness – and hence is describable *qualitatively*. As a result, subjective judgement is favoured and is in fact

at a premium. Another aspect of the disclosure is that the boundaries, both within the company and those that delineate it from the outer environment, become highly *ambiguous*.

- The aesthetic construction is fundamentally *non-conformist* and *contingent*. These are seen as the precursors to creativity. Being so, it is able to quickly adapt to *non-linear* processes, although its lack of structure and control systems can sometimes cause difficulties in managing the routine, linear processes.

- Rightness of management procedures and decisions is gauged by the degree to which the tension between the particularity and the consequent unity of details is self-evidently expressive.

- The effectiveness of the aesthetic organization depends on personal relationships and a social networking order, thereby relying on how well the employees can work together. In contrast to the scientific organization, the aesthetic organization is sometimes indistinguishable from the people who constitute it.

- At its best, it yields a *support* and *participative* culture where management style is channelled through sequences of networks, akin to the ecological networks in nature. At its worst, it can eventually degenerate into an *autocratic* culture, which could include wild subjective whims of individuals in power, unpredictable decision-making processes, and personalized anarchic structures.

- Finally, the characteristics of an aesthetic construction are: (1) effectiveness, (2) emergence, (3) unpredictability, (4) wholeness.

We can briefly summarize the essential differences between the scientific and the aesthetic modes *vis-à-vis* the organizational form and management styles:

Scientific Organization	Aesthetic Organization
Organizational Form	
1 Hierarchical/focused	Lateral/diffused
2 Pre-formulated pattern particular	Uniqueness of the particular
3 Rationally predetermined procedures	Emergent procedures
4 Precise goals	Flexible goals
5 Highly quantitative	Highly qualitative
6 Rules have to be followed	Rules may be bent
7 Clear-cut roles	Diffused/fuzzy roles
Management Style	
1 Clear accountability	Fuzzy accountability
2 Authority based on competence	Authority based on trust

3	Decisions emerge from empirical/rational basis	Decisions based on judgement
4	Highly objective	Highly subjective
5	Formal communication channels	Informal channels/word of mouth
6	Management based on competence/control	Based on inspiration
7	Tendency towards formal relationships	Tendency to informal relationships

Having outlined the differences that characterize the Eastern, 'non-entity' organization, it must be mentioned that these categories are hardly in strict either/or terms. Rather, most organizations seem to have a blend of both, with one or the other form predominating. For instance, the real strength of Japanese management lies in its rootedness in the emergent aesthetic form, but it also incorportates strongly pragamatic structures. On the other hand, Western organizations are just moving into the realm of such genuinely cross-cultural management. Eastern organizations seen more able to journey to the West; movement in the opposite direction seems more difficult. At least, until now.

From Physics to Psycho-Physics

Having established the fundamental differences between the two morphologies in terms of their respective scientific and aesthetic organizational forms, we now proceed to dig deeper into the Eastern archetype. As we shall see later, the crucial difference between the East and the West/North is the generic principle of *relationality*. Unlike in the scientific organizations which depend on physical metaphors, the Eastern organization is essentially 'psycho–physical', a term coined by Jung based on his studies of Eastern cultures. Such a structure is characterized by Joseph Needham as: '. . . spontaneous yet ordered, in the sense of patterned movements of dancers . . . none of whom are bound by law to do what they do, nor yet pushed by others coming behind, but cooperate in a voluntary harmony of wills.' Such a 'harmonic' organization is comprised of dynamic energy fields rather than static material entities whose basic stuff is neither solely psychological nor material, but an interplay of both. This is best expressed by *ch'i* in ancient Taoism, an infinite field of energy that links everything together. The chain of being is thus never broken. The continuous presence of the psycho-physical principle makes everything flow together as in the unfolding of a single process. To quote Chang Tsai: 'Ch'i moves and flows in all directions and in all manners. Its two elements, yin and yang, unite and give rise to the concrete. Thus the multiplicity of things is produced.' What are conceived as opposites in the rational and pragmatic modes are inseparable polarities in the holistic mode.

Managing an organization, from the psycho-physical perspective involves, in essence, a mastery of the *ch'i*. In fact, it is not so much a mastery over people or over processes that is seen as important, as over oneself. The very concept of 'control over' becomes redundant when a manager realizes that the 'multiplicity' of things (products, processes, people) are the unfolding of the same *ch'i* that also runs through him or her. Management turns into an art of balancing one's own *ch'i* with that of the organization. The sixty-sixth verse of the *Tao Te Ching* embodies this principle – substitute sage for the manager and you have:

> Why is the sea, king of a hundred streams?
> Because it lies below them.
> Therefore it is the king of a hundred streams.
> If the sage would guide the people, he must serve with humility.
> If he would lead them, he must follow behind.
> In this way when the sage rules, the people will not feel oppressed;
> When he stands before them, they will not be harmed.
> The whole world will support him and will not tire of him.
> Because he does not compete,
> He does not meet competition.

The manager's all pervasive psycho-physical context is thus able to dissolve the hard delineating boundaries that characterize Western and Northern organizations. Whereas the latter two focus primarily on the individual entity and its identity, the psycho-physical mode is based on a relationality that emerges out of there being neither entity nor identity. If the basic force flows through everything, then from a holographic point of view, each element contains the totality. Moreover, since the totality of the organization is a characteristic of the relationship between the inner spiritual world and the outer material world, the manager-sage attempts to embody this totality in his or her actions. In Buddhism, this is sharply characterized by the clear absence of separate identities. In fact, the dictum is that the essence (*svabhava*) of an entity lies in its relationality to all the other entities. *The Jewel net of Indra*, which illustrates this phenomenon, speaks of a wonderful net which has been hung in such a manner that it extends infinitely in all directions. In each knot of the net, there hangs a jewel and, since the net is infinite, the jewels are infinite in number too. The holographic character of this metaphor lies in the fact that in the polished surface of each of these jewels is reflected all the other ones. Finally, each of the jewels reflected in this one jewel also reflects all the other jewels in an infinitely recurring process.

It is as if a particular product, in itself, would not only reflect all the other company products, but also its very structure and systems, its core values and its philosophy. This is the basis of the Buddhist idea of *Sunyata* or emptiness, whereby, things are empty in that they lack an individuated self-essence. Their essence is only derived from their relatioship with and dependence upon the other. Since existence is an unbroken continuum and since every little bit is part of the flux, the bit cannot be understood in terms of its own nature outside of the wholeness of flow. In organizational terms, this whole is not to be mistaken for the pre-assigned pattern that characterizes scientific organizations. Rather it is the complex pattern that evolves out of the symbiosis between the part and the whole. If each part is not just a part, but has enfolded within itself the totality of the organization, the very basis of management goes through a radical shift in perspective. Is the conveyor belt worker, who adds another bolt to the fender of an unfinished car, in effect simultaneously working on the total car, and hence the totality of the company? Yes, would be the answer from an Eastern perspective. No, from a Western and Northern perspective. Rather than conceptualize the term 'empowerment' into a set of norms and policies, the Eastern approach is to transform the very context in which empowerment 'happens'. In an atmosphere where, a worker believes that he or she is participating in the wholeness of the company, empowerment has happened. Of course, for this to happen, everyone must be willing to be a non-entity because, paradoxically enough, only then does everyone have an identity! The manager who allows the empowering of the worker through his or her own 'non-entityness', is empowering the company and, as a consequence, is empowering him or herself as he or she is no different from the organization. That is Eastern organization in a nutshell!

As the *Tao Te Ching* says in its sixty-eighth verse:

> A good soldier is not violent.
> A good fighter is not angry.
> A good winner is not vengeful.
> A good employer is humble.
>
> This is known as the Virtue of not striving.
> This is known as the ability to deal with people.
> This since ancient times has been known
> As the ultimate unity with heaven.

Creative Management

According to the Taoist, each and every articular element in the organization has its own *te* but is also a principle of integration. On the one hand, water at rest is placid and plane enough to serve as a measuring gauge. On the other, it is fluid and totally indeterminate. When a vortex forms in flowing water, it is a manifestation of the same basic 'water-stuff'. Placidity and dynamic movement are but two interdependent parts of a whole.

The *manager-sage* knows, then, that his or her sense of self-ego or identity is nothing but the sensation of being only a 'part'. The individual's *te* expands to become coincident with the *te* of the company. As the *Tao Te Ching* states:

> The person of *te* takes charge of the tally;
> The person without it looks after collection.

This is perhaps the most fundamental characteristic of the harmonic, Eastern manager. By becoming co-extensive with the 'other', be it a product, a function or simply, a group of people, the manager of *te* is able to become extraordinary. The absence of a disintegrating ego makes him or her open to the *te* of his or her whole natural environment, so that the environment contributes to the manager, making him or her vital and productive. Such a manager, in turn, contributes to the environment, strengthening, enhancing and helping it to flow in its natural direction. The manager extends his or her self to become co-extensive with the natural way of things, and becomes a 'transformer' of things. Like the skilled potter whose hands express the clay and the clay expresses his hands, the manager of *te* transforms something other than him or herself and simultaneously, becomes part of the whole that is self-transforming.

This is the *Karma Yogi* in the Vedantic philosophy of India, the person who is able to work without attachment to the result of the work. Working solely for the purpose of end goals such as larger profits or better quality is self-defeating because the goal is always illusory, a theory or an abstraction. Having realized the interconnectedness of the world, the *karma-yogic* manager is able to detach him or herself from the demands of results and fruits of action that ego makes, and is consequently able to create with skill. As the *Tao Te Ching* says: 'Practice not-doing and everything will fall into place.' This is the quality of 'non-action'. The Sufi poet Rumi praises the connection between work and nothingness when he points out that, in our natural state, we seek out what needs working: or, we work at what needs work. He says:

> . . . every craftsman
> searches for what is not there
> to practice his craft.

> A builder looks for the rotten hole
> where the roof caved in. A water-carrier
> picks the empty pot. A carpenter
> stops at the house with no door.

> . . . if you were not friends
> with the vast nothing inside,
> why would you always be casting your net
> into it, and waiting so patiently?

For, paradoxically, only when the other is seen as 'valueless' (from the egoistic perspective) can it be made valuable in creative management. As the Indian epic poem *Bhagvad Gita* states:

He who sees inaction in action and action in inaction, he is wise among men,
he does all action harmoniously.

The *Karma Yogi*, the *Gita* insists, must understand the nature of both, the other
and the knower of the other. This mutuality of the totality and the particular,
the market and the product, the *tao* and the *te* is further elaborated in *Chuang
Tzu*.

> Now were you, in charioting *tao* and *te*, to go drifting and wandering, it
>   would not be so.
> Without praises or curses,
> Now a dragon, now a snake,
> You transform together with the times.
> And not willing to act unilaterally,
> Now above, now below,
> You take harmony as your measure.

The main emphasis is on the interplay – the fluidity among particular perspectives – 'now a dragon, now a snake'. The particular product or process is always
in the process of being reworked in the process of change. True to form, the
ultimate measure of the aesthetic order is harmony. The manager who 'knows'
when to cross over from playing the dragon to the snake is the one who knows
the value of 'appropriate action'. Unlike in rational action, there is no manual
that predetermines when the cross-over takes place. No amount of prior case
studies or previous benchmarks can prepare one for appropriate action. It is in
the nature of the aesthetic order of things for each action to be particular because
each case is itself so. The premise is psycho-physical, not physical, and therefore
unpredictable. What one can establish is the background necessary for appropriate action. After that it is a matter of relying on the creative moment that arises
from the depths of intuition. Such action, whether it be the '*karma yogic*' action
of the Vedanta, the 'action from emptiness' of Japanese Buddhism or '*wu-wei*' of
China, is irrepressibly participative and creative. David Hall elaborates on the
difference between such activity and the 'power-over' activity that generally
characterizes the world of action. 'Whereas power (over) often suggests the
correlative concepts of domination and control, "creativity" is a notion that can
be characterized only in terms of self-actualization. Unlike power relationships
that require that tensions among component elements be resolved in favor of one
of the components, in relations defined by creativity, there is no otherness, no
separation or distancing, nothing to overcome . . . creativity . . . requires that
each element of a relationship be continually in the state of creating the other.'

There is simply no pure creativity ('*wu*'), without a specific context, and vice
versa. There is nothing that is not subject to creative transformation. It must be
remembered that creativity in the Eastern context is coincident with an aesthetic
composition. There is no absolute ideal and no self-contained perfection. The
process of ongoing creative activity, in itself, keeps opening up possibilities for

further creativity. In this mode, there is no standardized structure that might provide a 'scientific' assessment of what is 'correct' and what is not. From Mair's book of 1983, we learn: 'People who really know what they are doing, such as crooks, boatmen, cicada catchers, whose intention is always available to any philosopher or emperor who has the sense to listen to them, do not go in much for analyzing, posing alternatives, and reasoning from first principles. They no longer bear in mind any rules that they are taught as apprentices. They attend to the total situation and respond, trusting to a knack which they cannot explain in words, the hand moving of itself as the eye gazes with unflagging concentration . . . The Taoist ideal is a spontaneity disciplined by an awareness of the objective. Let us say then that "Follow the Way" is translatable as "Respond with awareness." The awareness will be not only of the mirrored situation, but of how as a matter objective fact, things can be done, knowing how, knack, skill, art.'

Conclusion

'Respond with awareness'. This seems to be the Eastern management 'mantra'. Finally, the *Tao Te Ching* has this recipe for managing creatively, in its sixty-seventh verse:

. . . I have three treasures which I hold and keep.
The first is mercy; the second is economy;
The third is daring not to be ahead of others.
From mercy comes courage; from economy comes generosity;
From humility comes leadership.
But men shun mercy and try to be brave;
They abandon economy, but try to be generous;
They do not believe in humility, but always try to be first.
This is certain death.
Compassion brings victory in battle and strength in defense.
It is the means by which heaven saves and guards.

Bibliography

Bateson, Gregory (1973) *Steps to an Ecology of Mind*. London: Paladin.
Moore, Charles (ed.) (1967) *The Japanese Mind: Essentials of Japanese Philosophy and Culture*. University of Hawaii Press.
Hall, David (1987) *Thinking through Confucius*. New York: State University of New York Press.

Needham, Joseph and Ling, Wang (1969) *Science and Civilization in China*, Vol. 2. Cambridge University Press.

Tsai, Chang (1969) 'Correcting Youthful Ignorance', published in Wing-tsit Chan (ed.), *Source Book of Chinese Philosophy*. Princeton, NJ: Princeton University Press.

Lao Tsu (trans. Stephen Mitchell) (1988) *Tao Te Ching*. New York: Harper & Row.

Rumi, J. (trans. Coleman Barks) (1991) *One-handed Basket Weaving*. Athens, GA: Maypop.

Hall, David (1982) *The Uncertain Phoenix: Adventures Towards a Post-Cultural Sensibility*. New York: Fordham University Press.

Mair, Viktor (ed.) (1983) *Taoist Spontaneity in the Dichotomy of 'Is' and 'Ought': Experimental Essays in Chuang-tzu*. University of Hawaii Press.

4

Communal Roots

Introduction

From the creative spirit of the Eastern 'non-entity' organization, we now turn to the deeply elemental roots of the Southern organization. From a Southern perspective, the *vital forces* of the community create the ground for individual existence. It is for this reason that the Bantus of Africa understand the word 'force' without ascribing any attributes to it. For them, 'Being is Force', in its very essence, the two terms being perfectly mutual and interchangeable. Moreover, force is perceived as a value. Not surprisingly, in the language system of the Bantus of Africa, there is a conspicuous absence of attributes. A Bantu directs all of his or her efforts towards increasing the 'vital force'. All the forces of the universe have a mutual influence on each other: 'The world of forces is like a spider's web of which not one thread can be disturbed without shaking all the meshes.' This chapter outlines why the notion of force and energy forms the philosophical basis of the Southern world. As an illustrative example we have chosen the *Ifa* belief system from Africa which gives a vivid depiction of this energy system.

The Southern Notion of Oneness

In general, the Southern mode is primarily based on an ontology of 'oneness'. It is a clear nature-focused tradition, and the quest begins with an emphasis on discovering reality through a spiritual and physical networking relationship with the natural environment. The Southern world, although diverse and marked by differences, is bound by universally common symbols that suggest an underlying cultural and philosophical unity. Like the tree, the roots of Southern culture go deep into the body and blood of the land.

Not unlike the Eastern perspective, a society of people or an organization is perceived to be a complex chain of events. What you do influences the whole, and the whole, in turn, influences your actions. The only meaningful way to live in a community or manage the organization you are in is to strategically increase the 'vital force'. This involves a total involvement of the person with the organization. Increasing the vital force involves spirit, body, mind and relationships. Strategy then, is not so much a matter of rational planning and forecasting, but bringing oneself into resonance with the chain of events.

Time, especially the link between the past and the present, acquires a very different significance in the South. In the West and the North, the past is important too because, after all, knowledge is perceived to be a cumulative process. If we see farther than others, to paraphrase others, it is because we have the advantage of learning from the errors of the past. In the East, the past is seen as an impediment to innovation and the emphasis is on being in the here-and-now. In the South, the past is a living force functioning through a spirit-medium. The spirits of our ancestors are always with us and can be consulted in order to guide us to the future. As a result, the Southern view of an organization is cyclical and not linear. It is a product of past forces that have shaped it and now have become part of the larger totality. Thus, cultural ancestry of the place is of value to the vital force of the organization. Moreover, since the organizational cycle also runs into the future, managing the organization involves sustainability and a sense of vision.

The organization also has a sacral basis. It is experienced as personal and, therefore, must be approached in a personal manner. The personal nature of the organization demands that each and every person in the organization seek and sustain personal relationships. Moreover, each relationship has a moral content, and since the organization itself is an open system, the radius of involvement is necessarily global and all-encompassing. Managing it from this perspective is to empower oneself and the others.

Vital Force and Transformation:
The Native Perspective

In Southern thinking, the universe consists of a network of living forces. Man and woman, dog and stone, societies and organizations, beauty and laughter – all these are forces related to each other and in continuous interaction. The universe is a unity. If you take possession of part of a thing, you thereby participate in its life force. If you tear a leaf from a tree, not only does the tree quiver, but the whole universe is affected, since nothing stands alone. While in Western and

Northern terminologies, an organization may 'have' force, the native perspective maintains that the organization is force itself. To be part of an organization is therefore to partake in its potency. It has to be nurtured, sustained and perceived as being one with one's own force. From the native perspective, managing an organization is the singular act of finding the right attitude. That is both the means and the end. Discovering attitude is to find rhythm, which has the task of properly ordering everything. Rhythm is the architecture of being, the purest expression of force and the ground of every activity.

In organizational terms, the Southern manager can either 'increase' the vital force by managing the organization in the spirit of the community or decreases it by doing the opposite. He or she must never forget that like all else, the organization is cyclical. It is a product of past forces that have shaped it and now have become part of the larger totality. For these reasons, the Southern mode is fundamentally transformative. The purpose of rhythm is force itself and to apply it is to transform what you are doing from being an act of triviality to one of vitality. That is the reason why in African poetry, a poem is not considered complete if it is not accompanied by at least one percussion instrument. Meaning is achieved not by climax, which is usually the case in the linear Mentational mode, but through repetition, whereby the multiplicity of recurrent rhythmic tensions transform the word by infusing it with power. The poem, when it is sung and danced to the beating of a drum, is then not just a string of words, but a centre of power. Once again, its transformative intensity emerges from attitude.

From the Southern perspective, the purpose of management is to transform organizations at the grass-roots level. Like the limbic nervous system that grounds our faculties of thinking, sensing and Intuiting, the elemental power of an organization runs through its nervous network, co-ordinating all the other functions and activities. As a result, this mode is connected to setting up a humanistic, communal network of forces in the organization that transforms it into a centre of power. The function of the manager becomes one of being a crucial, affective link to the vital force. This force is the proof of legitimacy of any community or organization.

Managing Sustainably

Basic to the fourth world of the South is the notion of sustainability. This is the key concept through which the structural features of organizing people, land and societies are worked through. This was the basis of the concept of the Sun-God and the deities of Osiris, Isis and Horus in ancient Egypt, the notion of matriarchy and motherhood in Africa and that of relatedness in the native American Indian cultures. Nature and every element that emerges from this mode is associated with preserving the life force that runs through Nature's myriad forms. That is why it is significant that the elemental ideas in Africa and in the other Southern parts of our world came to be concerned with issues of land management, agriculture and the central notion of sustainability.

In the turbulence that is around, one of the critical arenas in which change is both imperative and ongoing, is precisely that of our relationship to nature. The dominant belief that nature exists only for the use of humankind has reached its limits and any further, indiscriminate use of it can only lead to an environmental and human crisis. Developing a sustainable and ecological model for economics, technology and business is not only imperative, but unavoidable. With the concept of *Gaia*, James Lovelock was able to give an ancient 'elementational' notion of the Earth as a living organism, a scientific basis. The roots of Gaia reach deep into the Southern axis that once linked Greece to Africa.

> The earth is a goddess and she teaches justice to those who can learn, for the better she is served, the more good she gives in return.

Xenophon's words echo the elemental link to the Earth and the very roots of our Southern heritage.

A Southern Cosmology: The Forces of Energy

To illustrate what we have so far attributed to the Southern world, we take the example of the *Ifa* belief system of the Yoruba peoples of Nigeria, drawing on the work of Philip Niemark. *Orisa* are energy forces that, for the most part, represent the different aspects of nature, for the Ifa people. In their world view, we are not merely human, but we are simultaneously all other things both, living and non-living. We are also the rock, the lion, the tree, the sky and the ocean. Similar to the concept of *ch'i* in the East and to the unifying principle of modern ecology, traditional African cosmology is closely in line with James Lovelock's contemporary planetary outlook on Gaia, whereby organic and so-called inorganic organisms are all alive together. Through engagment with the energy forces of Orisa, then, we can each take our own small quantity of the energies that prevail within us and combine them with the concomitant energies in nature. *Ifa* also teaches that each of us has a single Orisa energy from the universe that predominates. Niemark calls this our 'Guardian Orisa'. Learning to be comfortable with attributes, and to tap into them in a meaningful way, is an important step towards successfully travelling the paths we are meant to take. The sources of energy and power that drive the community spirit in the South, be it of an individual or an enterprise don't just belong to the present. They reside most importantly in the spirit of our ancestors.

The Nature of Spirit

Ancestor worship, according to Niemark, is a formalized structure for connecting the knowledge, wisdom, and power accumulated from our deceased blood relatives. It is not simply RNA or DNA, therefore, that links us to our past; it is an infinite road to energy and power. In fact the American management consultant, Harrison Owen, has identified such a road as representing the 'spirit', or mythos, of ourselves as well as our organizations. In that respect we might conceive of our organizations as sources of collective energy and power that draw upon their founding fathers and mothers, both dead and alive.

Unlike other cosmologies, such as astrology, i ching or tarot, *Ifa* divination tells us what is likely to happen if we do nothing to change our circumstances. The *Ifa* belief system, therefore, functions on the basic principle that our spiritual and worldly sides are not separate and competing entities. It believes that in order for either to succeed they must work together. We are neither born with sin nor born with guilt. Our only inherent obligation is to make the most of our potential. In *Ifa*, it does not matter what you choose to do, what matters is how you do it. If you do it well, in harmony with the universe, and in conjunction with your destiny, you will learn and grow along the way. It rejects a dichotomy of mind and spirit and embraces the concept that the linear and non-linear, practical and spiritual, analytical and emotional components of our being are neither separate nor antithetical. They are partners supporting the joyous process of living a full and wise life in harmony with the universe.

Ifa's world view, in other words, can be thought of as the spiritual representation of Einstein's theory of relativity. Its belief in, and practice of, ancestor worship bridges the time gap that Einstein believed must exist between the past, present and future. *Ifa* understands that the invisible world of deceased ancestors combines with the visible world of nature and human culture to form a single organic truth. Ancestor worship thereby provides you with the knowledge that life is a continuum. For it enables you to actually communicate with the energy of your departed family members – personal or corporate – and to feel the profound feelings that that engenders.

Death, sacrifice and rebirth

Ifa understands that you cannot be truly alive unless and until you understand death. And animal sacrifice is part of that understanding. In the intricate structure of rebirth, then, we visit Earth for specific growth and learning experiences, and when they have been achieved, we return 'home'. To leave before we have attained that particular wisdom and knowledge is disruptive. The teachings of *Ifa* believe in rebirth within the family. Through ancestor worship we can access or take advantage of the accumulated family wisdom that has been given us since conception. Through the act of creating children and the cycle of rebirth we – individually or corporately – continue the process, we increase the knowledge, and provide for the continuation of the flow for the 'crowning' of the next generation, or product line.

Destiny

In the Yoruba cosmology, then, the universe contains all possibilities, both good and bad. Individuals and organizations, therefore, have the opportunity to control their own destinies by working with natural forces. The failure to control one's own destiny is thus seen as an act of gross ignorance or stupidity with potential dire consequences. To those who work with and not against the natural order of the universe, who 'sacrifice' in both the literal and the philosophical meaning of the word, the potential is unlimited and the rewards beyond comprehension. The individual 'crowns his head', or makes their own 'natural' way.

The Way of the Orisa

The *Ifa* devotee is therefore constantly striving to open his or her own channels of all of the 401 *Orisa*, or energies, available. This is not a process that can be achieved only through understanding, it also requires the practising of ritual. Words and explanations can take us to the door, but if we are to enter, experience, and benefit from the vast reservoir of energy that is available to us, such literary devices must be transcended. Rather than suppressing or trying to modulate our emotions, moreover, we learn from *Ifa* that it is essential to feel intently. For it is these feelings which ignite and allow the non-linear side of our brain to perform its powerful functions. In harnessing our feeling capacities, moreover, seven of the Orisa, or channels of energy, are of primary importance. We start with the most powerful, namely 'Ori', or 'Oludmare'.

Ori – developing vision

The head of a company or organization, whom we might characterize spirit-wise as a 'rainmaker', is known as Ori; the supreme being is known as Oludumare – another form of the word. In the physical body, Ori has two roles, the physical and the spiritual. The physical functions involve the thinking brain, eyes that see, noses that smell, ears that hear. The spiritual functions are subdivided into character and destiny. Character is unchangeable. Destiny is more complex in that the *Ifa* followers believe that we choose our own. However, heads of southern African corporations are yet to enter into such realms of destiny, which transcend the mere exercise character, as exemplified by Stephen Covey's seven habits of effective leadership.

Destiny, in its turn, can be divided into three parts: what you would specifically like during your period on earth (your goals); those things given to you to help you achieve those desires (your capabilities); and your gender, or the family into which you were born (your identity).

Obtala – setting direction

- You are more cerebral than physical.
- You have a strong sense of justice and honour.
- You tend to analyse other people's behaviour and motives.

Obtala, whom we might liken to the spirit of divination, is king of the Orisa. He is the essence of purity, justice and clear thinking, in fact a Mandela-like character. He is the most rational of the Orisa, also representing a pure and clear way to transcendence. He has a sense of duty, attention to detail and personal integrity. Obtala's energy is derived from calm and space. He is the judge, making the right decisions. His is the humour of having seen so much that laughter becomes an extension of understanding; tolerance, for him, replaces impetuosity.

Sango – strategy formulation

- You are extremely articulate.
- You can talk people into whatever you want.
- You look ahead at the probability of people's actions.

Though best known as a warrior, and hence a 'hunter' spirit, Sango is in reality the quintessence of the strategist. Though he goes to battle furiously, he only does it as a last resort. Sangos like nothing better than to plan ahead – to set the stage and to pull the strings necessary to get the results they desire – by getting people to do what they want while leaving them with the impression that they made their own decisions. Conventional business leaders often conform to this Sango type.

Oya – being enterprising

- You love thunderstorms and lightning.
- Your life has been filled with sudden change.
- You resent discipline or confinement.

Oya's desire to guide or manipulate Sango from behind the scenes is a micro-cosm of the mystery in the energy of this powerful Orisa. Oya sets the course while Sango delivers the blows. More than anything, Oya represents the energy of sudden change. Her role as Orisa of the marketplace is a practical example of such.

In this constant ebb and flow, this shifting current of fortune, Oya is the predominant and guiding force. In fact, this Orisa of sudden change is respon-sible for opening the gate between the marketplace and our home, that is between Earth and Heaven. As such she has not yet been incorporated into the fabric of a conventional, southern African business organization.

Yemonja/Olukun – nurturing people

- You have a genuine caring feeling for other people.
- You forgive easily and often.
- People are drawn to you for comfort and understanding.

Each and every one of us – according to Niemark – is part animal, part vegetable, and part mineral. We are as much the water, rock, iron, tree or lion as we are human. It is in this sense that Yemonja/Olukun lives in us. Those who feel that Yemonja alone is their guardian tend to be too passive, too caring, often at the expense of their own well-being. Their nurturing female qualities can be pic-tured as the surface waters of the ocean and rivers.

The powerful Olukun energy lies in the bottom depths and will rise to the surface only after much disturbance or interference. Yemonja represents the 'feminine' component, and Olukun the masculine. This is an affirmation of the Yoruba view of the universe, where all things contain both female and male energy. Such a combination of receptive and assertive elements, both of which are associated with caring, are more latent than manifest in our current business organizations. Finally, there are no less than three of the primary Orisa which are concerned with the expression of joy, and with physical and sensual experiences.

Esu – having fun

- You enjoy good food, drink and sex.
- You love dancing, large groups and bright clothes.
- You don't like taking orders, or working in confined settings.

Zorba the Greek could well have been Yoruba, for Yorubas believe that life is meant to be enjoyed. It is the enjoyment of life that Esu symbolizes, and he himself enjoys every minute of every day. He wants what he wants, now. Life can be fun, rewarding, and exciting if you make the right choices. Such overt fun is yet to become integral to organizational life within the southern African business mainstream.

Ogun – making things happen

- You like physical things.
- You are quick to take offence.
- You prefer to 'do' rather than talk about doing.

Ogun, the Orisa of iron and metals, is a fierce warrior of brute strength, a loner by nature. It is his ability to work ceaselessly and with little rest that allowed him to create civilization. Such relentless activity is likely to be a necessary feature of the reconstruction and development programme in the new South Africa.

Osun – Constant Regeneration

- You are acutely aware of how you look.
- You are more comfortable being 'in control' of relationships.
- You make decision based on 'gut feel'.

Osun, finally, is an energy force focused on the present and intimately connected with all sensual pleasures. This sensuality is not hedonistic. It helps Osun and her children accomplish the single most important task of *Ifa* devotees: conceiving and bearing children.

In many ways, the single most important task in southern Africa today is to transform this desire for physical regeneration into an impulse for economic regeneration. This can only be achieved if the different Orisa are combined together, within a multicultural context. This is very much a feature of our post-modern era, in the world generally and in the new South Africa specifically.

Conclusion

African renaissance

In the 1960s, Niemark argues, the fascination was with yoga, meditation and the mantras of India. In the 1970s and the greater part of the 1980s, the trend in America moved Westwards and people sought the curative powers of the sweat lodge, through the wisdom of the native American, in the oneness with nature.

In the 1990s, Niemark predicted that there would be a renaissance of interest in Africa. Certainly the emergence of the new South Africa has fostered such an interest, at least of late, both materially through prospective economic renewal, and spiritually through programmes of healing and reconciliation.

Ifa extols both the spiritual and the temporal. The Orisa, or energy forces, it identifies are with you always. You do not need a church or a structure to access them. They are with you in the countryside and on the crowded urban thoroughfares. They can help you, Niemark maintains, achieve peace in one and success in the other. *Ifa* sees you as whole and provides the rituals for keeping you that way. Africa cosmology holds that the trees grow and flowers bloom not to become the biggest tree or the prettiest flower, but to express their joy at the energy of the sun, their pleasure at the nourishment of the rain and the soil. It is an integrated response to the universe of which they are a part.

Bibliography

Lovelock, J. (1991) *Gaia: The Practical Science of Planetary Medicine.* Gaia Books Limited.

Niemark, Phillip (1993) *The Way of Orisa.* San Francisco: Harper.

M'bigi, Lovemore (1996) *Ubuntu,* Knowledge Resources, South Africa.

ENVIRONMENT

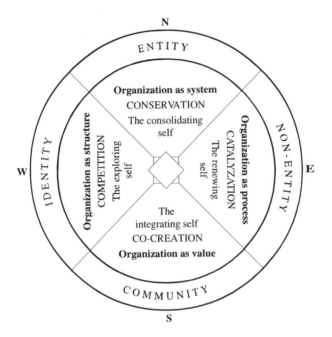

The universe is one whole, as it were, and is in some sense unbroken

David Bohm

Life . . . in this emergent point of view is not so much a property of the individual as it is a property of the entire planetary surface

Harold Morowitz

In the higher country of the mind, one has to become adjusted to the thinner air of uncertainty and to the enormous magnitude of the questions asked . . .

Robert Pirsig

The primary purpose of a company is to serve as an arena for the personal development of those working in the company. The production of goods and services and the making of profits are by-products.

Rolf Osterberg

Your Environment

Identifying the world in which you and your organization are located is a crucial starting point on the journey to the centre of the four worlds. However, it is not enough. You now need to start studying the terrain, the environment through which you will pass and from which you will derive your resources.

This section outlines four environments within which you and your organization are enfolded. They are: the *physical environment*, the *ecological environment*, the *psychological environment* and the *cultural environment*, each one forming a specific chapter.

At the end of the section you will have:

- Acquired an in-depth understanding of the relationship between management and (1) the natural sciences, particularly physics and ecology; and (2) psychology
- Acquired an ability to frame your work in terms of leading-edge concepts from science
- Discovered how to use strategically the managerial personality type you belong to: *hunter, herder, gardener* or *steward*
- Shifted your mind-set away from believing in stability and discover the world of instability and chaos.

5

Physical Environment

Introduction: The Unconscious Metaphor

Throughout history, all societies have guided themselves by some tacitly assumed answers to the great questions: Who are we? What is the purpose of all that we do? What kind of universe are we in? The accepted answers to such questions become the metaphysical foundations for societies, the unconscious metaphors that shape and mould the purpose, the attitudes and values of individuals and organizations. Eventually, they provide societies with a sense of their own destiny.

During the past three centuries, the chief metaphor that society has turned to has been the scientific world view that emerged out of the two philosophical centres of *empiricism* in the West and *rationalism* in the North. As we have said before, these represent in our four-worlds model, the archetypes of 'identity' and 'entity', or in Mitroff and Linstone's terms, the two worlds of 'agreement' and 'formula'. These two worlds have had a powerful impact on the evolution of our societies and organizations. The material success of our industrial civilization is matched by its failure to provide an intrinsic meaning to societies. Interestingly, the world of physics (and much of science) has already moved away from the first two worlds into the third and fourth worlds of 'non-entity' and 'community'. What this means for organizations is discussed in this chapter.

The Scientific World View

The scientific world view that emerged out of the Western and Northern worlds became the theoretical underpinning to our organizations and our attitudes to work and business. Nothing is still considered valid enough until it is 'scientific'. Science has became both the means and the end of all societal and organizational endeavour; the means are the usage of scientific methodology, while the ends are the construction of societies and organizations that are managed through the twin virtues of *prediction* and *control*.

The scientific world view that has prevailed until now has also been successful in shaping and implementing a comprehensive technological agenda. It has been broadly accepted as the nearest we can come to a 'true' picture of the universe. Where the metaphor of modern science has not been successful is in its inability to create a larger sense of meaning and value both for individuals and communities of people. The scientific metaphor seems to leave no room for the kinds of inner experiences and deep intuitions on which people base their most basic value commitments. Moreover, it has the tendency so often to portray a story of our origins around a series of random evolutionary processes, devoid of intrinsic meaning. The effect has been to deprive societies' and organizations' most fundamental values and meanings of any consensually valid intellectual foundation. This celebrated passage from Bertrand Russel echoes the story of the scientific world view based exclusively in the agreement and formula modes: 'That man is a product of causes which had no prevision of the end they were achieving; that his origin, his growth, his hopes and fears, his loves and beliefs, are but the outcome of accidental collations of atoms; that no fire, no heroism, no intensity of thought or feeling, can preserve an individual life beyond the grave; that all the labours of the ages, all the devotion, all the inspiration, all the noon day brightness of human genius, are destined to extinction in the vast death of the solar system, and the whole temple of man's achievement must inevitably be buried beneath the debris of a universe in ruins – all these things, if not quite beyond dispute, are yet so nearly certain, that no philosophy that rejects them can hope to stand.'

This was as official a statement of the prevailing world view as anything could get. Not only did this attitude dominate several generations of science-doing, it spilled over and became the predominating ethos in most aspects of society, most notably in the way organizations were perceived and managed. And the stronger this world view grew, the greater was the intensity with which 'natural' values and intuitions were sidelined out of the mainstream. So while on the one hand, business may have profited from using techniques of what came to be known as 'scientific management', it also became increasingly alienated from people and the natural environment. While on the one hand, it was able to reap the rewards of efficiency and profit, on the other hand, it led to a growing disempowerment of the human beings behind the calculated figures. Moreover, it led to increasingly dysfunctional societies, founded on the credo of 'jobs without purpose', 'work without meaning' and 'business without value'.

Undoubtedly, science is the singular definer of truth in modern society. It is vastly accepted as a cognitive authority, whose discoveries shape and mould everything we do, from raising children to managing businesses. However, there is every sign that points out that the 'scientific' definition of truth is no longer adequate to be the sole underpinning for organizations and societies, and that a 'new story' of science needs to be told urgently. What we clearly need is a new account of how things came to be as they are, within which we find a sense of life and purpose, a guide to learning and an impetus to transforming our lives, our societies and our organizations. At the heart of this new story will be, clearly, the insights of science and the facts of evolution. But this time, it will truly be a story, a narrative which will include the listener as a participator in the story. For ultimately, it will be about his or her life, this business or that, centred on the day-to-day world of work and play.

Let us, then, begin with an account of the 'old story' of science; why things came to be the way they are.

The First World of Science: The Universe as Machine

Writing in *The Reenchantment of the World*, Morris Berman describes the passage from medieval to modern times: 'The view of nature that predominated in the west down to the eve of the scientific revolution was that of an enchanted world. Rocks, trees, rivers and clouds were all seen as wondrous and alive, and human beings felt at home in this environment. The cosmos, in short, was a place of belonging. A member of this cosmos was not an alienated observer of it but a direct participant in its drama. His personal destiny was bound up with its destiny, and this relationship gave meaning to his life.' The main goal of pre-modern science was to understand the meaning and significance of things, rather than prediction and control. Ethical questions were considered to be of the highest significance. Fact and value originated from the same source; 'What do I know?' and 'How should I live?' were in fact considered to be one and the same.

The medieval world view went through a metamorphosis in the sixteenth and seventeenth centuries, replacing the notion of an organic, living universe with that of the world as a machine. A new scientific methodology came into prominence, shaped and formulated by two of Europe's greatest minds, Francis Bacon from England and René Descartes from France. Drawing from the pragmatically rich culture of of his home country, Bacon devised the empirical method of science, the 'hands on', inductive procedure. First experiment, then draw conclusions from them, and then test out the conclusions through further experimentation. Bacon was the essential pragmatist, who was one of the pioneers of the Western world of technology. The Baconian first world was based on the overall framework of scientific experimentation, the technological questioning of nature under duress.

Natura vexata

Bacon pointed out that nature had to be questioned directly by putting it in a position in which it was forced to yield its answers. He wrote: 'For even as in the business of life a man's disposition and secret workings of his mind and affections are better discovered when he is in trouble than other times, so likewise the secrets of nature reveal themselves more readily under the vexations of art [technology].' What Bacon was saying was that the knowledge of nature comes about under artificial conditions. His conviction was that *knowledge is power*, and *truth is utility*. Although technology had existed before the seventeenth century, this was the first time that it was elevated to the level of a philosophy, through its embodiment in experiment. As Morris Berman points out, despite the extreme sophistication of say, Chinese technology down to the fifteenth century, it had never occurred to the Chinese to equate mining or gunpowder manufacture with pure knowledge.

Technology and economics

As Berman says, 'The collapse of a fuedal economy, the emergence of capitalism on a broad scale and the profound alteration in social relations that accompanied these changes provided the context for the Scientific Revolution.' What was crucial to the process was the equating of truth with utility and cognition with technology. The new framework was of experimentation, quantification, prediction and control. Commerce began to influence industry in a way that had never existed before. The old relationship between guild master and customer broke down. A new merchant class began to emerge as credit became necessary to sell to distant markets. The merchant was able to first secure exclusive disposal on produced output and later became the creditor to the artisan for buying raw material. Eventually, the merchant became the manufacturer as artisans fell into debt and peasants became wage earners. Money and credit became the motors of economics. As is often pointed out, the main characteristic of Western industrialization was the birth of a new 'individual will', which became the pioneering spirit of the renaissance. Interestingly, this development was closely tied up with a new technological model that was dependent on quantification. As the universe began to be viewed through technological lenses, it led to greater control over nature which in turn led to the creation of wealth, credit and individual success. This cyclical connection between the three elements of the time is represented in figure 5.1.

As Berman points out, even the notion of time underwent a fundamental transformation from the pre-modern cyclical conception that was based on seasonal changes to a new linear notion based on technological control. This had a great impact on people like Galileo who based an entirely new science by

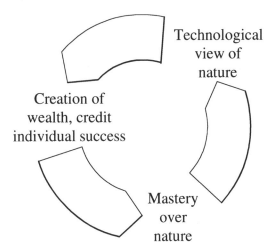

Technological
view of
nature

Creation of
wealth, credit
individual success

Mastery
over
nature   Figure. 5.1

emphasizing the 'how' of things rather than the 'why'. Galileo's method involved distancing himself from nature in a non-participative way. Although an academic himself, Galileo's inspiration for science came from technology and engineering.

The Second World of Science:
The Universe as Method

While Bacon focused on the pragmatic side of science that would allow 'common men' to find agreement with each other on the basis of observed sense data and experimental results, Descartes wanted to formulate a method that would allow him to construct a complete science based on *certainty*. 'All science is certain, evident knowledge,' he wrote. 'We reject all knowledge which is merely probable and judge that only those things should be believed which are perfectly known and about which there can be no doubts.' So while Bacon chose the way of accumulating hard data through rigorous experimentation, Descartes chose the method of analysis: break up a problem into pieces and then arrange the pieces in a logical order. According to Descartes, it is no use collecting data or examining nature on Baconian lines. The real need is for a system of 'clear thinking' which can then be applied to every phenomenon under study. Descartes called for the external world to be blocked out while the nature of right thinking was studied. With this in mind, Descartes pronounced that it was necessary to disbelieve everything that one thinks one knows. 'My whole purpose', he pointed out, 'was to achieve greater certainty and to reject the loose earth and sand in favour of rock and clay.' Since the only certitude that existed, according to Descartes was mathematical, 'science', he said, 'must become a "universal mathematics".' Descartes' method of acquiring knowledge was based on geometry and involved the following steps: (1) state the problem in its complexity; (2) break down the problem into its simplest units, its component parts; (3) re-assemble the whole structure in logical fashion. For Descartes, this was the only key to knowledge. 'Those long chains of reasoning,' he wrote, 'so simple and easy, which enabled the geometricians to reach the most difficult demonstrations, had made me wonder whether all things knowable to men might not fall into a similar logical sequence.'

The second world of Descartes was that of a mathematical philosophy, which followed directly from his methodology. In the *Principles of Philosophy* (1644) he showed that such logical thinking led to the notion of the universe as a vast machine, consisting of two basic entities: matter and motion. So everything in the universe could be explained in terms of the arrangement and the movement of its parts. With the method, he postulated that mind and matter were distinct entities; while one was *res cogitans*, the thinking thing, the other was *res extensa*, the extension. These two developments in Cartesian thought were to exercise a profound impact on all aspects of society. From now on, everything would be described and understood in terms of matter and motion.

Quite clearly, in spite of the basic differences between the first world of Bacon and the second world of Descartes, one dove-tailed the other. Bacon's goal of 'utilizing' truth was realized by Descartes' means: the precision of measurment was not just restricted to a methodology but it involved setting into motion a technological agenda. In the words of Morris Berman, '. . . another seventeenth century departure from the Greeks: the conviction that the world lies before us to be acted upon, not merely contemplated.' A new Faustian modernity was emerging in sixteenth century Europe based on 'doing', rather than 'being'. Between the empiricism of Bacon and the rationality of Descartes, a new scientific revolution was being created. What is relevant to note is that the implications of this revolution were as much psychological as physical, probably more so. If to manage your organization, it needs to be treated mechanically, then your mind must behave mechanically as well. The laws of mechanistic science became both, externalized as well as internalized. According to Descartes, '. . . the mind itself be from the very outset not left to take its own course, but guided at every step; and that the business be done as if by machinery'. The essence of man, according to him was 'his activity as a thinking being'.

Moreover, this activity is purely mechanical. As Morris Berman puts it: 'The mind is in possession of a certain method. It confronts the world as a separate object. It applies this method to the object, again and again, and eventually it will know all there is to know.' What Descartes did was to provide Bacon's utilitarian agenda with philosophical teeth. Gallic panache for systematic theory combined with Anglo-Saxon pragmatism to create the most pervasive world view of all times.

The metaphor of modern science

This French–English alliance that postulated that matter and motion were the basis of everything, soon became the singular metaphor for managing organizations and societies. On this foundation, the scientist and manager alike had to make three assumptions and then rearrange his or her world view on that basis. These assumptions are as follows:

1 *The notion of objectivism* The assumption that there is an objective world which the observer can hold at a distance and study separately from himself. *The implication of objectivism for management* That organizations are best managed when they are held at a distance and treated by the manager as being separate from him or herself. The manager is called upon to assume the guise of an observer, so that observations can be made without subjective interpretation.

2 *The notion of positivism* The assumption that the real world is that which is empirically measurable in terms of facts and figures. *The implications of positivism for management* That the only 'reality' of an organization is that which is measurable through figures. Anything that cannot be measured is in turn, invalid and unreal. It is the manager's job to quantify as much as possible, for that leads to effective controls.

3 *The notion of reductionism* The assumption that any phenomenon is best understood by reducing it to its smallest constituent parts and then studying the parts. *The iimplication of reductionism for managament* That organizations can be managed best by reducing them to their elemental parts. Management is then all about managing each of the constituent parts as is.

Newton's mechanics: straddling the West and North

The ultimate success of the scientific revolution in the West and the North owes itself to another Englishman, Isaac Newton, who realized the Cartesian dream and completed the work began by Bacon. Born in 1624, he was able to develop a complete mathematical formulation of what came to be known as the mechanistic view of science. Praised as 'perhaps the greatest advance in thought that a single individual was ever privileged to make' by Albert Einstein, Newton's lifetime achievement was the *Principia*, a comprehensive system of definitions, propositions and proofs. Unifying the empiricism of Bacon and the rationalism of Descartes, Newton reduced all physical phenomena to the motion of material particles. This motion was caused by the force of gravity, whose effect is described by the equations of motion. Newton was thus able to explain all physical phenomena in terms of what were therafter referred to as the Fundamental Laws of Motion.

The three-dimensional stage of Newton's universe, in which all physical phenomena took place, was an absolute space, always at rest and unchangeable. All changes in the physical world were described in terms of a separate dimension called time, which again was absolute, having no connection with the material world and flowing smoothly from the past through the present to the future. Matter for Newton was essentially passive with an ability to remain conserved. All that happens in the world, according to Newton, has a specific cause and gives rise to a definite effect, and the future of any part of the system can – in principle – be predicted with absolute certainty. This mode of perceiving reality, had far-reaching consequences for not just science, but for the whole of industrial society. In Newton's universe, there is no room for uncertainty. Under the influence of such a world view, we have built and managed organizations using similar means and ends: avoiding subjectivity in management and avoiding questions of purpose and usefulness to society. This mode became the bedrock of management philopsophy not only in the Western and Northern world, but in all the industrialized areas of the world. This world view had enormous successes in the eighteenth and the nineteenth centuries. As Fritjof Capra writes in *The Turning Point*: 'Newtonian mechanics was able to explain the motion of the plants, moons and comets to the smallest details, as well as the flow of the tides and various other phenomena related to gravity . . . The picture of the world as perfect machine . . . was now considered a proved fact and Newton became its symbol.' The world view that we have inherited from Newtonian physics continues to have a profound effect on our whole lives; it is still our most important window on reality, permeating our attitudes and value systems, influencing the way we manage our businesses, our societies and our relationships.

Beyond predict and control

As we have seen, the world view of modern science encompasses the first two worlds of empiricism/pragmatism and rationalism. In the first world, meaning is defined by agreement over experimental results and placed squarely at the centre, and a *structure* is built around it. It was precisely this approach that was utilized by the manufacturing enterprises of the UK and USA in the last century and this one. In the second, Northern world, an abstract concept, such as the second law of motion becomes the definer of a universal *system*, around which structures are built. This style is more prevalent in continental European organizations.

However, in both modes, management is defined as the science of the predictable and the manager is at once the classical scientist who is able to shape future events on the basis of tested laws. The symbols of this joint mode, the machine and mathematical theory, occupy centre stage. The manager's role is to manage the machine through the use of the mathematical theory. In the legacy of this paradigm, the management of organizations is governed by management laws that are a spin-off from Newton's world of particles and objects in motion. In such a scenario, organizations become the mass-points that Newton's model suggested, isolated in their apparent objectivity both, from the self of the manager and from the external environment. Since success in such a model can only be measured in terms of acceleration and mass, this became the agenda for the big businesses that dominated the Western and Northern worlds.

However, the risk of depending exclusively on the predict-and-control mode is that it works only as long as the environment in which it is used stays stable and predictable. It becomes obsolete when the environment becomes unpredictable. In the 1980s, this is precisely what happened and traditionally strong organizations that were squarely grounded in the first and second worlds suddenly found themselves incapable of functioning as before. The formation of a new world view became imperative; one that could reflect the dynamism and change that was taking place in the environment. This new world view did not come from the world of management; once again, it was science that sowed the seeds for a new metaphor. It came from such areas as relativity, field theory, quantum physics and ecology. In terms of our four-world model, this new science was profoundly holistic and reflected the Eastern world that had eluded science so far. And in the last two decades, a Southern, humanistic perspective has also been emerging. We have chosen to focus on quantum physics in this chapter and ecology in the next one.

Beyond fragmentation

The third world of holism helps in taking organizations beyond the endemic fragmentation that arises out of the Western and Northern worlds of technology and science. Of course there are areas where it is appropriate to break up wholes into parts. As physicist David Bohm points out: 'if we crush stones into parts with a hammer, in order to make concrete, that's appropriate. But using the same hammer to "break" a watch would not produce parts, but fragments that are separated in ways that are not significantly related to the structure of the watch.' The point is, in the legacy of the machine and the mathematical theory, we have latched on to a way of thinking that produces irrelevant fragments rather than seeing the parts in their right perspective, which is their relation to the whole.

A similar fragmentation takes place in organizations. As a result of this approach, countless managers ultimately cease to give the divisions in their organizations, the significance of being merely convenient ways of managing and indicating relative autonomy; instead they begin to perceive themselves and the organization as made up of nothing but separately and independently existing components. Guided by this fragmentary view, the manager acts in such a way as to (1) divide him or herself away from the organization and (2) divide up the organization into simpler, more manageable parts. Forgetting that we have built our organizations as a reflection of this manner of thinking, we delude ourselves into thinking that is how organizations and people naturally are. The manager therefore obtains apparent proof of his or her fragmentary self-world view, because it now seems to have an autonomous existence independent of his or her will or desire. What the manager doesn't notice is that it is he or she, acting according to his mode of thought, who has brought about the fragmentation.

Fragmentation is therefore an attitude of mind that disposes the manager to regard the divisions between the various relative 'parts' of the organization as absolute and final, rather than a limitation of his or her thinking. As a result, any actions are partial and limited in their scope and impact. Boxed in and insulated from the outer environment and fragmented internally, such an organization is not able to respond fluidly to change. Decisions are usually formed within closed-loop thinking patterns that serve no other purpose than to reinforce the first principles on which they were based. It is with this in mind that we now examine the third, holistic world that shows us a way out of this predicament.

The Third World of Science:
The Universe as Paradox

As physics turned to the investigation of subatomic matter, the neat and tidy world of Newtonian physics began to get turned over by new discoveries. Every time nature was asked a question in atomic experiments, the answer was a paradox. The more accurate the experiments got, the sharper the paradoxes became. The first of the baffling paradoxes was the discovery that the subatomic units of matter appeared randomly as particles and as waves. It was impossible to predict when it would appear as what. Finally, Niels Bohr, the Danish physicist turned to the Chinese notion of 'yin' an 'yang', the opposites that complement each other, and postulated his theory of complementarity (as illustrated in figure 5.2).

While the old physics had made a sharp division between a particle (material) and a wave (amorphous), they now seemed to be interchangeable. Quantum physics, then, bridged the gap between matter and energy, pronouncing that the two were different sides to the same phenomenon. Gary Zukav, who along with Fritjof Capra compared the organic, unified and spiritual world of the East with emergent discoveries in physics, wrote: '. . . something very exciting is happening. Physicists have proved rationally that our rational ideas about the world in which we live are profoundly deficient.' Zukav went on to postulate that we may be approaching the end of science the way we know it. Physicists were hinting that only direct experience can give us a sense of the realm of connectedness in the universe. Erwin Schroedinger, one of the founders of quantum theory said:

Figure 5.2 Complementarity

'Western thinking is still trying to objectify everything. It is in need of blood transfusion from Eastern thought.' The Taoist saying, 'The real is empty, and the empty is real' was echoed by English physicist Paul Dirac's statement: 'All matter is created out of some imperceptible substratum . . . nothingness, unimaginable and undetectable. But it is a peculiar form of nothingness out of which all matter is created'.

Secondly, it was found that matter does not exist with certainty at definite places as per Newton's laws, but rather shows 'tendencies to exist', and events do not occur with certainty at different times and in definite ways, but rather show 'tendencies to occur'. A new element of uncertainty and 'non-local' interconnections was beginning to enter physics.

A physics of interconnectedness

Experiments have shown that if paired particles (identical twin particles in polarity) fly apart and the polarity of one is changed by an experimenter, the other changes instantaneously. The two particles remain mysteriously connected. Known as Bell's theorem after it was proposed by J. S. Bell, it proves that all objects constitute an indivisible whole.

A careful analysis of the process of observation in atomic physics by the scientists has shown beyond doubt that the subatomic particles make meaning as isolated entities, only *vis-à-vis* their interconnectedness. Over the last two decades, this principle is found to be true not only at the atomic level, but at all levels of matter and life. As we shall see in the next chapter, this is the governing principle for our ecosystem. An example of this phenomenon is the vortex, which is a recurrent, stable pattern that forms within the flow of fluids. Although on the one hand, we may choose to perceive and define the vortex in autonomous terms, in actuality the existence of the vortex depends upon the flow of water. Stop the flow and the vortex disappears.

To take another simple example of this phenomenon, let us consider the motion of some of these building-block particles in a piece of metal. We shall refer to these as free electrons (the ones that are not bound to atoms). These free electrons in, say, a piece of metal normally tend to move around randomly and independently, doing their own thing, as it were. However, the situation changes dramatically as soon as more energy is added to the metal. Suddenly a chaotic situation sets in, and a wild electronic dance ensues. But beyond a

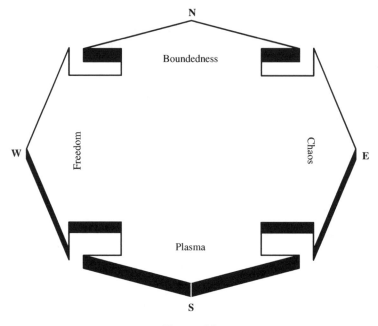

Figure. 5.3

critical point, the chaos changes to a new kind of behaviour, and the electrons
suddenly begin oscillating as a self-organized whole, with what are called plasma
vibrations. What is revealed through this simple phenomenon is that the individuality of these electrons is enfolded within a larger wholeness which reveals
itself under certain conditions.

It is as if the free electrons exist in four worlds and depending on what the
external conditions are, a certain world manifests itself. Firstly, the electrons
behave as individual particles. This is the Western world in our model. Secondly, they are bound to one another as members of a system, which is the
Northern world. Thirdly, the electrons are part of a chaotic whole which is
catalysed by external energy input. This is the Eastern world in our model. And
finally, the electrons are a collective plasma, which is the Southern pole of our
model. This can be represented as shown in figure 5.3.

Evidently, the West–East axis is clearly the dynamic axis while the North–
South axis is the static axis. The real nature of the electron is to be found at the
confluence of all four states, which is at the centre of the four worlds.

Similarly, the phenomenon of superconductivity arises from a form of co-
operative and collective order. At a critical temperature, the vibrating atoms
within an electric conductor stop impeding the flow of current through a process
of self-organization. The system now starts behaving as a whole. Within this

superconductor, a current once established, can continue to flow for hundreds of thousands of years. Similar holistic behaviour is also to be found in the laser beam and in superfluidity. All resistance to flow vanishes as previously random molecules suddenly act as one quantum entity.

According to English physicist and thinker David Bohm, who pioneered the movement towards a holistic science, the notion of isolated material entities turns out to be an abstraction and their properties observable only in their interactions with other systems. What quantum theory did was to open up a new perception of reality, based, not on a collection of physical objects, but on a web of relations in an undifferentiated and interconnected whole.

'I am because I am not': 'non-entity' revisited

These interconnections are an indelible characteristic of holistic science and always involve the observer as an essential component of science. The properties of any object can be understood only in terms of the object's interaction with the observer. The Cartesian division between the I and the world, between the observer and the observed cannot be made in quantum physics. What the new physics is saying is that we can never talk about reality (which includes our organizations), without speaking about ourselves. In the words of atomic physicist John Wheeler: 'We had this old idea, that there was a universe out there, and here is man, safely protected from the universe by a six-inch slab of plate glass. Now we learn from the quantum world that even to observe so miniscule an object as an electron we have to shatter that plate glass; we have to reach in there. . . . So the old "observer" simply has to be crossed off the books, and we must put in the new word "participator".' In a participatory universe, the manager is no longer the objective, classical scientist. Instead he or she becomes inextricably linked to the organization in a deeply subjective way; by the sheer act of being a member of the organization, he or she alters the organization fundamentally! Neither the individual nor the organization can be regarded as separate entities. Their separateness is only an abstraction, at best a convenient notion.

Wholes and sub-wholes

One of the most important developments in modern physics was the discovery that there exists an order of wholeness that lies beneath the surface of ordinarily perceived reality. To take an example: while on a perceived level the collision of two billiard balls can be explained in terms of Newton's physics (i.e. by treating the two balls as distinct, autonomous objects), on a deeper, underlying level the conditions for their collision arise out of the general global conditions of the whole system. Similarly, the meanings of the gestures of a ballet dancer are contained in the whole movement of the dancer. While it is possible to analyse the motion of a dancer's body by means of photographs, it is clear that each element has its origin in the entire gesture and any static element is incomplete. Electrical fields and rivers are continuous things that defy analysis and vary smoothly from place to place. What the new physics says is that *all motion and change emerge out of the whole* and that the patterns and events of nature are the expression of an *underlying unity* of form.

So, from a Newtonian perspective, it is possible to abstract causal connections in an organization in a linear, one-to-one correspondence way. A company flow chart tells you exactly which department precedes which, who supersedes who and where the buck eventually ends. From a quantum dynamical perspective, such a flow chart is at best, only an abstraction. At worst, it is an impediment to perceiving reality the way it is: in flow and filled with simultaneous multiple possibilities. To take another example, you may define your company product (say, personal computers) in terms of various boxes such as research and development, marketing, financing and sales, but this fragmentation is useful as long as it does not become a hindrance to the evolution of the product. From the point of view of this Eastern world of quantum physics, the product is a 'process', and not an 'entity' the way we usually assume it to be. Being a process, it is a flowing movement and involves a multitude of causes that precede it and a multitude of effects that are a result of it. Moreover, these interconnections are probabilistic in the sense that they cannot be determined or predicted by any laws. Rather they emerge spontaneously out of the unique conditions at any given time. From this Eastern world view, the most effective approach is therefore not to force abstractions on a flowing whole; rather management becomes the art of staying open to and working through these multifarious factors that emerge out of the whole. From a holistic point of view, the product is a manifestation of the wholeness of the company, which is like an invisible ground, including both, the material and the non-material aspects of the organization.

From the Baconian and the Cartesian point of view, a whole is something that is constructed when all the parts are put together. Moreover, the putting together has to follow certain definite laws. So the 'wholeness' of an organization is the result of putting together all the constituent structures of operations, heirarchies, marketing, sales, product-development and the many other structures in a typical organization. The imagery is typically of building blocks locking into one another to form the whole.

From the perspective of the West and the North, *it is the parts that organize the whole*. From a quantum physical point of view, it is precisely the contrary: *it is the state of the whole that organizes the parts*. According to this principle, it is not the departments and the various 'parts' of the organization that put the company together; rather, the parts are synchronicities, or synchronous events in the organizational space-time that arise out of the underlying field of the organization. The problem in comprehending this totally is that when we think of the wholeness of our organization, we are thinking through the lenses of an outside observer who is looking at the company and questioning what wholeness is. This creates a fundamental division taking us back to where we started from. From a quantum physical perspective, there is no point at which the manager is divided from the rest of the organization. Rather the manager and the organization are part of an unbroken and seamless whole. They are like vortices in flowing water, relatively autonomous objects and forms that have emerged out of the whole. So are all the various departments and structures that we mistakenly perceive as being parts that combine to make the whole. These are not parts in the old sense of the word, but *sub-wholes*. These sub-wholes are stable, the way vortices are stable. The stability of a vortex is a function of the wholeness that is enfolded in it. If it were not for that, it would simply collapse. Applied to organizations this means that the departments and sections enfold the wholeness of the business in themselves. The accounting department is not just an individual entity; it is simultaneously a sub-whole, enfolding the unbroken wholeness of the organization.

Moreover, because each sub-whole enfolds the totality of the organization, the relations between them are internal rather than external. Wholes, like cells, divide naturally into sub-wholes on the basis of internal relationships. The important thing is that the whole, say the organization, and a sub-whole, say operations, are correlated categories: each implies the other. This is not because operations is 'part of the organizational structure'. Rather, operations has emerged out as a relative part (sub-whole) by virtue of the particular way in which it actively enfolds the whole and all the other parts.

The relationship between each sub-whole, be it marketing, sales, operations, accounts or whatever else, is thus prior to their being structured. But this is not the way we think and manage. Our tendency is to see them as separated. This is reflected in traditional management which is the science of bringing the disconnected parts together. From the quantum physical perspective, management is more of 'letting-go' of abstract notions of what constitutes order. The simile is of managing an organization as if it were a vortex.

Entering the Fourth World:
From Holism to Humanism

The initial notion of interconnectedness as provided by the new physics has serious implications for organizations and societies. If we consider the Eastern notion that individuality is an abstraction of a deeper underlying wholeness, it radically affects four organizational dictums:

- firstly, that the organization is an autonomous unit
- secondly, that the manager is an objective, detached observer capable of 'objective management'

- thirdly, that management is exclusively scientific in the classical sense
- fourthly, that organizations are predictable entities.

While the Eastern perspective focuses on 'undoing' the notions of identity and entity, that are so much a part of the Northern and Western worlds, it is left to the South to raise the question of where the spirit of community enters the realm of science. From a Southern angle, quantum physics also opens out the question of the relationship between the organization and its environment, both human (employees and members of society) and natural. From a Newtonian perspective, an organization is a collection of facts, and management is the effective usage and control of the body of facts to maximum advantage. The dictum of mechanistic science was that things do not possess purpose and meaning. They instead possess behaviour which can and must be described in an atomistic, mechanical and quantitative way. As a result, this affects the very substance of all relationships – between human and human, organization and community, organization and nature. In the Newtonian world, there is no room for reciprocity. The whole structure of Western and Northern science is grounded in a sharp distinction between *fact* and *value*. Consequently, the science of management tells you how to manage by providing you with a technique; it does not tell you what to do or whether you should do it. It is left to the fourth world to reopen the case for value in science.

As Morris Berman writes, 'what is really "real" for Newtonian science is what is abstract.' The various mathematical symbols and equations, the classification and generalization, the so-called facts of science, all make for a presumed absolute truth. Questions of value and meaning have no place in such a structure. This has had a direct bearing on the way organizations are still perceived and managed. For so many managers and executives, numbers still count for more than human empowerment; downsizing is seen as 'effective' because it reduces overhead costs; shareholder profit supersedes value for community; techniques find favour over values and exploitation of the environment is seen as 'natural' to industrial goals. According to many contemporary scientific thinkers, the reason why science dichotomizes fact and value and opts for the former is because, traditionally, scientific knowledge has identified singularly with prediction and control. It ignores the realms of subjective experience, transcendent knowledge and spiritual commitment. Ironically, these are precisely the realms in which all societies have found the basis for their deepest values and a sense of meaning.

Other voices

Our societies and our organizations have traditionally depended on an 'imbalanced' scientific metaphor which did not include the East and the South. As we have seen, areas of inquiry such as quantum physics have in the last few decades provided the impetus to move Eastwards. To complete the balance we need a Southern dimension of value, the plasma electronic state that we referred to earlier, which will provide the metaphor for a value-based approach in our organizations and societies. One of the strongest proponents of uniting fact and value was the German philosopher and scientist Goethe, who interestingly was a contemporary of Newton. Goethe's goal was 'to free the human spirit from a hypothesis which causes it to see falsely or partially.' He saw scientifc hypothesis and methodology as a scaffolding that must be dismantled when the building is completed. Goethe continually sought to bring back the element of human spirit into science. The highest purpose of science is the formation or cultivation of human sensibilities – the transformation of the human psyche. As Rudolph Steiner wrote about Goethe's approach to science: 'One of the most important consequences of Goethe's concept of science is that values, ethics and science are part of a single, whole knowledge.' For Goethe, facts and values had to be part of the same phenomenon.

Another dissenting voice was that of Douglas Fawcett who attempted to fuse value and fact through what he called 'Imaginism'. In his philosophy, the most fundamental power to be found in ourselves and in the universe is that of 'Imagining', which is both the activity of creating and what is created. Like a deep vision, it is simultaneously, a creation at a subliminal and collective level, and is based on conscious awareness at the conscious level. Fawcett saw imagining as fundamental to reason, for the process of reasoning involves imagining concepts, experimenting and coming to trust through experience.

In contemporary times, the person who has been pushing science and the description of physical reality towards the South has been physicist and philosopher David Bohm, who we introduced in the previous section. In Bohm's view we have inherited a belief that our thought is of an inherently different and higher order than matter. This belief has nurtured a faith in what we referred to as 'objectivity' – the capacity to observe an event without affecting it or being affected by it. From a Southern perspective, this is not possible, as our very existence is based on the existence of the other. Bohm thinks that our emphasis on being objective has been at the expense of a subjective mode and therefore has been lop-sided. Too much of West and North and too little of East and South. Bohm asserts that thought and knowledge are primarily collective phenomena. The notion that thoughts come to us from our individual 'selves' is a myth from our Western and Northern traditions. It is interesting to note that Bohm spent many years of his life in association with J. Krishnamurti the man who was once proclaimed as the world teacher and who disbanded an entire organization built around this assumption. Krishnamurti repeatedly asserted that the observer and the observed are one and that the division between them is a product of our conditioning. Thought is thus a communal whole, including emotions, reflexes and artefacts in its 'unbroken field'. What one individual thinks, from Bohm's Southern perspective, emerges out of a collective whole that is humanity. And vice versa, everything that an individual thinks and does affects humanity.

Science is no different. It may be considered to be an 'objective' body of knowledge for reasons of convenience, but at a deeper level, it embodies the spirit of community.

Together, the wave-like amorphousness linking the psychological space of the manager and the physical space of the organization creates a new approach to understanding and managing organizations. The manager can no longer assume that the organization only exists objectively, to be controlled as a fragmented mass-point through simple linear equations that fortify a rigid, predictable structure. What emerges instead is a combination of objectivity and a deeply subjective participation in the creation and sustenance of a *social* and *psychological* network. Secondly, if all organizations, and society at large are not just autonomous entities, but are part of an undifferentiated community, the earlier hard and clear notions of competetion and unending growth come under a new challenge. If the existence of individual particles is an abstraction of human thinking, then so is the consequent psychological formulation of competetion. If what gives meaning to particles is their complementary wave-like nature, similarly, what gives credence to competetive behaviour is its complementary co-operative behaviour! What follows is a phenomenon that is already beginning to manifest itself through alliances and joint ventures: in order to compete, you've got to co-operate.

To summarize, a Southern–Eastern approach to organizations includes the following characteristics:

• The organization is basically an undivided whole within which every 'part' is connected and interdependent upon every other 'part'. The wholeness also includes you, the manager.
• From the perspective of the first and second worlds, given the initial conditions, you can definitively predict the outcome of decisions and the direction your organization will take. However from the Southern–Eastern perspective, your organization is enfolded in a non-local, global field and what events and phenomena will shape its destiny are not fully predictable.
• While an objective approach to science, and consequently to organizations, is important from a factual perspective, a subjective approach is necessary from a value-laden perspective.
• Your organization is, above all, a community that is a member of a larger community. As such it has a shared destiny with its natural and social environment.

Conclusion: The Centre of the Four Worlds

The rethinking that the new physics has brought in has to move to centre stage into the world of organizations and of business. If we assume that our organizations will continue to coast along as before and that the old mechanical paradigm will continue to be applied, we are only deluding ourselves. Organizations that have hitherto grown and prospered on the basis of the mechanical metaphor have already started noticing the first signs of trouble. Fluctuations and factors that cannot be explained by the prediction and control mode of the first two worlds are already in our midsts. Well-oiled, old solutions that once worked with certainty now no longer seem to work. The old fix that worked on the notion that all problems are licked with advancing technology, growing production and hard work, seem to be obsolete in the chaos that is emerging all around us. It is as if the corporate equivalent of electrons had reached the stage of the collective dance.

Moreover, in other parts of the world, notably the Far East, a whole new concept is achieving results that are clearly eluding Western and Northern organizations. What Japanese and other Eastern companies are doing is to ride the stage at which the electron plasma takes over. In other words, they have hitched their organizations to another level of order where wholeness and collectivity has become a business principle. From our perspective, what is necessary is a balance of the four worlds, in which the structure of objectivity is complemented by subjectivity, predictability by flexibility and the individual by the community.

From a paradigm of certainty and predictabilty, we have come to a stage of the synergy of opposites. What quantum physics teaches us is that particle-like structures continually depend on wave-like processes for their sustenance. And vice versa. Being polar opposites, East and West and North and South constitute the total organization of our physical universe.

Bibliography

Mitroff, I. and Linstone, H. (1993) *The Unbounded Mind*. Oxford: Oxford University Press.

Berman, Morris (1981) *The Reenchantment of the World*. New York: Cornel University Press.

Descartes, Rene (1644) *Principia Philosophiae (Principles of Philosophy)*.

Capra, Fritjof (1982) *The Turning Point*. New York: Simon & Schuster.

Zukav, Gary (1979) *The Dancing Wu Li Masters*. London: Rider.

Steiner, Rudolph (1972) *World Economy*. London: Steiner Press.

Bohm, David (1994) *Thought as a System*. New York: Routledge.

6

The Ecological Environment

Introduction: Beyond Stability and Equilibrium

A so-called commonsense principle in the Western and Northern management worlds is that organizations need to be highly stable if they are to develop and grow. In fact, the search for stability and equilibrium has been the management equivalent of the search for the holy grail for most organizations. The requirements of stability and equilibrium have been traditionally associated with results such as growth, development, product quality, etc. According to Ralph Stacey, this need for stability has given rise to the following four 'navigational principles' of doing business. Readers will recognize that these principles are once again a spin-off from classical science and the laws of Newtonian physics and Darwininan biology.

- *Control*:   Always control your organization through a concrete vision, long-term plans and systems of rules and regulations.
- *Uniformity*:   Maintain a common and unified culture and make sure that all managers adhere to it.
- *Profit*:   Always focus on the bottom line first and everything else later.
- *Adaptability*:   Adapt as closely as possible to your business environment and deliver what the customers want.

However, in a rapidly changing environment, these principles, which are geared towards 'reaching equilibrium', are fast becoming obsolete. Organizations that could once use these strategies successfully are suddenly no longer sustainable. On the other hand, those that are prepared to drop the above 'mind-set' are proving to be successful. Control and stability are useful as far as they lead to identifying solutions to problems and applying systematic, formalized types of planning, implementation and control. But what is not often understood is that opting for exclusive stability results in highly brittle structures that ossify over time. As we saw in chapter 2, the reason for the decline and eventual failure of the 'classical' American organizational form was rooted, paradoxically enough, in the very factors that made it successful. If organizations do not alternate between stability and instability, they are apt to run down. Stable structures necessarily have to be complemented by unstable processes that undermine the very structures that epitomize stability. It is this paradoxical tension between stability and instability that we shall be exploring in this chapter.

Between Stability and Instability: The Ecological Principle

'To shake a tree is to shake the Earth,' goes an ancient East African saying, vividly evoking an image of nature as an interconnected whole. In a world of networked, global markets, financial systems that transcend national boundaries, and planetary satellite communication, the notion of interconnectedness acquires an even deeper significance. Yet, while the world in which we do business and manage our organizations has altered radically, the mental and physical models that we use have not. In the previous chapter, we saw how depending exclusively on mechanical models that arise out of the mechanical world view of classical physics is not only irrelevant, but counter-productive. The same holds true for classical biology. However, in spite of all scientific evidence about interconnectedness, we continue to hang on to outdated biological models of absolute competition and survival of the fittest. In this chapter we shall enter the world of the new ecology and seek out a coherent model based on it that will provide an apt metaphor for transforming our organizations.

As we shall see when we look deeper into the organization and dynamics of ecosystems, the 'navigational principles' of stability, control and adaptability do apply to ecosystems, but in a limited sense. Ecosystems do seek stability and equilibrium. But that is only one-quarter of the story of nature; it represents one of the four worlds. The need for equilibrium and stability is held together in a larger network of four worlds in which stability and instability co-exist. When we deal with an interconnected system such as a lake or a forest in which every part (or sub-whole) is in unbroken contact with every other part of the system, the system as a whole needs to be simultaneously stable and in a state of instability.

Business as a state of non-equilibrium

What we see repeated time and again in business organizations is the 'failure of success'. Called the 'Icarus paradox' by Danny Miller, successful companies become highly specialized over time, basing their strategy upon one asset. Seduced into following the 'done thing', they start seeking equilibrium at the expense of innovation and creativity. Very soon, they become ossified and the very factors that made them successful now lead to their downfall, like Icarus who flew too near the sun and melted his wax wings.

If our Earth's ecosystems, the coral reefs, the rain forests, the atmosphere, had followed the dictates of seeking equilibrium alone, life would have stopped evolving. The story of evolution is in fact, one of a continual tension between stability and instability. From an ecosystemic perspective, equilibrium can be defined as a state of stability from which no more energy can be extracted, like a brick lying flat. If it was on its side or its end, it could still 'fall' further, which means there is still energy available. When lying flat the brick is in its lowest energy state – equilibrium.

Ecologically, a state of complete equilibrium is closer to a state of death since it is reached only when all energy is used up. So organizations that are in a state of equilibrium are those that are traditionally waiting to be bailed out, taken over by a new management, or have simply declared themselves bankrupt. Nothing on our planet is in a state of equilibrium. Contrast that with say, Mars whose atmosphere is in perfect chemical equilibrium. Rather than equilibrium, it is disequilibrium that suggests the presence of life! The Earth's atmosphere is an extraordinary and unstable mixture of gases, but at the same time this composition has stayed the same over quite long periods of time. For instance the air we breathe is an impossible mixture of reactive oxidizing and reducing gases. The atmosphere is 21 per cent oxygen and 1.7 parts per million of methane. Oxygen reacts with methane in sunlight to form carbon dioxide and water. In an equilibrium state, the methane would soon be used up. That has never happened because methane is being continually replenished by methane producing organisms at the rate of 500 million tonnes a year.

Organizations too are like complex ecosystems that need to be sustained in states of non-equilibrium. The strategy for success is in being able to maintain a contradiction within your organization, where one part tends towards stability and the other towards instability. Richard Pascale explains the continuing success of Honda along similar lines. On the one hand, Honda management is all about traditional Darwinian and Newtonian principles: coherence, centralization, tight controls, and most importantly, adaptation to the environment. But on the other hand, these traditional perspectives are continually being shattered through individual and counter-cultural freedom to seek out instability. Through this meeting of opposites, Honda has been able to move to a higher order state of 'bounded instability' which is the hallmark of all ecosystems. We also refer to it as an 'autopoetic' state. An autopoetic organization is like a living system whose true identity is derived from the paradoxically simultaneous existence of instability and stability. Erich Jantsch defines it as the state reached once a structure has gone through the turmoils and turbulences of youth and adolescence and established its identity in the 'far-from-equilibrium' environment. Autopoesis literally means 'self-productive'. An autopoetic structure is able to resonate between using new inputs to dissipate into higher orders, and being stable in the presence of a rapidly fluctuating environment.

Organizational life-phases

The classical principles of straightforward competition, adaptation and control are geared towards a start-up, *youthful* organization. In the beginning, for organism and organization alike, there is a need for bodily growth and higher use of energy. Managers have to keep on their toes, quick to seek out new opportuities, cashing in on quick returns, similar to organisms that *exploit* the environment and struggle to survive on their own. Successful strategies become genetically and behaviourally adapted and organizations develop their own formulae and systems. A new order evolves, one of stability based on successful strategy. Resources are now used at a lower rate, and the organization, now in its *adult* stage, acquires *control* of itself and the environment. It 'settles down' and stops exploring, seeking instead to reap the benefits of the stability it has acquired. Around *mid-life*, there is the onset of turbulence and a dissolution of the old identity. Instability appears in the nature of end-of-the-line product cycles, diminished sales, divergent problems that cannot be fixed as before and conflict. The organization is in a state of dissonance and old structures come down to be replaced by new processes. As in life, the organization seeks out a return to a state resembling the youthful stage through a new identity, and *letting go* of old mental and physical models, thus changing the course of the organization. The tight order that was established is replaced by a loose structure. Finally in the last stage, the organization becomes *mature* and evolves to becoming a *legacy*. It is stable once more, but in contrast to the control mode, its stability is the result of spreading out its resources and gains macroscopically. The organization is now indistuingishable from the society it is in and it works towards the benefit of larger wholes. This is illustrated figure 6.1.

As is evident, the area of 'bounded instability' or autopoesis is one that is enfolded at the centre of the four worlds and which is the overlapping area at the centre of the two axes. When we say that ecosystems are in a state of bounded instability or autopoesis, it means that they are able to maintain themselves in a state of perpetual resonance within the four worlds of exploring, settling down, letting go and leaving a legacy. While they continue a pioneering, exploratory existence, they are equally well tuned into unpredictable, catalytic modes of being. Similarly, while they are highly stable as individual units, they are simultaneously responsible in maintaining the overall system of the Earth.

Positive and negative feedback

What is important from the point of view of formulating new management strategies that are not based on the old models of stability and equilibrium, is an understanding of how exactly these four worlds operate in an ecosystem. Firstly,

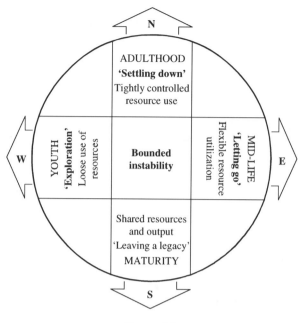

Figure 6.1

a prerequisite to stability is that you perceive your organization as abstracted out of its environment. It then becomes an autonomous entity with a high need for control and stability. It has a definite physical structure, it utilizes specifc mechanisms that are structured into various heirarchical orders within itself, and it has a need for accumulating energy to its advantage. To gain and consolidate its stability, it has to compete with the other organizations and adapt to changes in the external environment. New policies, laws, deadlines, etc., have to be followed. Fixing targets for profits and then preparing annual budgets, setting time paths for product development, frequent monitoring, corrective action are all aimed to keeping your business on a stable, predetermined equilibrium path. This is known as the path of *negative feedback*, a stabilty-seeking mechanism which dampens any deviation from the norm. A frequently quoted example of negative feedback is the central heating system in a house. A desired temperature is preset in the control mechanism, which also contains a mechanism to sense room temperature. The control system turns the heat on when room temperature falls below the preset mark, and does the opposite when the temperature rises above the level. By responding to the deviation away from the standard, the control system dampens any deviant movement. In other words, the emphasis is on maintaining a preset condition of stability.

Similar to what is observed in natural systems, your organization is simultaneously open to external and internal fluctuations and develops by being permeable to its environment. To counterbalance the forces of negative feedback, it has to remain continually unstable. This goes against conventional wisdom which says that instability is bad for the organization. Without instability, as we said before, the organization is apt to run into decay. The thermodynamic balance that prevents the running down of a closed, stable system is generated by instability and loops of positive feedback that create vicious and virtuous cycles that amplify small changes. Life creates conditions for life that creates more life, which is an example of positive feedback. Similarly, organizations must continually create through change and instability, conditions for organizational evolution. The organization is a set of open-ended interdependencies that link it to suppliers, financiers, retailers, consumers, the community that you serve, and the natural environment through vicious and virtuous cycles. These relationships flow in and through the company, identical to the chemical processes and cycles that flow in and through all ecosystems. The open-endedness demands instability through continual change.

'Far-from-equilibrium' stage

As a result, an ecosystem is a highly sensitized system. This means that if there is the slightest change taking place in any one part or aspect of the system, the change gets amplified over the whole system. Later on in this chapter, we shall be calling this a 'far-from-equilibrium' stage. Secondly, interconnectedness is only possible when the lines and boundaries that divide 'individual' systems turn amorphous and permeable. So, for that matter, where does a leaf begin? And where does it end? Likewise, what are the boundaries of a lake, or a sea? When systems are seen from the ecological perspective, clear-cut demarcations and boundaries just stop making sense. If a leaf, for instance, 'ended' at what we traditionally perceive to be its contour, it would die instantaneously. And so would the entire ecosystem. The so-called edges of leaves are, in fact, highly amorphous linkages with the environment, and the sun itself. What every schoolchild learns to define as 'photosynthesis' is basically a scientific description of the leaf's relationship with the sun. And our's too, for every time we breathe in a lungfull of oxygen to keep us alive, we are breathing in the relationship of leaf and sun. Where do we end, then? Certainly not at the contours of our body. Our skins too are highly porous linkages to the outside, without which we would not survive. What digests the meal you have just eaten is not 'your' digestive system, but a highly sophisticated alliance between your body and millions of microbes that live in your intestines. Nothing in nature can be demarcated into individual entities.

From a traditional, equilibrium perspective of management, your organization is best managed if it is perceived to be an isolated, autonomous entity. So we traditionally demarcate our companies with hard boundaries, both inside and outside, under the impression that a cartographed organization provides for stability. In reality, a cartographed organization is no more stable than the map of a country, or a stuffed animal in a museum. All three are examples of complex systems that exist only in continual interaction with the external environment. While the animal depends on sun, water, plants and life-forms for its development, nations depend on free flow of information, social, economic and political institutions and organizations depend on managing the linkages with suppliers, retailers and consumers. From this perspective, a state of complete equilibrium is simply unsustainable; stability has to be counterbalanced by instability and it is in the dynamic tension between the two that organisms and organizations alike survive, grow and develop.

A plant for instance is able to respond immediately to a change in the acid level of the soil it is in, by changing its own pH value. This response is the outcome of an inherent instability in the plant that makes it open to fluctuation. Similarly, the very existence of the plant is the outcome of its permeability, its lack of clear boundaries. However, this is not to ignore the fact that ecosystems and living organisms are also highly stable entities. The same plant that has an inherent instability about it is also highly stable, in the sense that it is able to withstand a great deal of external perturbation. Trees in a forest are able to expand their size and numbers precisely because of a need for greater stability. Similarly, ecosystems are able to conserve themselves by being individualistic, or non-permeable. Your own organization cannot be permanently unstable. Rather it has to balance itself between phases of stability and instability. What strikes as being a paradox, namely the co-existence of stability and instability, is in fact a generative ecological principle. Moreover, as we shall see in this chapter, it also becomes the generative principle for a four-world approach to managing organizations.

Tansformation phases in ecosystems

According to the emergent ecosystemic model, to manage your organization as a purely stable and isolated entity that competes with other such stable entities simply does not work any more. There is no absolute stability in the natural world. Rather, stability goes hand in hand with instability. Looking closer at the natural world, it appears that the dynamic state of 'hanging' between stable structures and destabilizing processes takes place at the centre of four worlds of:

1 Competetion
2 Conservation
3 Catalyzation
4 Co-creation.

This is shown schematically in figure 6.2.

Let us take an example from an ecosystem first and work this model through. After that, we can apply this model to organizations and their management.

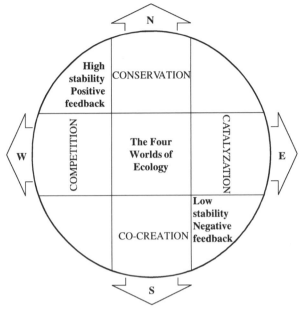

Figure 6.2

The Four Worlds of Soil

A handful of soil from your garden reveals the extraordinary life-support systems of the Earth. Beneath the thin layer of soil covering the continents of our world lies the ecosystem that governs the existence of every species on earth. It houses the bacterial and the microbial powerhouse, containing billions of microscopic organisms. This same handful of soil also contains the strands of the four worlds of ecology.

The first world of competition: pioneering and exploration

At first glance, the top soil provides nutrition for plants and trees and consequently to all the other species. A 'good' patch of soil allows plants and trees to colonize itself. It provides the ecological milieu for the pioneering stage of bodily growth in which plants, trees, shrubs and weeds increase their body mass. In their growth phase, all plants and animals use resources from their environment to build their tissues. They increase in size through a high intake of energy. This leads to a build-up of biomass in the system, characterized by a factor called *gross production* (*P*).

Gross production is a bit like the gross national product (GNP) that measures the financial well-being of a nation. Like the GNP, this factor only measures the expansion of biomass and the number of species. It does not take into account the overall qualitative well-being of the entire system, very much in the same way that the GNP does not take into account the quality of living in societies. The world of competition is the world of survival. It is all about individual plants, trees and animals trying to get maximum access to the initially plentiful resources available.

The second world of conservation: settling down and organization

Left to itself, the pioneering, competetive aspect of life would completely over-run the soil and, very soon, it would be reduced to rubble. Not unlike in the economics of societies and countries where the pioneering spirit and competetion has to be supplemented by some kind of conservation of resources, soil needs to be 'kept going' by some built-in system. So, the Northern European societies of Scandinavia have a built-in high taxation system that allows them to run a welfare state in which all citizens receive benefits of free housing, hospitalization, and an education for life. In conservation, something is 'put back' into the pool of resources for the benefit of all.

In the case of soil, this Northern world is made operable through millions of nitrogen-fixing bacteria in the soil. This mechanism of nitrogen fixation, trans-forms free nitrogen, which is otherwise useless for life cycles of plants and animal species, into ingestible nitrogen compounds. There are two types of nitrogen-fixing bacteria: (1) symbiotic bacteria, those that attach themselves to the roots of plants and (2) non-symbiotic bacteria, those that live free in the soil. It has been estimated that in a single season, in an acre of soil, the symbiotic bacteria which form small nodules on the roots of plants may add about 150 pounds of nitrogen to that acre. The asymbiotic bacteria, on the other hand remain ceaselessly active in breaking down dead organic matter, to release again nitrogen and the other nutrients of life into the soil and the atmosphere. The soil is thus able to conserve its nutrients and maintain its life cycle over a longer length of time.

The third world of catalysation: creative destruction

The symbiotic and asymbiotic nitrogen-fixing bacteria prevent the pioneering stage from completely depleting the soil of its nutrients. As we saw, the ecosys-tem is thus able to better sustain the demands made on it by the pioneer stage. But over time, conservation of the soil through nitrogen fixation alone is not enough. Conservation by itself is akin to a bureaucratic structure which although necessary at a certain stage in the development of an organization or a society, becomes an impediment to further evolution. By becoming desensitized to the real needs and demands of the environment, bureaucratic structures become ossified. If it were left to only the conservation world of the ecosystem, life would over time, settle into predictable, highly organized structures. In the case of a forest, after having passed through the tribulations of the pioneer stage, it settles into maximum homogeneity and becomes specially adapted to specific niches. This is again true of the Scandinavian societies which over time have become so highly homogenized that it is diffiult for them to adjust to the emergent multiculturalism that is sweeping the world.

The effect of conservation is to build up the *entropy* level in an ecosystem. Entropy is like life-energy which is either accumulated and stored, or dissipated. In the pioneering mode, entropy is spent on exploration and the system is loosely bound in the sense that resoures can flow in a diversity of ways through the system. In the conservation mode, energy is conserved and entropy thus accumulates in the system as a result of homogeneity and organization. But excessive entropy build-up – which is another word for equilibrium – is fatal for any living system. Under these conditions, the system simply buckles under and collapses. What usually happens in nature is that this tendency to accumulate entropy and move towards full equilibrium is offset by certain processes that engage in what can be termed as catalytic destruction. To prevent entropy from building up, ecosystems 'discover' another level of order, in which the structures that have been built up are destroyed to prevent ossification.

In the case of the soil ecosystem, other bacteria invade the plants and trees and start causing disease. The more homogeneous a forest becomes, the more susceptible it is to the disease-causing bacteria. The plants and trees that the bacteria invade are called the 'host species'. The association between bacteria and the host results in an abnormal condition in the host which causes blight and rot. These bacteria are carried from one tree to another by the very mechanisms that are part of the tightly bound structure, namely bees, pollinating insects and rain. Hurst, writing in *Crisis and Renewal*, uses the forest fire phenomenon as another example of 'creative destruction'. In the case of a fire, a system is not destroyed completely; it is partially destroyed in order to be renewed.

Catalysation is a phenomenon through which a number of 'tag-on' processes undermine the existence of the previous conservative order of stability and increasing equilibrium. Whether they are the invading bacteria, forest fires or typhoons, these catalysts alter the earlier structure and create new situations in which the energy blocks are removed. In contrast to the 'desensitized' state of the ecosystem at conservation stage, the system becomes highly sensitized at the catalytic stage. As we shall see later, positive feedback loops amplify small changes and push them through the entire system, keeping it in a 'far-from-equilibrium' stage. This is also the stage where life can take new directions and lead to the development of new species and behaviour. Our own evolution from our anaerobic bacterial ancestors to oxygen-breathing ones was the result of a similar far-from-equilibrium stage. Chaos and creativity seem to have a partner-ship in the ecosystemic model. It goes without saying that as far as our organi-zations are concerned, this is the part that we have most trouble with!

The fourth world of co-creation: evolution

Whereas catalysation disrupts the ecosystem to shift it to another level of order, co-creation is the re-ordering of the system. This re-ordering is at the very heart of life's evolution. Like a mountain spring from which a river is eternally born, co-creation is the very fountain head of all the patterns, relationships, structures and processes in life. From the point of view of the old biology, life evolved by adapting to the environment. But as we saw, this is only one-quarter of the truth, applicable to the competetive, pioneering aspect of ecosystems. What we now know is that life does not merely adapt to the environment, rather life and its environment are partners in co-creation.

So, for instance, in our example about the soil ecosystem, we saw that the soil sustains life on earth. We also saw how the nutrients are recycled back into the soil with the help of certain bacteria. But where does the soil itself come from? In the old biology, it was taken as a given, something that exists as the environ-ment. What we now know is the soil is continually being created by the plant and animal life that lives off the soil. So carbon dioxide is pumped down by life on the surface after dissolution in water near the rock surface. The water may have come from rainwater or fed by nearby spring and rivers. This solution now causes rocks to weather. The micro-organisms aid this process and more soil gets created. Without life there would be no soil, only the rock rubble of dead planets.

The emergence and the maintenance of life is an ongoing transformative process. *While life emerges out of its environment, the environment needs to be continually transformed by life so as to remain life-supportive.* Moreover, this is achieved by life being in a state of continual change itself, not opposing the forces of the environment, but flowing with them. Life and the environment can be said to be partners in co-creation. To take another example of this co-creative aspect: blades of hydrophytic grasses reduce stream velocity, thereby forcing the waters to drop the silt load and the decaying plant material they carry along. This increases channel deposition, which creates more soil and nutrients for plant roots. Plants grow stronger, denser. This reduces velocity further, creating more deposition. Deposition displaces water. The stream overflows and spreads out, greatly expanding its surface area as it flows over. The water's energy drops drastically. Nourishing water and silt are spread over a broad channel, nourish-ing more lush growth. This growth creates greater accumulations of spongy, absorbent, plant material, spreading the slowing water even wider.

The interaction between natural energy and life's energy is the chief principle of co-creation. The interaction is often so subtle, so insignificant that we don't even see it. Each small shift in equilibrium creates another small shift. Each new equilibrium covers the tracks of the previous change. The power lies in the accumulative consistency with which these changes shift equilibrium in life's favour. Life creates conditions for more life, which in turn create conditions for more life. These loops create change, not stability. *By shaping the development of its environment, life allows itself to be shaped by the environment.*

Likewise, the purpose of business from this fourth-world perspective, is to co-create a common future in which resources and benefits transcend the four walls of the organization and encompass as wide an area as possible. Organizations that do so, develop; the ones that don't eventually die out. From a co-creative perspective then, on the one hand your business depends on the external environment for its growth and development. But curiously enough, on the other hand, it must participate in the creation of an environment that is sustainable and conducive to doing business.

Business and the Four Worlds of Ecology

Organizations are like blades of grass, trees, coral reefs, forests. They streamline the flow of resources and make it amenable to humans in the form of goods and services. They too are contained within the four directions of *competetion, conservation, catalysation* and *co-creation.* Each of these four ecological worlds which isomorphically pervade our organizations therefore require different strategies on the part of the manager. We now consider each of these four worlds, juxtaposed on the four global axes, and outline how different strategies need to be adopted by the manager based on the lessons of ecology.

The Western world of territorial management: the manager as hunter

The conventional hands-on management that is so much a characteristic of Anglo-Saxon enterprises is one that favours freedom and individuality over collective behaviour. The emphasis is on structured, yet autonomous organizations that are able to adapt to the environment and create maximum profit through a dissemination of products and services that sell.

The Western archetypal world is fundamentally a pioneering one. It is exemplified by rapid industrial and technological growth and a spirit of entrepreneurship. As we saw in the chapter 2, it demands an empirical, hands-on approach that is more than comfortable experimenting in trial-and-error situations.

The manager here is clearly the hunter–gatherer who stakes claims to unoccupied territory and the market that it offers. The attitude is highly competetive and the learning process is *reactive*. The aim of the hunter–gatherer manager is to try and build structures that can strengthen the organization's hold on the territory and the product. Change is not welcome unless it is predictable change for which the hunter is prepared. The hunter is mainly a sensate human being using instinct and a finely honed hunting acumen to advantage. Rationalization is often retrospective and is used only to build a successful recipe. But the action is primarily instinctive and based on a sensory reading of the situation at hand. The strategy of the hunter–gatherer manager is to try and cash in on the recipe by using it to exploit as many situations as possible. The recipe can both involve a product like Coca-Cola which is then marketed successfully across the globe, or a management strategy of sensing out emergent territories in the maket and then quickly moving in to occupy them.

Territorial management depends on physical resistance to opposing forces. The strength of this mode is its extraordinary ability to venture into difficult market conditions by playing hard and using one's natural instinct. The disadvantage of this mode is that it works best only as long as the organization is at a youthful stage. Entrepreneurship, the stronghold of Western organizations, is all about going 'against the wind' and erecting strong structures that can take the impact. The pragmatic, hands-on model of the West searches for identity in the world of structure. Like pitching one's tent or putting up a flag, the identity of the youthful organization comes from territorial advantage and competetion. This mode works efficiently as long as the company does not become 'over-adapted'. Texas Instruments once set the standards for semiconductors and were pack-leaders in the consumer electronics industry. But TI kept selling on price alone, having adapted to a market notion that low prices meant maximum consumption. This adaptive mind-set, once the cause of its success, became the cause of its decline. It was slow to move into the more sophisticated chip market and faster rivals moved into the niche. What happened with IBM is more or less a similar story. Hunting–gathering management is based on the premise that once the fences are erected around a territory, the company can coast along in a predictable world. But as the Texas Instruments case tells us, the real world of business is anything but that.

A territorial organization is a *structural* organization, composed of one-to-one correspondences, strict linearity, and the for-every-effect-there-is-a-cause logic. The bottom line is the deciding factor for all structures and for all practical purposes the organization has no connectedness with the outside world, except in terms of goods sold and services rendered. The balance sheet is all about profit and loss, the core values of the territorial organization. The environment of such a business is restricted to commercial parties, interested purely in the financial state of the organization. Correspondingly, the balance sheet of the territorial organization makes explicit the singularly financial relationship of the firm to the world outside.

The Northern world of niche management: the manager as herder

The Northern management form of the Scandinavians, unlike that of the Anglo-Saxons, is highly rational. In contrast to the hunter who is essentially a sensate manager, relying on instinct and trial and error more than reason, the Northern manager is a herder who operates entirely through reason. Whereas the Western organization adapts to the environment, the Northern organization depends on the environment adapting to it. Rather than capturing territories, the emphasis is on developing and implementing systems that find a specialized niche in the market. It is not immediate profit that is the main concern now as the system is assured of its survival. Rather it is to specialize in function and conserve resources as much as possible through a standardization of policies, procedures and species types. For instance, two of Denmark's biggest national dailies, *Politiken* and *Berlingske Tidende*, share a common spare parts inventory. They also have a system whereby in case of shortage of staff in either newspaper, they 'borrow' human resources from the other for the day. On all other counts, the two papers are competitors: they compete on price, quality, layout, readership, etc. But at the same time, being associates involved in a common business, they 'herd' together and conserve resources.

Herding organizations invest in technology and formal organizations procedure as a way of increasing specialization. Unlike the recipe method of the Hunter manager, the Herder manager works with a formulated theory that is applied to situations. This is the world of the 'formula' mode that Mitroff and Linstone refer to in chapter 9. The computer industry is an excellent example of how companies that were hunting successes were forced in the 1980s to adopt a herding policy. Hurst refers to the story of Compaq which in 1987 made it into the *Fortune* 5000 after only four years of operation. Very much like Texas Instruments, Compaq was squarely a hunting organization with a closely guarded territory. Prices were kept high as the territory was relatively safe. But during the early 1990s, sales started falling and the first losses began to register at Compaq. For the first time since its inception, there were lay-offs. What was once a unique Compaq territory had been invaded by many other competitors, who were selling similar products at much cheaper prices. What was clearly needed was a niche formation and a conservation of resources. Costs were cut drastically, the workforce was cut by 25 per cent and procedures made more efficient. In two years, Compaq quadrupled its output and improved sales growth.

The danger with herder organizations is that like homogeneous forests and other ecosystems, they are highly susceptible to catastrophe. Efficiency is bought at the expense of flexibility and resilience, which are the characteristics of the territorial organizations. The herder manager therefore needs to be able to upgrade existing systems constantly to offset the brittleness of the Northern organization.

These Northern, niche organizations are then systematized organizations, constructed on rational lines. The herder manager is a resposive and a deliberative learner and is able to conceptualize the organizational process better than the hunter manager. But on the other hand, the herder manager lacks the instinct, the individuality and the sensory acumen of the hunter.

The Eastern world of symbiotic management: the manager as gardener

In stark contrast to the highly stable niche organization of the North, the Eastern organization operates best in conditions of instability. The approach is neither to resist the flux of matter and energy in the environment, or submit to it. The middle path principle is that of the blade of hydrophytic grass, which prevents run-off not through direct opposition but by allowing the water to split and flow around it.

The emphasis here is on maintaining a highly fluid organization that is able to create changes both within itself and in the environment. This model tends to rely exclusively on generating processes that result in loops of positive feedback. The assumption that the gardener manager of the East makes is that turbulence cannot and should not be controlled. Moreover, unlike in the niche organization, turbulence is perceived in positive terms, as a precursor to creativity. So Honda, for instance, purposely provokes instability by hiring large groups of managers in mid-career from other organizations. The aim is to prevent the crystallization of one corporate culture. Counter-cultures are encouraged to provoke instability and consequently, innovative management.

So, the hunter manager adapts the territorial organization to the environment, and the herder manager creates a fit for the organization within the environment in the form of a specialized niche. In contrast, the gardener manager perceives both the organization and the environment as dynamic phenomena, incapable of being abstracted into a condition of stability. Eastern organizations generate conditions for their sustenance by 'losing themselves', letting go of previously held boundaries of 'in here' and 'out there' and the strict heirarchies within.

The development of a living system is the interaction between the life and the environment. To illustrate this, we use a term given by C. H. Waddington, the *epigenetic landscape*, which is a multidimensional world of valleys and hills. This landscape is a picture of both the individual organism and the external environment it develops in. The epigenetic landscape consists of what Waddington called 'chreodes', well-worn pathways that represent previously used genetic tracks. Like a ball rolling down a landscape, the developing organism is set in motion. It tends to follow the old chreodes. But the landscape itself is a dynamic one, it is alive, full of perturbations, and the organism may be influenced by the landscape to make a detour. But what happens is that the detour etches out a new chreode on the epigenetic landscape. So when future organisms use this new chreode, the eventual result is the formation of a new order of organisms. One organism therefore cycles-in the other through an interactive relationship between the organism and the environment. Open-ended, Eastern organizations maintain themselves in a state of development through a similar cycling-in process. The tendency in the territorial and the niche organizations is to resist perturbations and the demand for detours, and depend exclusively on negative feedback loops. But what is vital to the Eastern organization is to the invite the detours and allow new chreodes to develop. Sony's success with the *Walkman* and the *Camcorder* are examples of how product-chreodes develop through spontaneity and perturbation in the system.

Crucial to the gardener manager's approach to management is a phenomenon of symbiosis. It can be defined as an association of two or more living systems within a larger ecosystem that creates a situation of mutual advantage for themselves and for the larger whole. Japan's legendary relationships between producers and suppliers are an excellent example of symbiosis. At the Toyota plant in Takaoka, no worker has more than one hour's worth of inventory at the work station. When a defective part is discovered, it is immediately tagged and sent to a quality control area for replacement. The 'just-in-time' inventory system of Japanese corporations is possible only because of a symbiotic link of trust and mutual benefit between the parties involved. As Lynn Margulis points out in Lawrence Joseph's book *Gaia: The Growth of an Idea*: '. . . symbiotic cooperation is at least as important as "survival of the fittest" competetion; in order to compete – in order to get in the game in the first place – you have to cooperate. We now believe that the doctrinaire Darwinian view of "nature red in tooth and claw" is naive and incomplete. Symbiosis means survival.'

Symbiosis, then, means that competitors are able to enter into harmony with each other. In natural systems, there are innumerable examples of microbes that have evolved amazingly complex symbiotic relationships. While some microbes lower hydrogen sulphide concentrations for others, the others in turn, provide organic compounds. Some microbes 'eat' but are anaerobic, which means they are not capable of 'breathing, oxygen, but they exist in symbiosis with others which can 'breathe' but cannot 'eat'. Margulis extended microbial symbiosis further to what she refers to as *endosymbiosis*. So when two or more species cooperate closely enough, eventually obsolete qualities no longer appear in the offspring. Margulis writes: 'The consortial quality of the individual pre-empts the notion of independence.'

Once again, the Japanese organizational model seems to be directed towards Margulis' endosymbiosis. Similar to the dropping off of redundant qualities as an evolutionary pattern, Japanese corporations place premium value on continually refining existing systems by eliminating those aspects that have become obsolete. This dynamic state of continually evolving products towards higher forms of order is achieved through symbiotic interplay between competitors and a deep interconnectedness between the organization and the consumer. An

endosymbiotic organization thrives and profits on its being part of an interconnected whole. The symbiotic interplay, both within the individual company and
within the bigger organizational network, is the result of the gardener manager
participating in the interconnection instead of being the objective observer.

The Southern world of homeostatic management:
the manager as steward

The Southern world is characterized as being able to maintain itself in a state of
dynamic equilibrium. In biological terms, it seeks to maintain a state of
homeostasis. The Earth for instance, is bounded on the outside by space with
which it exchanges energy, sunlight coming in and heat radiation going out. It
is bounded on the inside by inner space, the vast volume of plastic hot rock that
supports the crust and with which the Earth exchanges matter. Within this
boundedness, it maintains itself through the presence of life.

All ecosystems are endowed with the necessary mechanisms for homeostasis,
which include energy flows, material cycles and invisible information networks
that connect all parts and regulate the system as a whole. Homeostatic management involves treating the organization as a macroscopic entity, like the self-
regulating Earth itself. On a macroscopic scale, boundaries become unimportant
and the steward manager both draws in resources from as wide an area as
possible and spreads services out across an equally wide area. The steward
manager's starting point is the notion that the organization can never exist as an
isolated entity. Like all ecological phenomena, it stays alive and healthy only as
long as it maintains a web of relationships, both within itself and with its
environment. For the steward manager, unlike the hunter or the herder, organizational operation is not a matter of formulae or theories. Rather, it flows in and
through a web of relationships that bind the organization to society and the
environment. The bond is a porous one, similar to the kind of amorphous link-
edges that characterize a leaf or a lake. Products have to be developed and
improved through a constant interlinking of people, ideas, skills and resources,
and they have to reach the market through a network of processes. Resources
enter the organization through link-edges, and wastes have to be disposed off
through other links. But within the old organizational logic, particularly in the
Anglo–Saxon organizational model, we go about our jobs as managers convinced
that the organization functions best when perceived as a fragmented entity.

According to the new biology, rather than competing for survival, early
chemical matter structures evolved through co-operation. So, what was the
reason for the co-operation? These early non-living microstructures were part of
a very large macrostructure, the chemical system of the whole Earth. As the
microstructures evolved, they changed the chemistry of the macrosystem. This
in turn produced more fluctuations and new microstructures emerged. *Micro
and macro produced each other, like reflections down a hall of mirrors.* So, co-

evolution is a holistic unfolding towards a future, not a random interaction of parts. Later when bacteria appeared as the dominant life on Earth, there was no free oxygen. Some of the bacteria created fluctuations in their own (micro)structures and subsequently in the macrostructure of the Earth's atmosphere and restructured into forms capable of photosynthesis. For the next 2000 million years, they went about totally transforming the earth's atmosphere by filling it with free oxygen! According to Jantsch, there was a curious selflessness and *vision* in the way they went about it. Already adapted to the oxygenless environment, how did the bacteria 'know' that they had to restructure themselves to becoming oxygen-dependent, so that life could evolve further? According to Jantsch, the goal is the extraordinary intensification of life. In his scenario, the universe as a whole is an autopoetic structure. 'Life appears no longer a phenomenon unfolding in the universe – the universe itself becomes increasingly alive.'

Your organization – a microstructure – is enfolded within macrostructures of societies, cultures, the Earth and life itself. Micro- and macrostructures are reflections of each other. The organization participates in the intensification of life. From the homeostatic perspective, the organization has no beginning and no end. A business organization is like a biological organism which thrives on its being a part of a larger interconnectedness; and functions best, when managed as one. From the ecological perspective, homeostasis is the natural path of the universe.

The Southern homeostatic pole provides a sense of direction to the organization by rooting it in a universal legacy of shared value. The Southerness explicitly manifests itself through a 'mission' and a visionary need to express deeply rooted values and desires to change the world through products and services. The business world still awaits a fully developed manifestation of the Southern, value mode. Perhaps that will be the path of all future organizational evolution.

Partners in Evolution: The Legacy of 'Oikos'

The term ecology originates from an ancient Greek word, *oikos*, that simply meant home. Ecology (*oikos* + *logos*) thus became the 'study of one's home' and consequently, of one's relationship to all that constitutes 'home'. Interestingly, the word economics has also been derived from the same root. Since 'nomics' means management, economics translates as the 'management of the household', which involves an increase in 'value' for the benefit of the household*.

---

* Aristotle made a distinction between 'oikonomia' and 'chrematistics'. Oikonomia is the management of the household, whereas chrematistics is manipulation of wealth for short-term benefit to the owner.

Accordingly, ecology and economics originate from a common ground and as such are inntrinsically linked in their meaning. While economics without ecological value would make for unsustainability, ecology bereft of economic structure would lack structure and consistency. Each is enfolded within the other. This is ironic considering that the situation as we have traditionally known it has been precisely the opposite. The generally widespread notion – both within the business community and outside – that ecological considerations violate the very basis of economic well-being, and vice versa is familiar rhetoric. In the mechanical world view, success is measured in economic measures and not ecological ones, although the two are intrinsically connected. In effect, we are supposed to 'manage' our organizational household without 'valuing' it.

The dysfunctional organizational form of today, struggling to retain a foothold in the slippery world of contextual change is a consequence of precisely the same problem: managing without valuing. The first effect of this is to alienate the manager from the 'ecology' of the organization: the systemic networks and invisible processes that hold the company together. Secondly, the organization itself ends up isolated from its environment. Economic progress becomes a pendulum-like movement between production and consumption, within a completely closed system, governed exclusively by its own laws, rather than the systemic pattern and processes that govern value in nature.

However, this model seems to have reached the limits of its sustainability and there is considerable evidence that a paradigm shift is on its way in. In the turbulence that is shaking up old structures of thought and beginning to produce unprecedented changes in our organizations and societies, a transformation in the traditional dualism between ecology and economics is imminent. Any new understanding must necessarily provide a framework that articulates a new coherent system in which ecology and economics return to being complementary forces. The return to one's home, the *oikos*, is simultaneously emotional and pragmatic. For to return is to renew, to gather sustenance for the future; it is to reach deeply into one's roots and tap the wellspring of belonging. From the primeval carbon atoms that continue to exist and sustain our individual bodies, to the natural fossil-fuel resources and the elemental energy that we utilize and mould in every fibre of our organizational systems, our links with *oikos* are undeniable and irrevocable. Whether it is an organization, a society or any of the other myriad forms that we forge, each of these, in one way or other, is rooted in *oikos*. An understanding of these indelible links is the singular act of understanding a universal system at work, through an array of complex relationships, chains, linkages, alliances and interdependencies that make us and our environment a fountain of energy flowing through a circuit of soils, rocks, microbes, plants, animals, the atmosphere, our societies, and our organizations. Consequently, it provides a powerful model and metaphor for the alternative so badly needed to produce far-reaching changes in our societies, organizations and lives. And, in the return to one's home, there is a genuine possibility for change.

Conclusion

As we move into the closing years of this century, the need for a new, coherent world view for businesses and societies becomes more and more important. We believe that the four worlds of ecology are able to provide such a world view. From the pioneering spirit that marks the human need to explore and further existing knowledge to the spirit of value that creates a context in which all can benefit, our evolutionary record carries the imprint of both ventures. Gaia, the name used by scientist James Lovelock to symbolize the planet Earth, is an embodiment of the four worlds that prevail in our organizations and the four cultural corners of our world. From our physical environment that we have been examining in this chapter and the previous one, we now turn to the inner world of human beings: our psychological environment.

Bibliography

Stacey, R. (1992) *Managing the Unknowable*. California: Jossey-Bass.

Miller, D. (1990) *The Icarus Paradox: How Excellent Organizations Can Bring About Their Own Downfall*. New York: Harper Business.

Pascale, R. (1990) *Managing on the Edge: How Successful Companies Use Conflict To Stay Ahead*. London: Viking/Penguin.

Jantsch, E. (1980) *The Self-Organizing Universe: Scientific and Human Implications of the Emerging Paradigm of Evolution*. Oxford: Pergamon Press.

Hurst, D. (1995) *Crisis and Renewal: Meeting the Challenge of Organizational Change*. Boston, MA: Harvard Business School Press.

Joseph, L. (1991) *Gaia: The Growth of an Idea*. New York: Arkana.

7

The Psychological Environment

Introduction: The Process of Individuation

In the previous chapter, we proposed that the dynamics of our organizations are an extension of the four worlds of ecology. In this chapter, we propose that business and management can be recognized, as an extension of the psychological nature of the human being. In that respect ecology and psychology move to the centre stage of the management of an organization, while economics and technology shift to the wings. More specifically then, the ecological and psychological goals of companies become an existential as well as a physiological imperative. A new ecology of management overtakes the traditional pragmatic and rational approaches to organizations and a dynamic orientation supplants a static one.

Construction and development

This shift to an ecology perspective is not only a management movement. It also reflects a shift in the development of modes of scientific thought as we saw in the chapter on our physical environment. In biology too, the first step was that of classification, which was the chief characteristic of the first and second worlds. Botany and biology spent 2500 years on the taxonomy of plants and animals. The next step, after classification, was so called 'ontogeny'. This marked the emergence of the third and fourth worlds in which attention turned to the origins, development and direction of a phenomenon. In the past 150 years, therefore, nearly every social and natural science has been transformed from a structure and system oriented perception of the phenomena under investigation to a process and value oriented one. This occurred in astronomy with Laplace, in logic with Hegel, in history and political economy with Marx, in biology with Darwin, and in psychology with Piaget and with Jung.

The renowned French-Swiss psychologist Jean Piaget's vision derives from a so called 'open systems evolutionary biology'. Rather than locating the life force in the closed individual or environment as is characteristic of pragmatism and rationalism, it locates a prior context which continually elaborates the distinction between the individual and the environment in the first place. It does not place an energy system within us so much as *it places us in a single energy system of all living things*. Primary attention is paid to the *progressively individuated self and the bigger life field*. Piaget's principal loyalty, therefore, was to the ongoing conversation between the individuating organism and the world.

Development then involves the transformation of such 'structures of the whole' in the direction of greater internal differentiation, complexity, flexibility and stability. A stage represents a kind of balancing relationship between a knowing individual or organizational subject and his, her or its environment. In this balanced position the person or institution *assimilates what is to be known* in the environment into his, her or its structures of thought. When a novelty or challenge emerges that cannot be assimilated into present structures of knowing then, if possible, the person or institution *accommodates* (i.e. generates new structures or systems).

A stage transition has occurred when enough accommodation has been undertaken to require, and make possible, a transformation in the operational pattern of the individual or corporate whole. This leads to what the organizational psychologist Elliot Jaques has called 'requisite organization', that is a matching of individual and organizational cognitive capacities, or to what Jung has termed 'self-regulation'.

Self-regulation

For the Swiss-German contemporary psychologist Carl Jung, all the essential functions of the physical body, and of the human psyche, operate in accordance with the principle of dynamic opposition. In other words they are arranged in opposing systems which, in health, are kept in balance through a process of positive and negative feedback. Thus hunger is balanced against satiation, sexual desire against gratification, sleep against wakefulness. Jung was convinced, moreover, that the human psyche, like the body, was a self-regulating system. The same, of course, could be said for an entire business enterprise.

You strive then, as a person and as a manager, to perpetually maintain a balance between opposing propensities, while, at the same time, seeking your own individuation. A dynamic polarity exists then – as individual or as organization – between your surface personality and your deep *self*, between your masculine consciousness and your femininity, between our extraverted and introverted attitudes. Thus the greatest and most important problems of life and work are all fundamentally insoluble. They must be because they express the necessary polarity inherent in every self-regulating system. They can never be *solved*, only *outgrown*. Jung saw the whole life cycle as a continuing process of metamorphosis which was commissioned and homeostatically regulated by the Self. While conducting you through the life cycle, the Self causes you to experience the images, ideas, symbols and emotions that human beings have always experienced since our species began. That is why management as an art form, whenever it expresses archetypal reality, speaks to universal principles of human existence.

Jung on individuation

At birth we are just like any other baby, or like any pioneering enterprise. Yet at the same time we, as persons or as organizations, are unique. All archetypes are at once universal in their basic forms and unique in their individual manifestations. All *life*, for the individual and for the institution, *is a balancing act between the personal and the collective*, through which each one of us sustains his, her or its unique version of those universal regulators, which govern all humanity. As we pass from one stage of personal or organizational life to the next, new aspects of the self/enterprise become salient in the psychic economy and demand expression. All those aspects of self which have yet to be lived provide a prospective dynamic which gives to human and organizational existence a purpose and a meaning.

What matters is not so much what we are, or what we have been, but what we are in the process of becoming. That is is the very essence of the individuation process. Jung saw individuation, to be primarily the responsibility of the second half of life, that is of the maturing individual or organization. In our four-world model, this translates itself as the third and fourth worlds. If you go on living biologically and economically into the second half of life, without becoming conscious of yourself existentially, then you are missing the point of becoming as complete a human being as it is in you to become. Coming to selfhood then, in the second half of life, is more than a cultural commitment to be a good individual or corporate citizen. It is an ethical choice to fulfil your individual or institutional humanity, to transcend your fear of death and to recognize yourself as a unique expression of all creation. That realization made, you enter the religious or 'metaphysical' dimension. You attain wisdom. For the more conscious you become, as a person or as a corporation, the more the universe becomes conscious of itself.

Jung's so-called 'number 2 personality' (the Eastern and Southern) then, the individual and organizational Self, is there in each of us from the beginning, all the way through, and at the end of life. It is both the origin and the goal of its own realization through the intermediary of the travelling ego – number 1 (Western and Northern). From earliest infancy the individual self or corporate

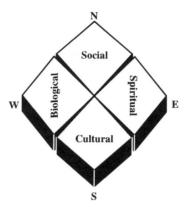

Figure 7.1

vision seeks to become manifest through working in equal partnership with your individual ego, or corporate competencies. In a way the self is to the ego what God is to man, for the ego is, in a manner of speaking, the self's representative on earth. At first the ego exists only as latent potential, as a component of the self. Then, as maturation procedes, the ego gradually differentiates itself.

Moreover, the inner programme imparted to the second half of life, according to Jung, has a quality quite different from the first. The problems of the first and second quarters of life he saw as essentially biological and social, and those of the third and fourth quarters as essentially cultural and spiritual. This can be represented as shown in figure 7.1.

'The human has two aims,' Jung wrote. 'The first survival orientation, the begetting of children and the business of protecting the brood – to this belongs the economic and technological position. Only when this aim has been achieved does the new aim – the ecological and psychological one – become feasible.' The diagram is then modified to include these dimensions, as shown in figure 7.2.

Transition from one world to the next, moreover, is a time of potential crisis for every individual, organization or indeed society. It was precisely in order to help the individual through these critical periods that 'rites of passage' emerged in primitive societies. French ethnologist Arnold Geneep demonstrated that the rites proceed through three stages – *separation, transition* and *incorporation.* Each rite is a death and rebirth ritual through which the individual or institution 'dies' to his, her or its previous world (separation) and is 'born into' the new one (incorporation). Development of the personality and organization, however, is not a simple, linear progression but a spiral with progressive ascents and regressive descents through the four worlds. Probably the best contemporary exponent of such adult development is the American developmental psychologist Daniel Levinson and his work on the four seasons of life.

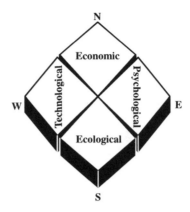

Figure 7.2

Life's Seasons

Structure-building and structure-changing

For Levinson the components of your life are not a random set of items, like pebbles washed up at the shore. Rather, like threads in a tapestry, they are woven into an encompassing design. Recurring themes in various sectors of your life and work help to unify the overall patterns of the tapestry. Individual's lives, as well as those of institution's, differ widely in the nature and patterning of these themes.

Your life structure consists of a series of alternating *stable* (*structure-building*) and *transitional* (*structure-changing*) periods. The primary task of every stable period is to build a life structure. You must make certain key choices, form a structure around them, and pursue values and goals within that structure. A transitional period terminates the existing life structure, and creates the possibility for a new one. The primary tasks of every transitional period are to question and reappraise the existing structure, to explore various possibilities for change in self and world, and to move towards commitment to the crucial choices that form the basis for a new life structure in the ensuing stable period.

The task of a *developmental transition*, then, is *to terminate a time in your life*. This involves accepting the losses such a termination entails, as well as reviewing and evaluating the past world. You thereby decide which aspects of the past to keep and which to reject, and consider your wishes and possibilities for the future. You are suspended between the past and the future, struggling to overcome the gaps that separate them. Much of the past must be given up, separated from, cast out of your life, and there is much that can be used as a basis for the future. Changes must be made in self and world. The decision to 'stay put' in one world is not always based on a reaffirmed commitment. It may stem from resignation, inertia, passive acquiessence or controlled despair – a self-restriction in the context of severe external constraints. This kind of surface stability marks the beginning of a long-term decline unless new factors intervene – perhaps in the next transitional period – and enable you to form a more satisfactory life structure. In fact the same kind of developmental logic, as we have seen with Piaget and with Jung, apply to an organization as to an individual.

No matter how satisfatory a structure is, in time its utility declines and its flaws generate conflict that leads to modification or transformation of the structure. As Marx said: 'Every system contains within itself the seeds of its own destruction.' The once stable structure passes into a new transitional period. The seasons change. Developmental tasks are undertaken anew, and the lessons of growth are gathered and stockpiled against the new period coming. The pattern of individual and organizational development continues.

The First World of the Novice: Western Exploration

Exploratory stages

Early adult transition (17–22)   The first task is to move out of the pre-adult world, to question the nature of the world and your place in it, to modify or terminate relationships with important persons. The second task is to make a preliminary step into the adult world, to explore its possibilities, to imagine yourself as a participant in it, to consolidate an initial adult identity, to make and test some preliminary choices for adult living. The first task involves a process of termination, the second a process of initiation. Both are essential in a transitional period.

First adult life structure (22–28)   As a young person, says Levinson, you have two primary yet antithetical tasks. First, you need to explore the possibilities for adult living, to keep your options open, to avoid strong commitments and maximize your alternatives. This task is reflected in a sense of adventure and wonderment. The second task is to create a stable life structure, to become more responsible and 'make something of my life'. If the first predominates, life has an extremely transient, rootless quality. If the second predominates, there is a danger of committing yourself prematurely to a structure.

In every period the several developmental tasks are contrasting and antithetical. Just as the 'early adult transition' requires a young person both to terminate one era and to intitiate the next, entering the 'adult world' requires of you both to explore freely and to make firm choices. You must take on adult responsibilities and make something of your life. Externally there are pressures to 'grow up', get married, enter an occupation, and lead a more organized life. In the self there are desires for stability and order, for lasting ties, for fulfilment of core values. At the same time the exploratory stance requires the young person to 'hang loose', keeping your options open and avoiding strong commitments. Also your own youthful vitality generates a sense of adventure and wonder, a wish to seek out and discover all the treasures of the new world you are entering.

Age 30 transition (28–33) At about 28 the provisional quality of the twenties begins to end and life becomes more serious, more for real. A voice from within the self says 'if I am to change my life, if there are things in it I want to modify or exclude, or things missing I want to add, I must now make a start, for soon it will be too late'. In most cases then, the life structure of the late twenties is incomplete or fragmented. The 'age 30 transition' therefore provides an opportunity to work on the flaws in the life structure formed during the previous period, and to create the basis for a more satifactory one. For some the transition proceeds smoothly; for most it takes a more stressful form.

You fear you might not reach the future. You feel you can move neither foreward nor back. The integrity of your enterprise is in serious doubt. Young people speak then of the age 30 crisis, whereby you experience the imminent danger of chaos and dissolution. As the age 30 transition ends, you move towards major new choices or recommit yourself to existing ones. If they are well made from the viewpoint of your dream, values, talent and possibilities, they provide the centre for a relatively satisfactory life structure. If the preparatory work has been poorly done and the new structure is flawed, life in 'settling down' will become increasingly painful. The same, incidentally, applies to a business organization that, as new management attempt to consolidate its pioneering enterprise, suffers from its flawed entrepreneurial foundations.

Exploratory tasks

Forming a dream

The vicissitudes and fate of the 'dream' have fundamental qualities for adult development. In its primordial form, the Dream is a vague sense of self-in-world. It is associated with a sense of identity, the 'I am' feeling, the experience that 'I exist', that self and world are properly matched. I can be myself, as a person and as a manager, and can act in accordance with myself. It has the quality of a vision, an imagined possibility that generates excitement and vitality. At the start it is poorly articulated and only tenuously connected to reality, although it may contain concrete images such as winning the Nobel prize or making the national sports team. It may take a dramatic form as in the myth of the hero, the great artist, or the business tycoon performing magnificent feats and receiving special honours. It may take the mundane forms of the excellent craftsman, the husband-father/wife-mother in a certain kind of family, the high performing manager, or the greatly respected member of your community.

Many young people, in fact, develop a conflict between the life direction expressing the dream and another that is quite different. You may be pushed in the latter direction by your parents, by various external constraints – such as lack of money or opportunity – and by various aspects of your personality – such as guilt, passivity, competitiveness or special talents. You may thus succeed in an occupation that holds no interest for you. The conflict may extend over many years, evolving through various forms. Those who betray their dream in their 20s will have to deal with the later consequences. Those who build their life structure around the dream in early adulthood have a better chance for personal fulfilment, though years of struggle may be required to maintain the work and commitment towards its realization. *Your dream is your personal myth, an imagined drama in which you are the central character*, a would-be hero engaged in a noble quest. It portrays a complex world, a natural landscape, a varied cast of characters, social institutions and conflicting groups. The plot involves elemental struggles between good and evil, truth and error, beauty and ugliness, and the outcome has portentious consequences for the entire world. The hero of the dream is but one of many figures in your self.

To the extent that this figure plays a predominant part in the evolution of the life structure during early adulthood, Levinson maintains, other internal figures and parts of the self tend to be neglected. *Whatever the nature of your dream, as a young person you have the developmental task of giving it greater definition and finding ways to live it out.* It makes a great difference in your growth whether this initial life structure is consonant and infused with this dream, or opposed to it. If the dream remains unconnected to your life it may simply die, and with it your sense of aliveness and purpose.

In the reworking of the dream, you also modify the meaning of the ladder. At around 40, when you reach the top rung of your early adult ladder, you have to reappraise the meaning of the ladder itself. It is not just a matter of evaluating how well you have done within the current definitions of success and failure. You have to question the basic meanings of success and failure in more complex terms, giving more emphasis to the quality of experience, to the intrinsic value of your work and products, and their meaning to yourself and others. Again the same applies to an organization as a whole as to an individual at this point.

Forming mentor relationships

A mentor may act as a teacher to advance your youthful skills and intellectual development. Serving as a sponsor, he or she may use their influence to facilitate your entry and advancement. Such a mentor may be a host and guide, welcoming the initiate to a new occupational and social world and acquainting you with its values, customs, resources and cast of characters. Through his or her own virtues, achievements and way of living the mentor may be an exemplar that the protégé can admire and seek to emulate.

The mentor has another function, and this is developmentally the most crucial one: to support and faciliate the realization of your dream. He or she fosters your development by believing in you, by sharing in your youthful dream and giving it his or her blessing. Such a mentor helps to define your newly emerging self in its newly discovered world, and creates a space in which you, as a young person, can work on a life structure that contains the dream. In the usual course of events you initially experience yourself as a novice or apprentice, then a more advanced, expert and authoritative adult. As the relationship evolves you gain a fuller sense of your own authority and your capability for autonomous, responsible action. The balance of giving/receiving becomes more equal. The shift serves a crucial development function, whereby you transcend the adult/child divide.

Forming an occupation

Young people who make a strong occupational commitment in the early 20s, without sufficient exploration of external options and inner preferences, often come to regret it later. On the other hand, those who don't make a commitment until the 30s, or who never make one, are deprived of the satisfaction of engaging in enduring work that is suitable for the self and valuable for society.

Forming love relationships

One of your first developmental tasks, as a young person, is to form the capabability of having adult, peer relationhips with the opposite sex. These relationships may have many components in many combinations: affection, sexuality, emotional intimacy, dependency, nurturing, romantic love, friendship, collaboration, respect, admiration, enduring commitment. It takes time for young people to learn about their inner resources in relation to the opposite sex and what they offer, demand and withhold from them.

You have a lot to learn about the characteristics of men or women that attract you, and what it is about the opposite sex that you find appealing. Your pre-adult development moreover, according to Levinson, prepares you partially, but never sufficiently to undertake this work. It also leaves you with a legacy of guilt, anxiety and mystification. In the light of these difficulties it is small wonder that relating to the feminine (as a man), or to the masculine (as a woman), within yourself, should be a life-long task. This is, in fact, an equally life-long endeavour for any organization, that is with respect to coming to terms with its respectively 'hard' and its 'soft' attributes.

The Second World of Settling Down:
Northern Consolidation

Settling down

As a young adult, or growing organization, your 'settling down' phase is your main vehicle for realizing youthful ambitions and goals. In this period a person or institution has two major tasks. First you need to establish a niche in society, to anchor your life or business more firmly, and to develop competence in a chosen field. You thereby seek to become a valued member of a valued world. Second you have to work to 'make it', or to seek competitive advantage, striving to advance, to progress according to a timetable. Whereas the first task contributes to the stability and order of a defined structure, the second involves a progression within that structure. Family and local community are the main forces making for stability; occupation is the main force for movement and change.

The imagery of the 'ladder' is central to the 'settling down' enterprise, again both for you and your organization. It reflects the interest in advancement and affirmation so central to this period. By 'ladder' Levinson refers to all dimensions of advancement – increases in social rank, income, power, fame. The ladder has both objective and subjective aspects. It reflects the realities of the external world, but it is defined by you and your institution in terms of your own meanings and strivings. The overall task then, in 'settling down', is to settle for a few key choices, to create a broader structure around them, and to invest as fully as possible in the components of the structure. These components incorporate work, family, community and the pursuit of long-range plans and goals within it, thereby affirming what is truly important, and shape your work, life and institution accordingly.

At this stage of consolidation, as a manager, then, *you are identified with the organization you are trying to run smoothly*. You are an 'executive' or business 'administrator' in the specific sense of the word, a person whose meanings are derived out of the organization rather than deriving the organization out of your meanings/purposes/reality. In consolidating your 'self', at this stage, the operational constraints of the organization provide the bounds within which you form your managerial identity. Similarly, an organization at this stage of its life is more inclined to offer 'me too' products and services than significant developments of these. Such developments are more likely prospects at mid-life.

The Third World of Mid-life: Eastern Renewal

Tasks of renewal

Every developmental transition, for Levinson, presents the opportunity and the necessity of moving forward towards a new integration of four key polarities.

This is most particularly the case, however, at individual or organizational mid-life. To the extent that a person, or institution, thereby renews itself you create a firmer basis for life and work in the ensuing phase. To the extent that either fails, you form inner contradictions that will be reflected in the flaws of a next life, or organizational, structure. The four polarities whose resolution is the principal task of mid-life are those of young/old, destruction/creation, masculine/feminine, and attachment/separation. They are not specific to mid-life transition, but they operate here with special force.

Young meets old

In every transitional period, to begin with, the internal figures of young/ enterprise and old/bureaucracy are modified and placed in a new balance. *The end of the preceding period stimulates old thought about being in a rut. The start of the new period stimulated young thoughts and feelings about being reborn.* The task in every transition is to create a new young/old integration appropriate to the time of individual and organizational life. An increase of old qualities of maturity, judgement, and self-awareness need to be vitalized by young qualities of energy, improvisation and spontaneity.

Attachment meets separateness

During the mid-life transition, in particular, a person or a corporation needs to reduce their heavy involvement in the external world. To do the work of reappraisal both must turn inward. You must discover what their turmoil is about, and where it hurts. *Having been overly engaged in wordly struggles, you need to become more engaged with yourselves.* In this period the archetypal self, that is the individual or indeed organizational core, takes on greater definition and vitality. It becomes a more active internal figure, with and to whom the conscious ego or self-aware organization must learn to talk and listen.

As such a person, or organization, you need to separate yourself or itself from the striving ego and from competitive pressures, so that you or it can better hear the voices, or core competencies, within.

The creative artist, as well as the truly innovative company, works on the boundary between attachment and separateness. You see yourselves as part of humanity, so that you care about the fate of your products in the future of humanity. To be creative, however, you must maintain some degree of separateness. Your work, individually or collectively, must express and be true to yourselves, to your personal calling or corporate purpose. Although your techniques and products are to some degree shaped by various external and competitive pressures, your ultimate source of growth and development is to be found within your selves. *If you cannot withdraw sufficiently from engagement with others, and draw upon their own creative sources, your work will become repetitive, dry and unconnected to yourselves.*

Creativity meets destruction

To construct anything, something else must be destructured and restructured. The balance of nature is a mixture of destruction and creation. Both are essential to the harmony and evolution of the world. Knowing that your own death is not too far off, you, at mid-life, are eager to affirm life for yourself and for the generations to come. You want to be more creative. Your creative impulse is not merely to make something. It is to bring something into being, to give birth, to generate life. This inevitably rubs off on to your organization.

Masculine meets feminine

The masculine form of creation is to produce something by making it according to your own design: planning, moulding, erecting, transforming raw materials into a new product. This specifically masculine form of youthful creation is to build a bridge, invent a mousetrap, or improve the design of a car. The feminine form is represented by the conceiving and raising of children. As such you do not 'make' the child grow. You enable it to grow, and you do this best when you accommodate to the inner laws of growth that govern evolution. In that respect, organizationally speaking, joint ventures and organic growth surpass mergers and acquisitions of the more aggressive kind.

Stages of renewal

Mid-life transition (40–45)

For the great majority of people this is a period of great struggle within the self and within the external world. The mid-life transition, for individuals as for organizations, is a time of moderate or severe crisis. *You question nearly every aspect of your lives and feel that you cannot go on as before.* You will need several years to modify the old path or to form a new one. The neglected parts of your self/organization urgently seek expression. Internal voices, or competencies, that have been muted for years now clamour to be heard. At times they are heard as a vague whispering, the content unclear, but the tone indicating grief, outrage or guilt. At other times they come through as a thunderous roar, the content all too clear, stating names and places and times, and demanding that something be done to right the balance. You hear the voice of a personal or corporate identity prematurely neglected, of a love lost or not pursued, of a an internal figure who wants to be an athlete or an artist, an entrepreneurial or an enabling organization. You must learn to listen to these voices and decide consciously what part you will give them in your work and life.

Such a 'geographical study' is a mapping expedition in a territory often experienced as a desert, with long stretches of sand enlivened by occasional oases. The individual or institutional traveller discovers that some of the perceived water holes are mirages, others real, and that the territory contains far more resources than you had hitherto been able to see. Slowly you learn how to look below the surface and to make use of the treasures you find there. In effect the same would apply to an organization seeking to rediscover its 'core competence'.

In the mid-life transition, moreover, an individual or an organization – as a way of seeing, knowing or committing –, moves beyond the dichotomizing logic of the 'consolidation phase'. You begin to see both sides of an issue simultaneously. *You attend to the pattern of interrelatedness in things.* The multiplex nature of the world is invited to disclose itself. Mid-life, then, will involve you in going beyond the clear boundaries of identity that you, in your individual or organizational consolidation phase, worked so hard to construct. Whereas your 'consolidation' in adulthood restricts itself to conscious awareness, in the course of your mid-life renewal you must come to terms with your personal or corporate unconscious – archetypal elements which partly determine of your actions and responses. The person or organization in mid-life, then, makes the experience of your truth the principle by which other claims of truth are tested. At the same time you assume that each genuine perspective will augment and correct aspects of the other, in a mutual movement towards the real and the true.

Individuation (45–52)

The rapidly lengthening life span in modern society has stimulated widespread concern with the era of late adulthood. We are beginning to seek ways of improving the quality of life for the elderly, and of managing the economic burdens involved. Much less attention has been given to a problem of equal or greater significance, that is the rapidly growing percentage of the population in middle adulthood? Unless the quality of life in this generation can be improved, the middle age will be under strain and society will continue to be short of creative leaderships. While occupational roles have become more specialized we need more people who can contribute as leaders, managers, mentors, sources of traditional wisdom as well as vision and imagination. Modern society, Levinson maintains, and modern corporations require a vital developing contingent in middle age.

A major developmental task of middle adulthood is to find a better balance between the needs of self (individual or organizational) and the needs of society. As a person who tends to become less tyrannized by your ambitions, dependencies and passions – like an organization or society less obsessed by the competition – you can play your social roles in a more responsible way than ever before. You can develop greater wisdom if you are less focused on the acquisition of specific skills, knowledge and rewards. An organization can develop greater scope for itself if it is less focused on developing itself as an independent entity. Something is intuited by you, in this case, which lies beyond the organization as a system, involving a self-or-organization that travels between systems, or exists in the dynamism between them. This represents a return to the relationship orientation of balance of the exploratory stage, but at a whole new level, a relationship between forms or systems.

Rather than expressing yourself in terms of loyalty to an abstracted system or institution you have an urge to take responsibility for the construction and even transformation of such a system. This amounts to a transcending of your identification with the product in favour of an orientation to the process that creates the product. Work organizations, therefore, that will not recognize your growth and development often force the employee to choose between the job and his or her own life-project. In fact, the great developmental task of this era is not to retire early from worldly responsibilities, or to try vainly to free oneself from all passion and destructiveness, but to *seek a new balance between power and love.* Again the same applies to organizations as to individuals. It is critically important to both society and to the individual that the person at mid-life learns to exercise authority with wisdom and passion. In order to care more deeply for others, then, you must come to care more deeply for yourself. It means that, while you enjoy the power and tangible rewards of leadership, you gain even greater satisfaction from creating a legacy, enjoying the intrinsic pleasures of work and having more individualized, loving relationships. *Beyond the concern with personal survival there is a concern with meaning.*

It is bad enough to feel that life will soon be over. It is worse to feel that you have not had – and never will have – sufficient value for your self. The wish for immortality, Levinson maintains, plays an important part in a man's reappraisal of his life at 40. In the remaining years he wants to do more, be more, bo give his life a meaning that will live after his death.

When you can judge your own accomplishments and recognize how well you are living up to your ideal, you provide yourself with a reservoir of self-gratification. You meet your own standards with contentment. Your actions are in harmony with your aspirations and you feel approved by your ego ideal for what you have done. This is not the self-inflation of the egocentric person or organization (which is a compensation for feelings of inadequacy and incompetence) but, rather, honest self-regard for what either one is and does.

Individuation, in sum, involves the integration into yourself of much that was suppressed or unrecognized in the interest of a prior self-certainty and conscious adaptation to reality. *Here there must be a reclaiming and a reworking of your individual or organizational past.* What the previous stage struggled to clarify, in terms of the boundaries of self or business, this stage now makes porous and permeable. Alive to paradox and the truth in apparent contradictions this stage tries to unify opposites in mind and experience. Ready for closeness to that which is different and threatening this stage's commitment to justice is freed from tribe, class or nation. You are ready to spend and be spent for the cause of conserving and cultivating the possibility of others' generating identity and meaning.

Yet at this stage your self remains divided. It lives and acts between an untransformed world and a transforming vision. In some cases this division yields to the call of radical actualization, which Levinson calls the 'legacy stage'.

The Fourth World of Integrity: Southern Legacy

Imagery of the legacy tends to flourish during the mid-life transition, as part of the work of the young/old polarity. Your legacy, as an individual or corporate entity, is what you pass on to future generations: material possessions, creative products, enterprises, influences on others. People differ enormously in their views about what constitutes a legacy. Although the real value of your legacy is impossible measure, in your individual or organizational mind it defines to a large degree the ultimate value of your lives – and claims to immortality. In every era, you normally have the need and the capability to generate a legacy. But subsequent to the mid-life transition the meaning of legacy deepens and the task of building a legacy acquires its greatest developmental significance. As we learn how to foster development in adulthood, 'creating a legacy' will become an increasingly important part of middle adulthood. This will add to the personal fulfilment of individual adults, to the innovativeness of large-scale organizations, and to the quality of life for succeeding generations.

For Erik Erikson, a prominent antecedent of Levinson, only those of us who have in some way taken care of things and people – and who have faced the triumphs and disappointments that come with being originators of products and ideas – develop what he terms 'ego integrity'. Such integrity, he maintains, is the ego's accrued assurance of its investment in order and meaning, as part of a world order and grounded in spiritual depth. *It is an acceptance of your own and only life cycle as something that had to be and that, by necessity, permitted of no substitutions.* As such, a mature person, or indeed organization, you know that all human integrity is at stake in the one style of integrity in which you personally or corporately partake. The absence of integrity and the danger in this stage is a sense of despair. The lack or loss of integrity is signified by the fear of death.

The virtue of old age, then, is that it can contribute to cultures out of such integrity and wisdom. In the embodied wisdom of genuine integrity the courage and vision of wholeness that animates persons in other stages are renewed and sanctioned. The integrity of old age thus contributes to the possibility of exploration in the youthful stage.

As is obvious, the four worlds of the individual human being are isomorphic with the four worlds of ecology that we saw in the previous chapter (see figure

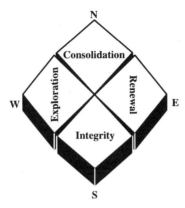

Figure 7.3

7.3). The first world of *exploration* is what we called *competition* when applied to ecosystems such as soil. This is the stage of pioneering and exploration that is marked by a high consumption of resources for the growth of an organism. In an organization, this is marked by the pioneering stage in which resources are utilized for the survival and physical growth. The second stage of *consolidation* is synonymous with the stage of *conservation* in which resources are no longer used up as before but are maintained by the system. The third stage of *renewal* is isomorphic with the stage of *catalysation* which is marked by creative destruction which leads to the evolution of a new order. Finally, the fourth world of *integrity* is isomorphic with *co-creation*, which is the stage of homeostasis of the ecosystem. Juxtaposing the ecological and the psychological worlds, we have the form shown in figure 7.4.

Conclusion

The whole process of individual and organizational development, ultimately, is dynamically connected, each successive spiral stage linked to and adding to the previous ones. Each stage marks the rise of a new set of capacities. These add to and redefine previous patterns of strength without negating or supplanting them. Certain life issues recur, though each successive stage addresses these at a new level of complexity.

Each stage represents a widening of vision and values, correlated with a parallel increase in the depth of selfhood. This all makes for qualitative increases, both individually and collectively, in intimacy with self-others-world. Transitions from one spiral stage to the other are protracted, painful, dislocating or aborted. Arrest can and does occur at each stage. Finally, your personal and

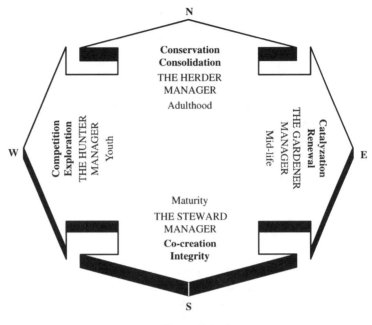

Figure 7.4

corporate characters are shaped by the master stories that we tell ourselves and by which we interpret and respond to events that impinge upon our lives. Our master stories are the characterizations of the power-in-action that disclose the ultimate meanings of our lives.

As a manager of corporate ecology, you will not see yourself therefore, or your organization, as a passive receptacle which needs training or consultancy programmes in order to stimulate learning or change. Rather, *as a developmentalist, you recognize the agenda upon which you or your institution is already embarked*, and which you can facilitate or thwart, but not yourself invent. Such an approach suggests a kind of life-long capacity to nourish and to keep buoyant your personal or your organizational 'life-project'.

Bibliography

Fowler, J. (1984) *Stages of Faith*. New York: Harper.
Jaques, E. (1991) *Executive Leadership*. Oxford: Blackwell Publishers.
Kegan, R. (1992) *The Evolving Self*. Cambridge, MA: Harvard University Press.
Levinson, D. (1979) *Seasons of Man's Life*. New York: Alfred A. Knopf.
Stevens, A. (1990) *On Jung*. London: Penguin.

8

The Cultural Environment

Introduction

Economic myopia

To manage naturally, across space and time, involves transforming matter into spirit, and vice versa, as well as developing from youth towards maturity. It is something of a cliché to declare that we have entered the information age. Yet already some four hundred years ago, with the dawning of the first Elizabethan age, the then English Chancellor of the Exchequer, Francis Bacon, declared that 'knowledge ought to bear fruit in works'. The same Bacon wrote a text on *The Advancement of Learning*, and gained subsequent renown as the father of scientific method. In some circles, moreover, he is believed to be Shakespeare. What definitely applied for him was that knowledge which bears fruit in works should be drawn from out of a nation's 'common clay'. Bacon was, in that sense, a man of the people.

While Bacon's prophetic words may have influenced some of the management literature of our day, they remain far removed from the corridors of power. British Chancellors of the Exchequer and American Secretaries of State for Commerce continue to focus on financial – as opposed to human – capital, alongside tax and interest rates. Similarly business leaders focus on the financial bottom line, rather than upon the human factor. Similarly in Europe, although the Germans now have a 'Minister for the Future', political and economic leaders are still substantively lodged in a past, where knowledge was identified with science and culture, on the one hand, and with education, on the other. Industry and employment remains set apart from what is becoming the major, and non-material factor of production, that is knowledge.

Furthermore, in the world at large, the triumph of capitalism, and supposedly of the market economy, has resurrected our collective faith in the powers of free enterprise. Alongside such enterprise, in our newly envigorated and classically based economies, stand the traditional, physically based factors of production. Land is represented in contractually based property rights; labour is embodied in a freely marketable 'workforce'; and capital is transacted in the global financial markets. Our overall economic, commercial and industrial perspective has not changed in any significant way in over two hundred years.

Business myopia

Within businesses, and business schools, the foundations have remained equally unmoved, at least over the course of the last century. In the early 1900s Henri Fayol, the French engineer and industrialist, wrote his seminal work, *Industrial and General Administration*. In it he divided up the business functions between technical activities, including production, and commercial ones, including buying and selling. Similarly he separated out financial and accounting activities, including the procurement, allocation and divestment of monies from so called security activities, including the protection of property and persons. Finally Fayol incorporated managerial activities as the integrating function, including planning and organizing, command, co-ordination and control. Aside from the transformation of the ill-fitting 'security' function into today's human resource management, the basic activities of business have not been substantively reviewed for a hundred years.

The era of human capital may be upon us, together with its constituent knowledge workers, but our underlying business and economic perspective has remained remarkably unchanged. It is our intention, here, to make due amends, with American Secretary of State for Labor Robert Reich paving the way, rather than laying the actual foundations for our business and economic renewal.

Knowledge work and the information economy

For Reich the era of 'human capital' is now surpassing the hitherto dominant epochs of enterprise and management. Reich's is not a voice in the American wilderness. No less an authority than Peter Drucker has added to the debate: 'Knowledge now has become the real capital of a developed economy'. While knowledge, then, is seen by both Drucker and Reich to be the real human capital of a developed economy, information has recently been viewed, by Californian economist Paul Hawken, as the critical factor of production: 'The mass economy is being replaced by an economy based on the changing ratio between mass and information contained within goods and services. While the former was characterized by economies of scale, by many goods being produced and consumed by many people, the latter is represented by people producing and consuming smaller numbers of goods that contain more information embodied in design,

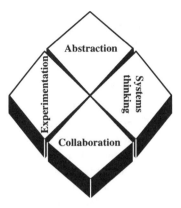

Figure 8.1   The functions of the symbolic analyst

utility, craft, durability and knowledge added to mass.' How, then, is this brought about?

The symbolic analyst in the work of nations

For Robert Reich, within the context of the information economy, the key player is neither manager nor entrepreneur, but a symbolic analyst, who engages in four key tasks (see figure 8.1).

These tasks have emerged, for Reich, out of the American blue. What significance do they have in the global businessphere? They relate directly to the major knowledge domains, or philosophical systems, that have emerged in the four worlds. Some of these systems are a few hundred years old, as in the case of the Western and Northern worlds, and others go back thousands of years, as in the case of the East and the South.

From enterprise to learning

The emergence of the information economy, the knowledge worker and the symbolic analyst are symptoms of a larger cause, that is the emergence of 'intellectual' – as opposed to material or financial – capital as the primary source of comparative economic advantage. In the process, the knowledge-based learning enterprise gains evolutionary precedence over the commercially or industrially based business enterprise.

As knowledge supplants land, labour and capital as the pre-eminent factor of production so the continuing renewal of our knowledge base – with a view to its commercialization – becomes a prime function of the learning, or knowledge-creating, enterprise. Such a knowledge base rests upon both the sciences, and the humanities. Whereas the former, embodied in modernity, is converted into physical and social technologies, the latter, reflected in tradition, is transformed into management style and corporate culture. The Japanese, for example, have developed knowledge-creating enterprises which have recombined Western technologies, such as microelectronics and statistically based quality controls, with Eastern philosophies, namely Confucianism, Taoism, Shintoism and Buddhism. The most productive learning enterprises – as has been the case for the large manufacturing establishments in Japan – manage to fuse together, and indeed continually resynthesize, modern technology and traditional culture. The challenge that an emerging economic player like India faces is then to recast modern business and technology in a genuinely Indian cultural and philosophical context. A company such as Shyam Ahuja (chapter 16) is intrinsically Eastern by virtue of its natural bias towards 'process' instead of 'structure' or 'system'. In the Northern world, a company like Oticon (chapter 15) is an excellent example of how modern technology can be combined with a generic philosophical and cultural base of rationalism. By the same logic, Southern companies have the task of rooting themselves in a people-centred, humanistic cultural tradition. Chapter 17 provides an excellent example of how this was turned into a winning combination. Within the European context, Southern companies such as Benetton have traditionally maintained precisely this combination. In the Western world, philosophical traditions and modern technologies, have become increasingly disconnected from one another. Therein lie the origins of lack-lustre economic and business economic performance. The time is therefore ripe for renewal, in the form of a collective-learning, or knowledge-creating, enterprise.

Business's Knowledge Foundations

Economic renewal: retracing knowledgeable steps

To convert the materially based factors of production into factors based on information or knowledge, it is necessary for us to go back to the grass roots of knowledge. In so doing we shall find that Adam Smith's classical economics – from whence land, labour, capital and enterprise came – derived from a so-called 'pragmatic' tradition. Such empiricism, utilitarianism, or pragmatism is only one of several knowledge bases that have prevailed within Europe since the renaissance.

As we have already described, the four most pervasive sources of knowledge, or historically based worldly philosophies, are pragmatism, rationalism, holism, and humanism. Those generic philosophies, in their turn, have spawned diverse economic concepts and applications that precondition business activity. English pragmatism underlies the market economy, and French or Scandinavian rationalism underpins their '*dirigisme*' or 'welfarism', Germanic or Japanese holism underlies their integrated economic systems, and Italian humanism its family based socio-economic network. As business and economy evolve, therefore, from a material to an information base, so a series of transformations takes place.

- A market-based enterprise, marked by a horizontal exchange of goods and services, is transformed into a 'learning enterprise' through which knowledge is *internalized*.
- A *dirigiste* bureaucracy, vertically stratified into functions, is transformed into a 'learning organization' through which knowledge is progressively *combined*.
- A business system, with interdependent functions and emergent processes, is transformed into a 'learning organism' through which knowledge is *externalized*.
- A family based network, with reciprocal personal and commercial relationships, is transformed into a 'learning community' through which knowledge is *socialized*.

During the course of this chapter we shall be introducing each of these in turn and, later, we shall be elaborating upon both their conceptual foundations and their practical implications. We start with the conceptual foundations of the commercial enterprise, set within the pragmatically based market economy.

Pragmatism – Internalizing Knowledge

'Relating to, or concerned with the practice or practical side of anything; the function of thought as a guide to action; one skilled in affairs of business; application of ideas or the practical bearings of conceptions or beliefs; truth is pre-eminently to be tested by the practical consequences of belief.'

'Pragmatism', the doctrine that all knowledge is acquired through experience, is firmly embedded in the philosophical soils of Great Britain, most particularly, as we have seen, in England. The seminal philosophers Hobbes and Locke, as well as the classical economists Smith and Bentham, were all of an empirical bent. Common law based on precedent, behavioural psychology based on directly observable phenomena, and classical science based on visible blocks of matter, all stem from this Anglo-Saxon 'feet on the ground' approach.

Classical economics, then, as preached by Adam Smith, and as practised by the empirically oriented Anglo-Saxons, converted the British experience – or rather what the British hoped would eventually emerge from the trend which they detected in their own story – into something very like the Platonic idea of capitalism. A picture emerged of a perfect market, unimpeded by the influence of any public authority, with a vast multiplicity of buyers and sellers, none of them strong enough to impose a desired direction on events. The marketplace, the small independent trader, and the non-interventionist public authority were, and still are, indissolubly associated with political freedom. Not so in *dirigiste* France, or the welfare systems of Scandinavia!

Rationalism – combining knowledge

> 'The notion that reason is in itself a source of knowledge superior to and independent of sense perceptions, as contrasted against sensationalism or empiricism; knowledge can thereby be deduced from a priori concepts; such rationality is opposed to emotion or intuition.'

Where pragmatism is inductive, rationalism is deductive. The seventeenth-century French philosopher Descartes was as seminal an influence on the latter as Francis Bacon was on the former. Beginning in philosophy with clearly perceived institutions which he regarded as comparable to the axioms of geometry, Descartes, a mathematician of the first rank, constructed by deductive reasoning his complete cosmic theory. Analytical method, cognitive psychology, and constitutional law all come naturally, therefore, to the rationalist.

In the economic arena the physiocrats, immediate predecessors of Adam Smith, were rationalists who set out to find self-evident truths in the light of reason rather than with the help of experience. However, the direct counterparts to the British classical economists were the French socialists. The best known is the nineteenth-century pamphleteer Saint Simon, who considered the forces of the market as conducive to anarchy rather than as instruments of discipline. Saint Simon saw all producers, employees and employers as a huge class of 'industrialists'. For the rationalists, then, whether in Paris or Stockholm, *dirigiste* style planning supplants free-market economics, constitutional law transcends common law, cognitive psychology replaces the experientially based variety. Holism, on the other hand, is oriented towards a idealistic, systemic approach.

Holism – externalizing knowledge

> 'Constituting an undivided unit; comprising the total sum or undiminished entirety; a coherent system of or organization of parts fitting or working together as one; constituting a person in his full nature, development or relations; involving body, mind and emotions; comprising moral, social and economic activities.'

From a European perspective, the holistic foil to the pragmatism of Bacon and the rationalism of Descartes was the idealism of the German philosopher Hegel.

For Hegel, every condition of thought or of thing, every idea and every situation in the world leads irresistably to its opposite, and then unites with it to form a higher or more complex whole. In a global business context, Holism begins with the notion that the factors of production are not land, labour and capital but nature, human and spiritual tradition. The last includes all capital, both physical and also spiritual, which has been built up in the course of time and is now available to help humans in production. 'Economists,' Adam Muller wrote in the nineteenth century, 'have tended to ignore spiritual capital. The fund of experience which past exertion has made available is put in motion by language, speech and writing; and it is the duty of scholarship to preserve and increase it. All these elements collaborate in production.'

As a result, industrial collaboration in pursuit of long-range objectives is fostered by powerful trade associations in certain industries in Germany, as is the case in Japan. Moreover, these spokespeople for the collective view have a direct entrée to the government machine. German *Verbande* (trade associations) have traditionally seen themselves as guardians of the interests of the nation's industries. Italy, too, has communal similarities.

Humanism – socializing knowledge

'Pertaining to the social life or collective relations of mankind; devoted to realizing the fullness of human being; a philosophy that asserts the essential dignity and worth of man, relating to the arts and humanities, to the "good" things of life.'

In Europe, renaissance humanism was first and foremost a revolt against the other wordliness of medieval Christianity, a turning away from preoccupation with personal immortality to making the best of life in this world. For the Renaissance the ideal human being was no longer the ascetic monk, but a new type – the universal man, the many sided personality, delighting in every kind of this earthly achievement. In the global context, humanism is the prerogative of all Southern cultures and companies, thereby including South African Cashbuild and the Brazilian Semco both of which draw upon the strength of human empowerment and shared value. The strength of the South lies in indigenousness in contrast to Northern generalization.

Ferdinando Galiani, an eighteenth-century Italian abbott in diplomatic employment in Paris, provides an example of Southern indigenousness and flexibility. He condemned the dogmatic rationalism of the French physiocrats, and called for flexible policies in line with historical and geographical conditions rather than for adherence to immutable principles of allegedly universal applicability.

Galiani's historical sense made him see value not as an inherent quality of goods, but as one that will vary with man's changing appreciation of them. He recognized the effect of social forces and stressed the role of fashion as a determinant of man's desires and thus value, as is eminently the case today in the textile industry. Employment today in Pratese textiles, based in middle Italy, has remained steady while the industry has declined in other developed countries. Prato's success rested on two factors: a long-term shift from standardized to fashionable products, and a corresponding reorganization of production. This involved a shift from large integrated mills to technologically sophisticated shops, specializing in various phases of production.

The story of Prato textiles can be retold, in Italy, for many industries: the mini steel mill of Brescia; the ceramic building materials industry of Sassuolo; the high-fashion silk industry of Como; the farm machine industry of Reggio Emilia; and the special machinery and motorcycle industry of Bologna. The humanistic Italian model, in effect, provides an example of an economic system whose strength derives, to a large extent, not from its differentiation, but from its integration with the social structure.

Each member of our philosophically based quartet, then, has a distinct part to play if they are to make good music together. The question is: how does such a process of integration come about? How does business renew itself in this knowledge-creating light?

Knowledge Intensive Business

Renewing the factors of production

Commercially based free enterprise, as we have seen, is a composite of the economically based factors of production – land, labour, capital and enterprise. In a rough and ready sense these are reflected in the major functions of business. The technical function represents an upgrading of land into technology; the personnel function reflects a conversion of labour into human resources; the finance function upgrades capital transactions into management control; and finally the commercial function represents the conversion of enterprise into procurement and marketing.

At this point, however, we remain imprisoned within an exclusively Western world of 'materially' based business, and economy. For a start, this world must work in tandem with the more 'informative' Northern world. As we move out of the purely material world into synchronicity with the 'informed' world, then, for Reich, physically based enterprise might be replaced by 'informatively' based experimentation. Moreover – in prospect if not in actuality – as the gold standard is replaced, according to financial analyst Adrian Hamilton, by an information standard, so finance becomes ever more an abstraction.

The two worlds of West and North are complemented by the East as linear mass-production is transformed into circular, and so called 'lean' manufacturing. As a result, technology lends itself ever more to Eastern, systems thinking.

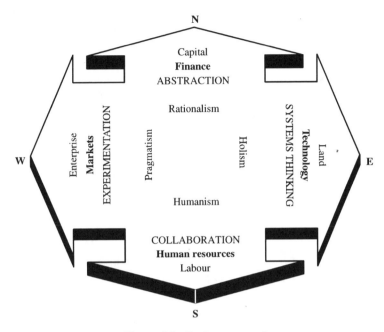

Figure 8.2   Business renewal

Finally, as the physical image of a 'labour force' is transformed into the Shoshana Zuboff's 'informated' image of a learning community, the Southern world enters the picture by transforming individually oriented personnel management into communally based collaboration.

As is indicated in figure 8.2, and in the final analysis, the four knowledge domains – pragmatism, rationalism, holism and humanism – repectively underpin our renewed factors of production.

Reconceptualizing business

As business academics, we have a continual responsibility for abstracting, or reconceptualizing business, albeit with a view to active experimentation, in collaboration with others, and in the context of the wider cultural and economic environment. Hitherto, the material grounds for conceptualization were contained within the proverbial business functions – of marketing, operations, financial and human resource management – with an overlay of organizational behaviour and corporate strategy. At the same time, the Anglo-Saxon world has predominated in codifying business and management, with the traditional, functionally based MBA as its most pervasive influence. In reconceptualizing business for the information age, we shall be developing Reich's basic framework, in the light of our newly discovered knowledge domains, thereby proposing:

- Firstly, *individually grounded* in the Western world of *pragmatically based experimentation*, the concept of *action learning* supplanting marketing management, and oriented towards *the learning company*.
- Secondly, *institutionally grounded* in the Northern world of *rationally based abstraction*, the concept of *organizational stratification* supplanting management control, and oriented towards *the learning organization*.
- Thirdly, *wholly grounded* in the Eastern world of *holistically based systems thinking*, the concept of *general systems* supplanting operations management, and oriented towards *a learning organism*.
- Fourthly, *societally grounded* in the Southern world of *humanistically based collaboration*, the concept of *informated work* supplanting human resource management, and geared towards *a learning community*.

The Western World of the Learning Company: Internalizing Knowledge

Action learning

Reg Revans in England, as the originator of 'action learning', has followed in the empirical and experiential footsteps of Francis Bacon and Adam Smith. For Revans, self and system, manager and organization, are irrevocably intertwined. Quoting from St. James's Epistle in the Old Testament, he urges us 'to be doers of the word, and not hearers only, thereby deceiving ourselves'. Revans' commitment to internalizing knowledge, through self-in-action, involving ongoing experimentation, assumes almost religious proportions.

Exchange of experience

Action learning, in effect, arises out of an exchange between fellow learners, individually engaged in projects, but regularly trading information, advice and ideas in so called 'learning sets'. Such action learning groups form a 'level playing field', whereby the free trade, of goods and services, amongst free enterprises, is supplanted by the free exchange of knowledge, amongst free spirits! For Revans, then, within the learning set, it is not a matter of 'the blind leading the blind', but rather a case of individuals learning more from their 'comrades in adversity' – each pursuing their commercially and psychologically risk laden projects – than from teachers on high! In other words managers, in the spirit of free inquiry, exercise their 'questioning insight' amongst one another, rather than looking up to experts for their 'programmed knowledge' from the educational establishment. So much for the marketplace for learning, as it were.

What about the concept of action learning, that is the personal analogy to the impersonal market mechanism?

Person-as-scientist

As we saw in chapter 1, for Revans, as for Francis Bacon before him, the process of learning involves, at the outset, a two way flow between *action* and *reflection*. The actor changes the system; the reflector changes the self. Neither can operate effectively in isolation of the other. You can only learn from experience if you reflect on it. Unless you have experience, you have no foundation on which to base your learning. The model of the learning process that Revans puts forward is a particular application of general scientific method. It encompasses a survey – reflective observation, an hypothesis – abstract conceptualization, a test – active experimentation, and an audit – concrete experience.

- *Survey* activity involves observing, collecting data, investigating, fact finding, becoming aware.
- *Hypothesis* making involves speculating, conjecturing, theorizing, design, invention, pattern formation.
- *Testing* involves trial and experimentation.
- *Audit* involves inquiry, inspection, scrutiny, verification.
- Finally, there is an integrating *control* phase where an attempt is made to improve general methods following the particular experiment.

Revans' approach to learning focuses on the managerial personality. Conversely, the French-Canadian organizational psychologist Elliot Jaques is oriented towards the impersonal, rationally based organization.

The Northern World of the Learning Organization: Combining Knowledge

Organizational stratification

The functioning of social institutions depends, for Elliot Jaques, on more than having the right individuals: it depends to begin with on having the 'requisite' *organizational stratification*. As far as leadership is concerned, moreover, it is impossible to describe or define what is meant by the right personal competencies until the nature of the task has been defined, and the organization designed and constructed to enable the work to be done. Finally, it is through his or her work at a matched level of individual and organizational cognition, Jaques argues, that a person maintains his primary sense of reality.

The stratified work context

Stratified work bureaucracies are, by definition, hierarchical. They contain a range of different levels, reflected in different strata of work. This work, moreover, mediates between an individual's internal mental processes and the external organization's requisite functioning. For Jaques therefore, the hierarchal levels of control are preconditioned, in such a 'requisite' case, by strata of information processing capacity. He maintains, as a result, that there is a universally distributed depth structure of levels of bureaucratic organization, whereby natural lines of stratification exist at 3-month, 12-month, 2-year, 5-year, 10-year and even higher levels still. The existence of the stratified depth-structure of bureaucratic hierarchies is the reflection, in social organization, of the existence of discontinuity and stratification in the nature of human capacity. The capacity is referred to as *work capacity*, which is further analysed in terms of both a person's and an organization's level of abstraction, or ability to cope with complexity.

Stratified orders of complexity

Orders of information complexity are the increasingly complex groups of data which an organization must take in, and subsequently use, to inform its cognitive processing, and thereby to solve its problems. The learning organization, therefore, is able to accommodate progressively more complex information, ranging from the specifically concrete to the universally abstract. There are, in fact according to Jaques, four orders of complexity. These are as follows:

1   *First order concrete things*, that is specific things that can be pointed to. The variables are clear and unambiguous 'use this tool'; 'employ him, not her' – they are not tangled together, and they are relatively unchanging.
2   *Second order verbal abstraction*, through which managers are able to run factories, to design new products, to discuss orders with customers, to produce financial accounts, to maintain information systems and generally carry out the activities necessary to run a business unit.
3   *Third order conceptual abstractions* involve, for example, balance-sheet values that bring together a wide range of accounting categories, which can in turn be translated into specific and concrete assets and liabilities. The abstracted values, are characteristically very ambiguous, continually changing and inextricably entangled.
4   *Fourth order universal abstractions* contain concepts that are grouped together into the universal ideas that are required for handling the problems of whole societies.

For Jaques, then, depersonalized structures and functions eclipse Revans' personalized attitudes and behaviours. The American Peter Senge, as we shall see, combines mental modelling with systemic thinking.

The Eastern World of the Learning Organism: Externalizing Knowledge

Introducing systems thinking

Peter Senge at MIT, drawing upon the spirit of holism that has predominated within a Germanic as well as oriental world view, has developed an approach to learning that befits large-scale systems. The *general systems* approach brings together disciplines for seeing wholes. When an idea moves from an invention to an innovation, Peter Senge claims, diverse 'component technologies' come together. Emerging from isolated developments in separate fields of research, these components gradually form an ensemble of technologies that are critical to each others' success.

Five new disciplines are converging, Senge claims, to create learning systems. A discipline, for Senge in this context, is a developmental path for acquiring certain skills or competencies, based on a body of theory that must be mastered. Such a discipline involves a strengthening or even perfecting of mental faculties and moral character.

The context of general systems

The general systems approach, in its turn, is the antidote to the sense of helplessness that many feel as we enter the age of interdependence. It is a discipline for seeing the structures that underlie complex situations, and for discerning high from low points of leverage. It is a framework for seeing interrelationships rather than things, for seeing patterns of change rather than static 'snapshots', for viewing causality in multidimensional and circular terms, rather than in unidimensional, linear ones.

Five new disciplines

Senge has developed a system of rules to cover five related disciplines. These embrace so-called 'personal mastery', the development of 'mental models', the evolving of 'shared values', and the exercise of 'team learning', all in conjunction with 'systems thinking' in itself.

1 *Personal mastery* is the discipline of continually clarifying and deepening vision, of focusing energies, of developing patience, and of seeing reality objectively. As such it is the learning system's spiritual foundation.

2 *Mental modelling* is the discipline of working with mental models – of people and institutions – starting with 'turning the mirror inward', that is learning to unearth their mental pictures of the world so to bring them to the surface and hold them rigorously to scrutiny. It also includes the ability to carry on 'learningful' conversations that balance inquiry and advocacy.

3 *Shared vision* involves the skill of unearthing shared 'pictures of the future' that foster genuine commitment and enrolment rather than compliance. In mastering this discipline, leaders in particular organizations, and in whole societies, learn the counter-productiveness of trying to dictate a vision.

4 *Team learning*, as a discipline, starts with 'dialogue', whereby members of a team, within and across organizations, suspend assumptions and enter into a genuine 'thinking together'. To the Greeks *dia-logos* meant a free flowing of meaning through a group, allowing the group to discover insights not attainable individually.

5 *Systems thinking*, then, is the fifth discipline. It is the discipline that integrates the four others, fusing them into a coherent body of theory and practice. For example, a visionary leader without systems thinking ends up painting lovely pictures of the future with no deep understanding of the forces that must be mastered to move from here to there. Systems thinking also needs the disciplines of building shared vision, mental models, team learning and personal mastery to realize its potential.

While Peter Senge, then, places considerable emphasis upon individuals (if not also organizations) 'thinking together' in systemic terms, Harvard Business School's Shoshana Zuboff is somewhat more concerned with the way people 'feel together' in communal terms.

The Southern World of the Learning Community: Socialized Knowledge

Philosophy of community

In his intricate study of communal activity the English political economist Ralph Glasser portrayed, in the 1970s, life in a typical village, S. Giorgio, in southern Italy. 'S. Giorgio insists that we see man in society in organic terms always, and that we demand to know, before anything else, what kind of emotional and spiritual life must underpin his workaday existence. It indicates compellingly that a certain type and size of small, self generating township – or growth unit – is the right social model to strive for, one that can be fully known to itself and

therefore helps the individual to maintain the reciprocal relationships of obligation and response required to support the community's emotional network.'

In fact, according to Harvard's economic historian, J. L. Badaracco, business
until the industrial revolution was enmeshed in relationships with families,
because households were basic economic units. 'The core of a firm,' was then
and still is – he says, as an Italian American – 'a dense web of longstanding
relationships.'

'Sentient' knowledge

Shoshana Zuboff, also based at Harvard, desribes how such long-standing relationships, for traditionally based craft workers, underpinned their involvment
with things, as well as with people. Such 'sentient' knowledge, she maintains,
was filled with intimate detail of material and ambiance, for example the colour
and consistency of metal as it was thrust into the blazing fire, and the smooth
finish of clay as it gave up its moisture.

By redefining the grounds of knowledge from which competent behaviour is
derived, new information technology, for Zuboff, lifts skill from its historical
dependence upon a labouring sentient body. While it is true that computer-
based automation continues to displace the human body and its know-how
(a process that has come to be known as deskilling) the 'informating power' of
the technology simultaneously creates pressure for a profound reskilling of
work. She quotes a paper mill engineer: 'You have to be able to imagine things
that you have never seen, to visualize them. For example, when you see a dash
on the screen you need to be able to relate that to a 35 foot square by 25 foot high
room full of pulp. I think it has a lot to do with creativity and the freedom to
fantasise.'

'Informated' work

Zuboff's learning community of colleagues and co-workers, as opposed to the
military terminology of line and staff, superior and subordinate, must engage in
four key functions:

1 *Informating strategy*
   For an organization or society to pursue an 'informating' strategy it must
   maximize its own ability to learn. In the process it needs to explore the
   implications of that learning for its long-range plans with respect to markets,
   product development, and new sources of comparative advantage. Some
   members will need to guide and co-ordinate learning efforts in order to lead
   an assessment of strategic alternatives, and to focus organizational intelligence in areas of strategic value.

2 *Technology development*
A new division of learning, for Zuboff, depends on the continuing progress
of 'informating' applications. These include maintaining the reliability of
the core, electronic database while improving its breadth and quality, developing approaches to system design that support an 'informating' strategy,
and scanning for technical innovations that can lead to new 'informating'
opportunities. This kind of technological development can only occur in the
closest possible alignment with organizational efforts to promote learning
and social integration.

3 *Intellective skill development*
The skills that are acquired at the data interface, nearest to the core of daily
operating responsibilities, provide a coherent basis for the kind of continual
learning that would prepare people for increasing responsibilities. The relative homogeneity of the total organizational skill base suggests a vision of
organizational membership that resembles the trajectory of a professional
career, rather than the 'two class system'. The interpenetration between
rings provides a key source of organizational integration.

4 *Social system development*
The abstract precincts of 'informated' work heighten the need for communication. New sources of personal influence are associated with the ability to
learn and to engender learning in others, in contrast to an earlier emphasis
upon contractual relationships or the authority derived from function and
position. The demands of managing intricate relationships reintroduce the
importance of the sentient body. The body now functions as the scene of
human feeling rather than as the source of physical energy.

Conclusion

In conclusion, as illustrated in figure 8.3, we have four world views. Each one is
comprehensive in its own right, but respectively biased towards individual,
organization, system and community. The concepts, then, of action learning,
organizational stratification, general systems and informated community sup-
plant the commercial, financial, technical and personnel ones to which Fayol
originally alluded. The knowledge domains of pragmatism (internalized knowledge), rationalism (combined knowledge), holism (externalized knowledge)
and humanism (socialized knowledge) serve to transcend the more narrowly,
and materially based factors of production, namely enterprise, capital, land and
labour.

Pragmatism, experimentation, and the *internalization* of knowledge through
the learning company, supplants sales oriented commercial management. Rationalism, abstraction, and the *combination* of knowledge through the learning
organization supplants finance based management control. Holism, systems
thinking, and the *externalization* of knowledge through the learning system

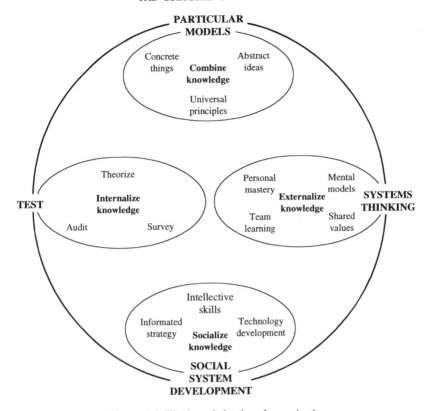

Figure 8.3 The knowledge-based organization

supplants technology based operations management. Finally humanism, collaboration, and the *socialization* of knowledge through the learning community supplants personnel oriented human resource management.

Bibliography

Lessem, R. (1993) *Business as a Learning Community*. McGraw-Hill.

Fayol, H. (1971) *Industrial and General Administration*, in the series 'Writers on Organizations', edited by D. Pugh. Penguin.

Drucker, P. (1989) *The New Realities*. Harper & Row.

Hawken, P. (1983) *The Next Economy*. Ballantine Books.

Lessem, R. and Neubauer, F. (1993) *European Management Systems*. McGraw-Hill.

Nonaka, I. and Takeuchi, H. (1995) *The Knowledge Creating Company: How Japanese companies create the dynamics of innovation*. Oxford: Oxford University Press.

Hamilton, A. (1986) *The Financial Revolution*. Viking.

Womack, J.P., Jones, D.T. and Roos, D. (1990) *Machines that Changed the World*. New York: Rawson Associates/Macmillan.

Zuboff, S. (1988) *In the Age of the Smart Machine*. Heinemann.

Revans, R.W. (1982) *The ABC of Action Learning*. Chartwell Brett.

Jaques, E. (1991) *Executive Leadership*. Oxford: Blackwell Publishers.

Senge, P. (1990) *The Fifth Discipline: The art and practice of the learning organization*. New York: Doubleday.

Glasser, R. (1977) *The Net and the Quest*. Temple Smith.

Badaracco, J.L. (1991) *The Knowledge Link*. Cambridge, MA: Harvard Business School Press.

KNOWLEDGE

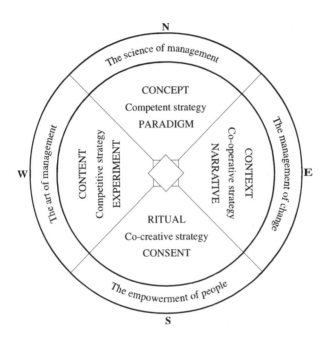

Knowledge is power

Francis Bacon

There are no national frontiers to learning

Japanese proverb

He who does not know one thing knows another

Kenyan proverb

All knowledge that is divorced from justice must be called cunning
Plato, quoted in Cicero's *De Officiis* (44 BC)

Your Knowledge Domains

First the four worlds of philsophy; second, the four environments; and now the four worlds of knowledge creation. To carry the metaphor of a journey further, you have studied the map, you know where you are and you know where you want to go. You also know the environment, with its various resources that you can draw upon. What you now need is the strategy that will enable you to travel on your own. This is the stage of *knowledge creation*.

This section introduces you to four 'knowledge strategies': the Western world of *competetive strategy*, the Northern world of *competent strategy*, the Eastern world of *co-operative strategy* and the Southern world of *co-creative strategy*.

Once you have reached the end of this section, you will be equipped to:

- Develop a specific model for knowledge creation in your organization, incorporating four worlds of *experiment, paradigm, narrative* and *ritual*
- Understand and apply leading-edge ideas and concepts of knowledge creation that have developed in the four worlds
- Customize and apply Nonaka's knowledge-creating cycle to your organization
- Start the process of transforming yourself from a *strategist* into a *symbolic analyst.*

9

Knowledge Creation

Knowledge: The fact or state of knowing; awareness; the body of truth or facts accumulated in the course of time.

Introduction

While the mass economy of yesterday was characterized by economies of scale, the emergent knowledge-based economy is represented by the creation and dissemination of knowledge in the form of products and services. So, intellectual capital replaces material or financial capital as the primary source of comaparative economic advantage. In the process, the knowledge-based learning enterprise gains evolutionary precedence over the commercially or industrially based business enterprise. In a new definition of knowledge, Peter Drucker calls it the 'real capital of a developed economy'.

With land, labour and capital – the trinity of traditional business – being replaced by knowledge on the centre stage of production, old ways of doing business are faced with obsolescence. Creation of knowledge and its commercialization now become the motors of organizational evolution. In the traditional mode of management, knowledge was assumed to be a 'given' entity, out there and absolute, made accessible by the laws of science. It was what we can refer to as 'prescriptive knowledge', the body of immutable, fixed laws and concepts that had been arrived at through a combination of empricism and rationalism. This is rapidly changing to a scenario in which knowledge is no longer seen as an absolute entity, but as something continually created. From the perspective of the four worlds, this creation of knowledge is rooted in four generic, cultural philosophies of the West, North, South and the East. Until now, organizations have just assumed the notion that knowledge was objective; now there is a growing consensus among scientists and humanists that what was termed as absolute knowledge was knowledge born out of tacitly Western and Northern philosophical and cultural modes. As the world turns global, we find that without the other two directions, our knowledge is fundamentally inadequate. It is with the intention of creating a new ecology of knowledge that this chapter is written.

The Decline of the Modern Management Mode

The proportion of US manufacturing capacity employed in production, which had reached 86 per cent in 1965, fell to less than 70 per cent in 1982. With resources being depleted at an alarming rate and an unprecedented increase in global pollution levels, the era of capital, land and labour was clearly on the decline. As other key players from outside the Anglo-Saxon and European world arrived centre stage, it became even more apparent that the existing knowledge base was inadequate. Science itself was moving into areas of uncertainty and chaos, and whereas traditional, classical physics had erected a structure on the notion that certainty and predictability were possible, new quantum mechanical principles favoured ambiguity, pluralism and diversity. Knowledge was no longer absolute but relative; what you saw and did depended on where you were and what your background was. Extended to social and cultural terms, this included your cultural conditioning and the mental models you used. The advent of quantum mechanics, relativity, cultural anthropology, and psychoanalysis destroyed all illusions of knowledge as an independently existing entity. Each of these disciplines were chipping away at the old edifice of objectivity and bringing back the subjective element into knowledge. Suddenly, the manager whose role was to observe and merely 'manage' the machine of the organization was faced with the responsibility of creating knowledge that would develop the organization.

As our knowledge-base changes from objective to participative, we enter what Reich calls the era of *human capital*, in which high-volume production will be replaced by flexible system production and in which integrated teams of workers will identify and solve problems from subjective perspectives. As a result, the new organization of work needs to be more collaborative, participatory and egalitarian than its scientific predecessor. The new enterprise can no longer afford rigid heirarchical chains since its success depends on quickly identifying and responding to opportunities in a rapidly changing environment.

In this new context, the creation of knowledge is no longer solely dependent on yesterday's scientific paradigm. On the contrary, knowledge itself moves out of its absolute, a priori status and becomes open to a range of diverse approaches. Going by Reich's analysis, since the key to economic, technological and commercial adaptation is held by the group rather than the individual, in the social rather the personal, standardized rules are replaced by culturally held philosophies that motivate and influence groups of people. Our knowledge-base, then, is no longer just scientific but is based on both, the sciences and the humanities, the proverbial 'two cultures' of the modern human. So modern technology must fuse together with ancient culture and, moreover, this fusion must be continually resynthesized. The problem with culture-derived knowledge is that, unlike scientific knowledge, it cannot be standardized. It is essentially pluralistic. There is no one right way of perceiving, thinking and doing. On the contrary, total meaning is constructed only when a phemomenon is perceived from a diversity of approaches, thereby making prescriptive knowledge next to impossible. This is the stage where the era of Modernity that began with the age of enlightenment starts giving way to the era of the 'post-modern'.

The Emergence of the Post-Modern Perspective

The theoretical discourses on modernity as an era, from Descartes through the Enlightenment and its progeny championed *reason* as the only source of progress in knowledge and society, and consequently in work and business. Reason was deemed competent to discover and apply norms upon which systems of thought and action could be built and society could be restructured. The extreme example of the modern view was the emergence of scientific management in America and to a certain extent in Europe. Post-modern theorists argue that in the contemporary world, dominated by rapid change, disappearance of ideologies, the all-pervasive media and electronic communication, the emergent processes of change and transformation in politics and society are producing a new post-modern society. The era of post-modernity constitutes a novel stage of history and novel organizational forms which require new concepts and theories.

The essence of the post-modern situation as it emerges from the humanities is that reality is essentially complex and ambiguous. Moreover, it is composed of ever-changing and interconnected patterns. The arena of business, from the post-modern perspective is not the predictable, manipulable entity it was once understood to be, but a network of changing patterns, affected and influenced by a variety of causes. *As a result there is no one single established way of managing organizations.* The prescriptive, logical manager of yesterday is being replaced by the one who can complement logic with intuition, rationality with value and create and manage companies using a knowledge base that incorporates more than just one cultural perspective.

Unlike the definitive modern mind that shaped the enlightenment and the scientific revolution, the post-modern mind may be viewed as being essentially open-ended, with an indeterminate set of attititudes, shaped by a diversity of intellectual and cultural curents. Yet out of this ambiguous, indeterminate situation, some fairly clear characteristics emerge.

- Knowledge is not something that is given by a priori principles.
- Knowledge is created through perpetual change and evolution.
- Concrete experience is prior to abstract principles.

- No single a priori thought can govern knowledge.
- All knowledge is ultimately subjective.
- Knowledge is always pluralistic.

What is therefore being questioned by the post-modern perspective is the old concept of the '*tabula rasa*', the empty slate that was seen to be an apt symbol of the human brain. This emptiness had to be filled in, as it were, with knowledge that was prescribed through authority, be it that of the church or of science. Learning became a matter of repetition and application, and knowledge a set of a priori dictates existing in absolute space and time. The classroom became the focus of learning because with the authority of the teacher and the book playing such an important role, that was where all prescriptive techniques could be used to maximum effect. One's working life was delineated from learning; that was seen to be the stage of application, not of learning. From the 'modern' perspective, business was the theatre of action, not of learning.

In the emergent perspective, there is never a stage when 'one has learnt'. Instead, learning is perceived to be an ongoing process, facilitated by life and interactions with circumstances and others. So business becomes the theatre of both learning and action. Moreover, action itself is infused with learning. In contrast to the '*tabula rasa*' phenomenon, learning takes place when one's tacit knowledge is fused with the a priori, prescribed knowledge. As we shall see, this is the genesis of knowledge creation.

The Four Sources of Knowledge

The first major source of knowledge in the industrial world is the pragmatic, inductive approach of the West, while the second is the deductive, rational approach of the North. While the former owes its legacy to men like Francis Bacon and Adam Smith, the latter is Cartesian. Both these modes are deeply ingrained in the scientific idiom of logical structure and routine tasks, aimed at producing maximum efficiency. But in an economy where the source of competetive advantage is no longer land, labour or capital but knowledge, the situation alters dramatically. If what Reich says about industrial nations entering the era of human capital is true, and if the new knowledge base includes the humanities, then our philosophical and cultural traditions must re-enter the picture. The Japanese for instance, have been able to create learning enterprises that have combined Western technologies such as microelectronics and statistical quality control with Taoism, Shintoism and Buddhism. Perhaps the origins of the current structural economic recession in Europe lie in the fact that the existing knowledge systems are totally disconnected from philosophical and cultural roots. And, consequently, perhaps therein lies one of the answers to the crisis of change. What is crucial, however, is that organizations learn to incorporate more than one philosophical and cultural mode in their management.

As we have said, the four most pervasive sources of knowledge, or historical based philosophies, are *pragmatism, rationalism, holism* and *humanism*. These generic philosophies have, in their turn, created diverse social forms and economic concepts and applications which form the preconditions of business activity. In Europe alone, English pragmatism (or empiricism) underlies the market economy, Scandinavian and French rationalism underpins networked bureaucracy, German holism anchors its integrated econmic system and Italian humanism is the family-based socio-economic network. The model of the four sources of knowledge, however, is not European alone but stretches across the four quadrants of the globe. Moreover, the model suggests that each of the four modes depends on the other three for reaching its fullest potential. In other words, Southern humanism is complemented by Northern rationalism, while Eastern holism is balanced by Western pragmatism as shown in figure 9.1.

These four parts of our new 'businessphere' – Eastern and Western, Northern and Southern – are underpinned by contrasting philosophies and hold complementary sets of values. They radically precondition the art of the possible, in management as in life as a whole. No longer land, capital and labour, these contrasting philosophies now become the generic factors of global production. The true knowledge-creating organization has to imbibe characteristics from all four bases, while being rooted in its home base. The emphasis is on organizations being able to fire on all four cylinders, thus being able to embody and enliven qualities from all four knowledge bases. Western Anglo-Saxon organizations have as their innate strength, the quality of pragmatism, as is borne out by the past successes of companies in utilizing this hands-on, entrepreneurial approach. This is precisely the quality that made Psion such a success. Northern and continental European organizations, however, are more

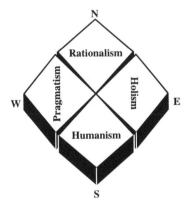

Figure 9.1

rational, drawing out of fixed concepts rather than the hands-on approach of the West, which is a fairly accurate description of the Danish company Oticon. Southern organizations have as their innate strength the quality of humanism and the strength of the organization lies in the human relationships it fosters. An example of this is South Africa's Cashbuild. Finally Eastern organizations are holistic and the emphasis is not on fixed concepts but on emergent situations, just as in the Indian Shyam Ahuja. Unlike Western companies, the Eastern ones do not assume a state of objectivity, but are highly subjective in their approach, as is evident in the Ahuja case. All companies mentioned here are included as case studies in the final section of the book.

The aim of this chapter is to find the connecting links between the West, North, South and East so that they become four parts of a dynamic *knowledge ecology*. We start with an account of each of these four modes and then bring them together. Our allies in this venture will be Americans Ian Mitroff and Harold Linstone who venture into similar terrain in their *The Unbounded Mind*, the European philosopher Michael Polanyi, and the Japanese management thinker Ikijiro Nonaka.

Western Pragmatism: The First World of Knowing

Mitroff and Linstone, writing in *The Unbounded Mind*, refer to their first way of knowing as the 'agreement mode'. The notion of agreement and observation are fundamental to modern science, the idea being that different observers must agree about data and thought-processes. In this mode of knowledge, the system attempts to infer a general conclusion from a limited set of observations through the process of induction.

Agreement is the world of 'sensing' that Jung referred to in his quaternity. For us, its home is the Western quadrant of the world. It relies on common observations gathered by the senses to 'define and structure' problems. Acording to Mitroff and Linstone, agreement begins the process of solving problems by defining the *identity* of the problem. This also requires that the boundaries of the problem be defined in terms of its 'supposed separation and unique existence independent of other problems'. The assumption made in this mode of problem-solving is the existence of a singular *truth*. A direct off-shoot of this mode is the specialist or the expert who works under the assumption that the problem has a singular identity and a single, prescriptive solution. The limitation of the agreement mode is obvious: it harbours a fundamental defect of not being able to establish any kind of connection between two observations.

Western pragmatism is the stuff that entrepreneurs are made of. The emphasis here is no longer on maintaining a paradigm that can be applied with consistency but on the notion that all knowledge is acquired through experience. Sensing rather than thinking is the operative term and there is a greater tendency for risk-taking than in the rational mode. The pragmatic mode is highly individual-based in contrast to the relatively higher group-orientation in the Southern and the Northern modes. As a result, competetion is highly favoured over co-operation and personal achievement is highly valued. This is made possible through the knowledge-creating process of experimentation which allows individuals and companies to travel on separate trails rather the proverbial beaten track of the paradigmatic 'formula mode'. Learning-by-doing is favoured over learning-by-thinking because the experimental/experiential mode, by definition, is highly action orientated. No longer systems of knowledge but specific applications take the centre stage in the experimental mode and content gains precedence over form. However, the assumption of an objective world is the same as in the Northern mode. Although different individuals may take up separate trails, the paths still converge at the point where observations are made. This is why Mitroff and Linstone call this mode one of 'agreement'.

Western knowledge or the knowledge that emerges from the agreement mode is *content-based* knowledge. It does not so much deal with interconnections or the context in which it is generated as it is with the immediate nature of what exists. As such organizations dominated by this mode are characterized by:

- *Structures* rather than systems or communal relationships
- A willingness to *take risks* so that explicit rules are often implicitly there to be broken
- Favouring *individuality* over the welfare of the group
- Breaking down work and organization into *specific tasks and roles*, all focused towards profitable business.
- Drawing upon powers of *sensing* and *experimenting*.

Such a knowledge mode typically tends to construct isolated structures whose strength lies in their sharp definition and the clear outlining of their boundaries, which is an apt description of some typical American or British businesses that are structurally very strong but systematically very weak. The weakness of this mode is the lack of a coherent wholeness that is the product of the interconnections and relationships of causality between the separate structures. This is the stage where the Northern world of *systems* enters the picture, what Mitroff and Linstone term as the problem-solving mode of the 'formula'.

Northern Rationalism: The Second Way of Knowing

Unlike the Western agreement mode, which is lodged in pragmatic and empirical traditions, the Northern formula mode is based on rationality. Although it shares the view with the empirical mode that truth is singular and that there is a single, clear truth that emerges at the end of an inquiry, in this mode the 'model' or the 'concept' precedes the hard data that were fundamental in the world of agreement. Like in Euclid's geometry, which starts off with basic postulates and axioms, the deductive, rational mode starts from clear concepts from which higher order propositions are made. The basic propositions of the kind that Euclid used become the formula that is then utilized to break down a complex problem to its constituent parts. The emphasis now shifts to *logical consistency* rather than agreement, and anything that violates the formula is ignored or dismissed.

The Northern mode of creating knowledge aims at being context-free and concept-rich. The pursuit of rationality is to transcend the network of all the possible causal relationships and abstract out details that will be of specific use. The rational mode seeks external coherence, the uniformity and standardization that is so necessary in future implementation.

Abstraction literally means, 'moving away from', and the rational form seeks to continually move away from the multiple-reality situation that is of vital importance in the Eastern mode. As a result, conceptual knowledge is specific to the system that is being used. Unlike the Eastern mode, the Northern form does not accommodate discontinuities and deviance away from the norm. It seeks to either establish a paradigm on the logic of rationality and consistency, or makes use of formal abstractions, constructs, stored information and prototypic knowledge to adhere to the paradigm or as Mitroff and Linstone refer to it, 'the formula'.

A paradigm, as the etymology goes, is like a pattern that repeats itself. The great developments in the information technology sector illustrate paradigmatic knowledge. Once a concept is developed, it becomes the paradigm for all future business. Within this paradigm, there occur a series of rapid developments, as in the computer world where microchip technology builds on existing knowledge through technological refinement and the use of better and more effective materials. Paradigmatic knowledge is invaluable in creating effective systems that can be standardized and replicated. Uniformity is useful when it comes to manufacturing or designing user-friendly systems. The limitation of the agreement or the conceptual mode, as we shall see very soon, is its tendency to become impersonal and rigid. Concept-based knowledge in organizations is characterized by:

- A *systematic* delineation of roles within the company
- Maintaining order and control, coupled with *uncertainty avoidance*
- Distinguishing between the *abstract* and the *concrete*
- Drawing heavily upon powers of *reason* and *thinking*.

Beyond the first and second ways

In spite of the relative differences in their philosophical home grounds, the West and the North share a conclusion that has become the touchstone of traditional management practice: that the world (and consequently, the organization) can be understood and managed as an *objective* reality. According to this principle, our minds do not alter the phenomena of the world; the world remains the same whether or not we are around. This belief therefore guarantees the two ways of knowing that we have just seen. For on the one hand, the conviction that the person has no influence on the nature of reality guarantees that reality will repeat itself consistently and, irrespective of who is observing, there will be an agreement as to its nature. This, as we have seen is precisely the Western way of knowing. On the other hand, for the same reason, objectivity guarantees logical consistency and so reality can be modelled on the basis of a singular truth, a formula.

This is where Mitroff and Linstone point out that in spite of the fact that the agreement and formula modes of knowledge have been highly successful in the natural sciences, they are inadequate when applied to fields such as the social sciences. As in management, 'Human beings do not start their inquiries into important social problems as geometry does with simple, . . . self-evident propositions.' They quote Russel Ackoff, for whom the 'starting points for all human inquiries are messes', where 'mess' represents the fundamental interconnectedness in which every problem is 'associated and involved inextricably with every other human problem'. They refer to Descartes, who we met in chapter 5, who believed that 'if one started with simple ideas and clear, precise definitions of problems, one would not be led astray in solving them'. However, the age in which this approach could work successfully is at an end. Today, according to Mitroff and Linstone: 'unless we start our investigations of complex problems with a clear recognition of . . . their inherent ambiguity and uncertainty, we end up misperceiving the problem. Precision and clarity may lead us deeper into deception and not rescue us from it.' In the choosing of a singular formula on which to base our decisions and management of the problem at hand, we, – in Mitroff's and Linstone's words, '. . . cut off innumerable other pathways that we could have chosen to explore the problem'.

This is the perfect place to bring in Michael Polanyi, whose major thesis was that observation and logical consistency (are the hallmarks of the Western and Northern modes) are not criteria of truth, as might be assumed to be, but criteria of stability. As Polanyi says: 'The attribution of truth to any particular stable alternative is a fiduciary act which cannot be analysed in non-commital terms.' This 'stabilized' view of reality as a result may equally be false or true. More an 'act of faith' than objectivity, it arises from an unconscious network in which bits of information are taken in from the environment. This is Polanyi's basis of 'tacit knowing', something that was adopted by Japanese management thinker Ikijiro Nonaka and turned into a powerful knowledge-creating model, which we shall explore briefly towards the end of this chapter and extensively in the next one.

To illustrate Polanyi's concept of tacit knowldge, let us use the illustrations made famous by philosopher Norwood Russel Hanson. What do you see in the pictures in figure 9.2?

In figure 9.2(a), do you see a bear climbing up the other side of the tree, or a tree trunk with burls on it? Similarly, do you see a flock of birds in figure 9.2(b),

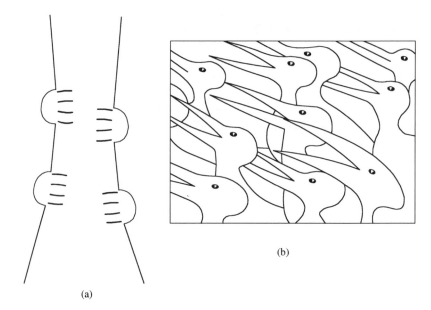

(a)

(b)

Figure 9.2

or a herd of antelope? Polanyi's point is that we see the world according to our mental models which we are trained to acquire from an early age. The process is both, biological and cultural. Thus for Polanyi, the notion of objectivity is a contradiction in terms. An organization is thus the product of unconscious biological and social process, and not just the objective entity that it is made out to be in the Western and Northern worlds. The manager and the employee are choicelessly implicated in the organization. Thus, taken by itself, the agreement/formula knowledge mode is intrinsically limited as a management tool. In these modes, the assumption is that management is an outside-in activity, in which the manager stands out and objectively creates order inside the organization. What Polanyi is saying is that it is equally an inside-out activity in which the manager is part of the chaotic messiness of multiple choices.

Mitroff and Linstone list some 'rules of thumb' that take us beyond the constraints of the two worlds of agreement and formula.

- Seek the obvious, but . . . challenge it.
- Question all constraints.
- Challenge as many assumptions about the problem as possible.
- Question the scope or the definition of the problem or the model.
- Question whether there is a problem to be solved, resolved or dissolved.
- Question logic itself.

With these pointers, Mitroff and Linstone take us into the sphere of complex thinking – multiple realities and multiple perspectives – which in our scheme represent the link from the North to the Eastern world of Holism.

Eastern Holism: The Third World of Knowing

As contrasted with classical physics in which light was considered to be either a particle or a wave, in quantum mechanical terms, both states are simultaneously possible. Rather than a single model or a set of observations, the focus now shifts to multiple combinations of models and observations. More than that, this mode takes into account the notion that both the experience of reality and its description are 'heavily dependent on the structures of our minds'. Mitroff and Linstone use the model of a computer to demonstrate this *multiple realities mode*. For a computer to utilize the hard data from the external world, it has to be carefully designed and built with the right hardware to read the incoming messages in the form of zeros and ones. Further, it is the software inside the computer that 'makes sense' of the incoming messages. In the same way, it is the 'structure of our minds' that decides the approach we take to solving problems and not the structure of the problem.

As a problem-solving or knowledge mode, the multiple realities mode incorporates more complexity than either the agreement or the formula modes. However, it is still too Northern and not sufficiently Eastern to work the notion of reality as a multiplicity all the way through. As Mitroff and Linstone also point out: 'In spite of [the] strong belief that single measures or single views of a problem are necessarily incomplete, multiple realities . . . still have the tendency to reduce all issues to numbers in the ultimate desire to produce a "single best" or optimal solution to a particular problem.'

It is with what Mitroff and Linstone term as 'unbounded systems thinking' that we truly enter into the Eastern mode of knowledge creation. In the unbounded systems thinking mode, there is a *holistic* awareness and knowledge of the fundamental interconnections and interdependencies that link everything to everything else. This mode not only takes into consideration the multiplicity of realities that are present, but also the multiplicity of perspectives. Problems cannot be reduced to scientific laws, because they have different story lines and different perspectives that could be based on history, politics and modes of thinking. Because organizations are complex systems and composed of people with different mental models, they can be viewed in terms of metaphors, such as machines, living systems, cultures and political systems, where each metaphor has a unique approach to thinking about the organization. Mitroff and Linstone provide an example of multiple perspectives that enter into complex systems such as organizations. 'A corporate executive must make an important decision on a new line of business. There is a detailed cost–benefit analysis from the executive's technical staff recommending a single "optimal" alternative or solution. The executive does not make the final decision solely on the basis of the report. The executive talks to various department heads to determine whether there is a strong support or opposition to the proposal. Over the weekend, the executive also talks with an old friend who runs a company in a different field. Valuing that person's judgement, the executive discusses his or her ideas. In addition, the executive draws upon intuition and experience. Only then does our executive decide in his or her own mind – presumably without a formal or mathematical weighting formula – between several different, probably conflicting, perspectives: technical, organizational, and personal or individual.' What Mitroff and Linstone are emphasizing is that different perspectives reveal unique insights about problems that are not 'obtainable in principle from the others'.

So, unlike the traditionally scientific mode which tries to be context-free in its search for universals, the Eastern, holistic mode is supremely *contextual*. By context is meant the entire network of causes, effects and relationships that determine an action or an event at any particular time. Rather than seek out convergent meanings and one-to-one correspondences in problem-solving, the holistic approach is to maintain multiple perspectives and divergences. From the Eastern viewpoint, logical consistency is structurally as useful as a tool for creativity as are a series of written instructions for learning to ride a bicycle. Genuine creativity and the development of now products and concepts is like learning to ride: both take place without pre-assigned maps as guides or instructions. The maps have to be drawn along the way as you seek to express the inexpressible.

Ikijiro Nonaka points out that in many Japanese companies managers handle this stage of learning not by dipping into formalized knowledge, but by drawing upon figurative language, symbols and metaphors. He mentions Honda as a clear example of a company where managers innovated through metaphor as much as through established concepts. 'The Theory of Automobile Evolution' was a term coined by Hiroo Watanabe, project team leader at Honda, to challenge what he called 'the reasoning of Detroit'. The term was coined in the spirit of the *koan*, a form of riddle used in Zen Buddhism that forces you to drop commonsense notions of reality through inconsistency. The inconsistency in Watanabe's term is that two different areas, the automobile, a machine and the theory of evolution, referring to living organisms, are metaphorically merged into one phrase. Nonaka refers to a metaphor as a distinctive method of perception, 'through which people can put together what they know, in new ways and begin to express what they know but cannot yet say'. To complete the story of the theory of automobile evolution, the result was the Honda *City*, the new, 'spherical' car, providing the most room for the passenger, while taking up the least amount of space on the road. The *City* became a concept that is now being used as a design analogy by almost all small car manufacturers.

Metaphorical knowledge is largely born out of intuition, something that the 'rational project' of the Enlightenment onwards, strictly abhorred. The question is, can intuition be learnt? More a process of unlearning than learning, intuition operates when the brain gives up trying to control events. Rather than 'trying to develop' a new car, Honda allowed the concept to evolve. Tacit knowledge must be allowed to 'flow out', creating the space and time for intuition and metaphor to flower. In work groups and teams, the most ideal form for allowing this to happen is the use of the story-telling form, the narrative.

Unlike what can be termed as the 'definitive' approach, the way of the narrative is based on the 'logic of plausibility', or 'on a logos of mythos that suspends commonsense categories and expands perception'. The strength of the narrative mode is in its ability to pull together contradictory strands of information and insight and then embody them in a network. There is an 'internal coherence' to the narrative mode that is in contrast to the 'external coherence' of the abstraction mode where there is consistency in the use of constructs, general information and prototypic knowledge. The narrative mode is also flexible and so can readily accommodate 'discontinuities, contradictions and exceptions' within its structure. In this way, managers can find expression in story telling and shaping new work realities using metaphors from other walks of life. Personal and professional spheres fuse together in the narrative mode and the manager is no longer conscious of the artificial divisions between the two. Even the divisions between the members of the team become blurred as a result, leading to an understanding of the often silent or implicit intentions of other players.

Causes in the narrative mode are divergent rather than convergent. Ideas, concepts and world views are not just that per se but events. To approach a problem narratively is to take part in it. To listen to the story of a colleague is to participate in it, see where you fit in: 'It invites the listener to play a part on the world of the possible, while at the same time it provides enough plausible manoeuvrability to include contradictions.' Narrative thinking is relational thinking, a mode of thought that is highly descriptive, linked to a total context and correlated to relationships within a group that is not formally organized but is organized around shared functions.

To summarize, narrative- or context-based knowledge in organizations is characterized by:

- Allowing *natural processes* to emerge freely
- Perceiving the organization in terms of *diverse events* rather than *specific things*
- Working through *contradictions* rather than *uniformities*
- Inviting *divergence* in place of traditional *convergence*
- Incorporating a desire to engage in *integrating* activities
- Learning through reflective *intuiting*.

Creating knowledge

The Eastern world is thus far more 'chaotic' than its Western or Northern counterparts. Knowledge is not a given, objective entity as in the agreement and formula modes, but emerges spontaneously out of a multitude of causes. Moreover, unlike in the empirical West where data and information play a major role, and unlike in the rational North which depends on concepts and models, the Eastern world is highly intuitive and thereby profoundly subjective. The communication networks that play a dominant part in any organization are shaped as much by people's tacit knowledge as by its explicit body of knowledge. A manufacturing company may have an extensive knowledge base in terms of technology, procedures, tried and tested benchmarks, but this 'explicit' knowledge base cannot 'create' knowledge. Knowledge is created first in the minds of people and then crystallized as an explicit system. Somehow, one person's tacit and personal knowledge must emerge out of the individual's mind and meet that of the others. To know how this happens, we now turn to Ikijiro Nonaka who lays the foundation for the Southern perspective on knowledge.

Southern Humanism: The Fourth Way of Knowing

According to Nonaka, the start-up point for knowledge creation is the conversion of tacit knowledge through interaction between people. Nonaka refers to the formation of a 'socialization field' in the organization in which employees allow their tacit knowledge to emerge out of themselves. Without this field in the long run, organizations lose their knowledge edge as potentially new products and ideas remain 'locked up' in the minds and experiences of its employees. According to Nonaka, there is a strong socialization field in many successful Japanese companies that is directly linked to their success in product development. A socialization field is not to be confused with 'socializing'. On the contrary, the field is about participating in the transformation of the world according to an ideal or a vision. This vision is like the organizational spirit which is imbued by every person in the organization. As Mitroff and Linstone point out: 'Ideals are fundamentally different from goals or objectives. Goals and objectives are desired end conditions that one either achieves or does not, within some finite time period . . . Ideals, on the other hand, . . . may not be achievable within any finite time period. This does not make them useless, for the fundamental purpose of ideals is to urge humankind in quest of a better end state.' For Nonaka, making tacit value explicit through the socialization field is a process of 'articulating one's vision of the world – what it is and what it ought to be'. As he says: 'When employees invent new knowledge, they are also reinventing themselves, the company, and even the world.'

The socialization field is the medium that allows *value* to be internalized by every employee in he organization. When this is done, the organization becomes a genuinely *humanistic* organization which puts knowledge in the service of humankind and the environment as a whole. This becomes the generative basis for the knowledge-creating organization. The four ideals that Mitroff and Linstone envision are:

1 Humane, whole person knowledge
2 Replenishment and restoration of the environment
3 Restoration of the dignity of the individual person and the total redesign of organizations
4 Aesthetic epistemology.

Value begins with the initial impulse and the *consent* to create. This 'Consentual knowledge' is similar to the initial 'feel' for a composition. The notes have yet to be written out, the intricacies and nuances are still very fuzzy but there is a gut-level feeling of what is to emerge. There is the consent to do good, deeply rooted in a commitment to the future in the form of an *ideal*. For organizations, this is the stage of the creation of *vision*. Deeply subjective but not individualistic, Southern humanism is rooted in the bringing together of many subjective viewpoints in the creation of consensus.

From the shared consent of many individuals emerges a path of action that creates a field of socialization: *ritual*. In fact, ritual is the oldest knowledge mode that we have known in the world. It is a way of creating and maintaining a body of shared information that is directly experienced. Notwithstanding the negative aspects of mindless ritual, it is at its root, a highly intelligent mode of communicating and sharing knowledge. In ritual, knowledge is neither described nor explained. It is embodied and sensually experienced in the form of a commitment. Ritual is knowledge in action and, as the etymology of the word tells us, it is the delineation of a time and space where sacredness is cyclically remembered. It is summed up by Deslauriers: 'In ritual, one lives through events, or through the alchemy of its framings and symbols, relives semiogenetic events, the deeds and words of prophets and saints, or if they are absent, myths and sacred epics.' Organizational ritual is intentional or consentual behaviour *par excellence*. It is culturally determined, functioning to connect the action of the managers with the greater story. A ritual is like a moment in space in time and space where a member is called upon to join in and partake of the intentionality of the group.

Rituals affirm the feeling of being part of a community and allow individuals to become members. Rituals in that sense are integrative, creating a cohesive direction for the company to move from. One may enter ritual space through remembering the deeds and words of past leaders and visionaries or the myths

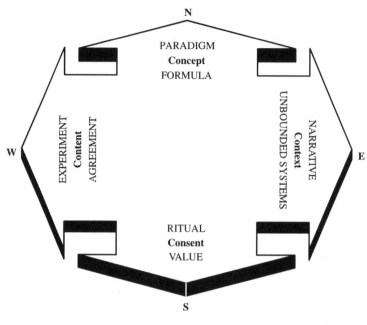

Figure 9.3

and epics of organizations. On the other hand, one may begin a new community by creating new myths and reformulating Ideals in which the rest are invited to consentually participate. The ritual mode of knowing allows the knower to experientially connect with a valued 'good' that is the true bottom line of the organization. Consent-based knowledge in organizations is, then, characterized by:

- Giving one's *consent* to *creating value* for the community
- Creating a communally based *family structure*
- Experiencing a profound sense of *social connection*
- Basing all one's actions in the bottom line of *value*
- Participating in shared *feeling*.

The Ecology of Knowledge

The four knowledge-bases can then be represented as shown in figure 9.3.

If these indeed are the new bases of knowledge of global production and economics, how do we access them? Where is the connecting line between philosophical principles and workable, knowledge-creating systems? This question is even more relevant when it comes to accessing the East and the South. While the Japanese have been able to take on Western technology by underpinning it with Eastern cultural and philosophical traditions, how do Westerners and Northerners achieve the reverse? If we are more at home with the philosophical traditions of the West and the North, how do we access the knowledge bases of the East and the South? This question becomes all the more serious because, in our existing 'civilized' societies, there are hardly any genuine aspects of the Eastern or the Southern modes.

The point is, there is an Eastern and a Southern side to each one of us. In other words, since the four-world model is an isomorph, it replicates itself at the macro level of societies and organizations and at the micro level of individual learning patterns. For instance, we utilize our Eastern side when we learn to ride a bicycle. For anyone who has learnt that 'art', the moment of learning occurs when we give up 'trying' to balance. In the cessation of all effort is then the discovery of balance. Therein lies one of the critical lessons on managing situations of turbulent change in our organizations. The idea from the holistic perspective is not to force equilibrium, but to allow the system to develop in a 'far-from-equilibrium' situation. It is not to try and force answers on questions but to ask the right question.

Similarly, we utilize our Southerness when we interact with others, trying to mobilize trust, co-operation and commitment for a common endeavour or towards a common cause. Holism and humanism are not incomprehensible when perceived in these terms: what we must understand is that for centuries we have invalidated these modes of knowledge as they have fallen outside of the traditional IQ knowledge system.

Conclusion: The Knowledge-Creating Process

As we have repeatedly stressed, the creation of knowledge needs to involve all four global factors of economics and production. Managers will have to learn to weave their organizations through the *ritual, narrative, paradigm* and *experiment* modes. Organizational creativity and learning is – according to Nonaka's model – the continual interplay between *tacit subjectivity* and *explicit objectivity*. This interplay should ideally work itself through all four knowledge bases of *humanism, holism, rationalism* and *pragmatism*. However, in most organizations, this does not happen. The traditional model of organizational management tends to over-emphasize either the rational or the pragmatic, leaving the remaining two worlds completely unexplored.

Deeply ingrained in traditional management is the view that the only useful knowledge is that which is formal and systematic, with codified data and universal principles. Whatever learning takes place within such a 'two-world' organization is essentially 'single-loop' learning. In this mode, existing information is used as both the means and the ends. All the organizational structures and systems are therefore utilized to basically retain the body of existing information. The idea is to continually preserve the traditional ways of thinking. All knowledge creation in such organizations is more 'renovated' than anything else. There is never any fundamental change taking place and a string of management fads and theories dominate renovation attemts in ordinary companies. The path of renovation is predictable: channel your energy and resources to putting the 'right' structures in place, and implementing effective systems. Although for a lot of organizations, the beginning is usually in the form of one person's ideal or vision, the real humanistic quality of the organization is very quickly reduced to a pat slogan or the now popular mission statement. Seldom is it maintained as the generative principle behind the organization, the real bottom line. The East is never explored and that remains the biggest blindspot in Western organizations.

Rather than renovation, the truly knowledge-creating organization is built on the lines of *innovation*. Rather than being lodged exclusively in the West and the North, the innovation route travels across all four directions.

Bibliography

Drucker, P. (1989) *The New Realities*. New York: Harper & Row.

Reich, R. (1982) *The Next American Frontier*. London: Penguin.

Mitroff, I. and Linstone, H. (1993) *The Unbounded Mind*. Oxford: Oxford University Press.

Polanyi, M. (1958) *Personal Knowledge*. Chicago, IL: University of Chicago Press.

Nonaka, I. (1991) 'The Knowledge Creating Company', *Harvard Business Review*, pp. 96–104.

Barfield, O. (1965) *Saving the Appearances*. New York: Harcourt, Brace and World.

Deslauriers, D. (1992) 'Dimensions of Knowing: Narrative, Paradigm and Ritual', *Revision*, Spring.

10

Knowledge-Creating Organization

Introduction

Ikijiro Nonaka and Hirotaka Takeuchi have devoted the past 20 years to studying the ways in which Japanese companies enhance the value of their products and services. In the process of what these two Japanese researchers have subsequently termed 'organizational knowledge creation', they portray a company as enhancing its capacity to create new knowledge, disseminate it throughout the organization, and embody it in products, services and systems. Faced with a crisis, moreover, they maintain that Japanese companies have historically used this proactive approach as a means of breaking away from the past and moving into new and untried territories of opportunity. This process of knowledge creation, they argue, is the key to understanding why the major Japanese corporations have gained their competitive advantage over the Europeans and, more often than not, the Americans.

Static and dynamic approaches to knowledge creation

Japan's comparative advantage, in fact, lies in the 'Eastern' way it views knowledge. As Nonaka and Takeuchi see it, in the West the theory of organization has long been dominated by a paradigm that conceptualizes the organization as a system that 'processes' information or 'solves' problems. This paradigm points towards an 'input–process–output' sequence of hierarchical information processing, or even business process reengineering. A critical problem with this approach is its passive and static view of the organization. Information processing is viewed as a problem-solving activity which centres on what is given to the organization, without due consideration being accorded to what is created by it.

While such a Western approach thereby emphasizes the absolute, static, and non-human nature of knowledge, typically expressed in propositions and formal logic, Nonaka and Takeuchi, as Easterners, consider knowledge to be a dynamic human process of justifying personal belief with a view to finding the truth. Any organization, in fact, that dynamically deals with a changing environment ought to not only process information efficiently but also creatively transform information into knowledge. Innovation, therefore, becomes a process in which the organization creates and defines problems and then actively develops new knowledge to solve them.

Moreover, innovation produced by any part of the organization in turn creates a stream of related information and knowledge, which might then trigger changes in the organization's wider knowledge systems. Why specifically, then, has such an approach emerged from Japan rather than from Europe or America?

The Japanese approach to knowledge creation

The essence of innovation in a Japanese context involves the re-creation of the world according to a particular ideal or vision. To create new knowledge means literally to re-create the company, and everything in it, in an ongoing process of individual and organizational renewal. It is not, therefore, just about putting together diverse bits of data and information, or even about generating 'wild ideas'. The personal commitment of the employees and their identity with the company and its mission are indispensable to such knowledge creation. For such creation is not the responsibility of the few – a specialist in development or marketing – but that of everyone in the organization.

Senior managers, as so-called 'knowledge officers', thus become romantics who go in quest of the ideal. Middle managers, as 'knowledge engineers', serve as a bridge between the visionary ideals of the top and the often chaotic reality of those on the front line of the business. Such managers mediate between the 'what should be' mindset of the top and the 'what is' orientation of the front-line 'knowledge pratitioners' by creating mid-level business and product concepts. They synthesize the tacit knowledge arising out of romantic ideal and pragmatic reality, make it explicit, and incorporate it into new products and technologies. This Eastern approach to innovation, then, draws upon a very different philosophical and, therefore, economic tradition from its conventionally Western counterpart.

Comparative Western and Eastern traditions

Western pragmatism and rationalism

The two fathers of Western philosophy were Plato and Aristotle. Plato built up an elaborate structure of thought from a rational perspective. He developed the notion of 'idea', as 'form' seen through the pure mental eye, and as an ultimate that the human spirit strives to reach and know. Human beings therefore seek the eternal, unchanging and perfect 'ideas' that can only be known through pure reason. Aristotle, a student of Plato, criticized his mentor. For Aristotle, such an 'idea' (or, more precisely, pure form) could not be isolated from a physical object, nor did it have an existence independent of sensory perception. Platonic and Aristotelian views were subsequently passed on, through intermediate philosophers, via continental European rationalism and British empiricism. The German philosopher Kant, in fact, argued that knowledge arises only when both the logical thinking of rationalism and the sensory experience of empiricism work together. For Kant, the human mind is not a passive 'tabula rasa' but is active in ordering sensory experiences in time and space, thereby supplying concepts as tools for understanding them.

Hegel, another noted German philosopher, argued that both mind and matter are derived from 'absolute spirit', via a dynamic, dialectical process. Karl Marx had a different approach to combining rationalism and empiricism, merging Hegel's dialectical dynamics and the emerging social sciences of the day. He refuted Hegel's abstract and idealistic philosophy because it could not explain the dynamic and interactive relationship between man and his environment. For Marx, in their pursuit of knowledge, both knower and known are in a continual and dialectical process of mutual adaptation. Finally, for the more contemporary German philosopher Martin Heidegger, our being in the world (*Dasein*) is not as a detached spectator – like Descartes' thinking self – but as someone with a close relationship between knowledge and action. The Japanese intellectual tradition, in fact, is closer to the German than to the French or English, and yet is still something that stands Easterly apart from this overall Western philosophical heritage.

Eastern holism and humanism

The pre-emphasis in fact, for the Japanese, is upon 'oneness' of man and nature, of mind and body, and of self and other. The most important characteristic of Japanese thinking, then, is the perceived 'oneness of humanity and nature'. For the Japanese, therefore, knowledge means wisdom that is acquired from the perspective of the entire personality. This orientation has provided a basis for valuing direct, physical and social experience over indirect, intellectual abstraction. Moreover, while Western societies promote the realization of the individual self as the goal of life, the Japanese ideal is to exist among others as a collective self. For the Japanese, to work for others is to work for oneself. The natural tendency for the Japanese is to realize themselves in their relationship with others.

The knowledge-creating businessphere

As a result of these different orientations, the major philosophical emphasis in the West is on pragmatism and rationalism, which duly outweighs holism and humanism. In terms of Nonaka and Takeuchi's 'knowledge-creating cycle', pragmatic 'internalization', and rational 'combination', thereby gain pride of place. Conversely, the major emphasis in the East, or at least in Japan, is on holism and humanism, so that the comparatively underdeveloped pragmatism and rationalism has been 'bought in', primarily from America. In the knowledge-creating cycle, holistic 'externalization' stands at an opposite pole to 'internalization', and humanistically based 'socialization' stands in contrast to 'combination'. As we shall now see, these four elements of the knowledge creating company, together with their underlying philosophical grounds, comprise different blends of so called explicit and tacit knowledge.

The Knowledge-Creation Cycle

Appreciating the nature of knowledge

Knowledge, epistemology and ontology

The combinations of tacit and explicit knowledge, originally brought to light by the contemporary Western philosopher Michael Polanyi, are described by Nonaka and Takeuchi as the epistemological dimension to organizational knowledge creation. In their terms, the continual dialogue between the two drives knowledge creation. Conversely, the extent of social interaction between individuals that share and develop knowledge is the ontological dimension. A 'spiral' model of knowledge creation shows the interaction between the two (see fig. 10.1).

While information is simply a flow of messages, for the Japanese knowledge is created and organized by the flow of information, anchored in the commitment and beliefs of its holders. As a result, as far as Nonaka and Takeuchi are concerned, attention should be focused on the active, subjective nature of knowledge – represented by such terms as 'belief' and 'commitment' – that is deeply rooted in the value systems of individuals.

The epistomological dimension: tacit and explicit

Knowledge that can be expressed in words and numbers, as in balance sheets and computer programs, represents only a fraction of the entire possible body of knowledge. Polanyi, as we have indicated, classified knowledge into two catego-

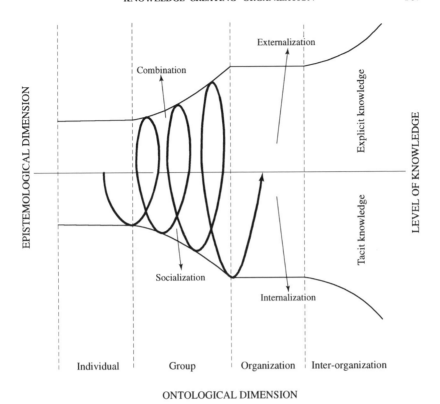

Figure 10.1 Spiral of organizational knowledge creation

ries. On the one hand 'explicit' or codified knowledge refers to knowledge that is transmittable in formal, systematic language. On the other hand, 'tacit' knowledge has a personal quality, which makes it hard to formalize and communicate. Tacit knowledge is deeply rooted in action, commitment, and involvement in a specific context.

Both tacit and explicit knowledge contain technical and cognitive dimensions. The tacit, cognitive elements centre upon 'mental maps' in which human beings form working models of the world by creating and manipulating analogies in their minds. These working models include metaphors, paradigms, beliefs, and viewpoints that provide 'perspectives' that help individuals to perceive and define their world. Explicit variations include codified systems of rules and
' regulations, policies and procedures, trading accounts and software programs. By contrast the technical element of tacit knowledge covers concrete know-how, crafts, and skills that apply to specific contexts. Similarly, specialized techniques in problem solving, negotiation and motivation form the explicit counterparts.

Tacit knowledge, then, is a continuous activity of knowing and embodies an 'analogue' quality that aims to share tacit knowledge to build mutual understanding. This understanding involves a kind of 'parallel processing' of the complexities of current issues, as the different dimensions of a problem are processed simultaneously. By contrast, explicit knowledge is discrete or 'digital'. It is captured in records of the past such as libraries, archives and databases, and is accessed on a sequential basis.

The ontological dimension: level of social interaction

Now we turn from epistemology to ontology. At a fundamental level, Nonaka and Takeuchi maintain, knowledge is created by individuals. Organizational knowledge creation, therefore, should be understood in terms of a process that organizationally amplifies the knowledge created by its people, and crystallizes it as a part of the knowledge network of the organization. In this context it is possible to distinguish between several levels of social interaction at which the knowledge created by an individual is transformed and legitimized.

In the first instance, an informal community of social interaction provides an immediate forum for nurturing the emergent property of knowledge at each level. Since this informal community might span organizational boundaries it is important that the organization is able to integrate aspects of emerging knowledge into strategic development. Thus the potential contribution of informal groups to organizational knowledge creation should be related to more formal notions of organization structure, both within the organization and without. This requires certain enabling conditions, within this ontological context, starting with purposeful intention.

Enabling conditions for knowledge creation

Organizational intention

Intention is concerned with how individuals form their approach to the world. While mechanistic information processing models treat the mind as a fixed capacity device for converting meaningless information into conscious perception, in reality cognition is the activity of knowing and understanding as it occurs in the context of purposeful activity. From the viewpoint of organizational knowledge creation, Nonaka and Takeuchi conclude that the essence of strategy lies in intentionally developing a corporate capability to acquire, create, accumulate and exploit knowledge. The most critical element of such corporate strategy, then, is to conceive of a vision encompassing the kind of knowledge and culture that should be developed, and to operationalize it into a management system for implementation. Such implementation is dependent, in turn, upon the establishment of conditions favouring individual or group autonomy.

Individual or group autonomy

The prime movers in the process of organizational knowledge creation are the individual members of the organization. Individuals, as Nonaka and Takeurchi have indicated, are continuously committed to recreating the world in accordance with their own perspectives. The principle of autonomy can, in fact, be applied at the level of individual, group or organization, separately or together. Autonomy widens the possibility that individuals will motivate themselves to form new knowledge. Autonomous individuals and groups in knowledge-creating organizations, furthermore, set their own task boundaries to pursue the ultimate goal expressed in the higher intention of the organization. Such intention is necessarily subject to fluctuation, and creative chaos.

Fluctuation and creative chaos

While intention is internal to the individual, and autonomy is intrinsic to one entity or another, knowledge creation involves continuous interaction with the environment. In this context chaos or discontinuity can generate new patterns of interaction, within and without. Individuals or groups have to recreate their own systems of knowledge if they are to take account of fluctuation. Specifically, when break-downs occur, they may be led to question the value of long-standing habits and routine tools. The role of top management, in this respect, at least according to the chairman of Canon, Ryuzaburo Kaku, is to give employees a sense of crisis as well as a lofty ideal.

This intentional fluctuation, which Nonaka and Takeuchi refer to as 'creative chaos', increases tension within the organization and focuses the attention of members on defining problems and resolving crisis situations. However, this knowledge-creating process takes place only when members reflect on their actions. Without reflection the introduction of chaos tends to produce 'destructive' tension. As the American organizational psychologist Edgar Schein has observed: 'When someone reflects while in action he becomes a researcher. He is not dependent on established categories of theory and technique, but constructs a new theory of the unique case.' The knowledge-creating organization, therefore, is required to institutionalize this reflection-in-action, in its processes as well as in its structures, to make it truly creative. Such reflection, moreover, is reinforced by what Nonaka and Takeuchi term 'redundancy'.

Redundancy of information

Redundancy is especially important at the concept development stage, when it is critical to articulate images rooted in tacit knowledge. At this stage 'redundant' information enables individuals to invade each other's functional boundaries and offer advice or provide new information from different perspectives. In short it brings about 'learning by intrusion' into each individual's sphere of perception. In organizational terms this means the conscious overlapping of company information, business activities and management responsibilities. Since members share overlapping information, they can sense what others are trying to articulate. There are two obvious ways to institutionalize such redundancy. First, internal rivalry encourages teams to look at a problem from a variety of perspectives. A second way is through strategic rotation, which helps members understand the organization from a variety of perspectives. Alongside the notion of redundancy, as an enabling condition for knowledge creation, is that of 'requisite variety'.

Requisite variety

According to the principle of requisite variety, an organization can maximize efficiency by creating within itself the same degree of diversity as the diversity it must process. To maximize such variety, Nonaka and Takeuchi maintain, everyone in the organization should be assured of the fastest access to the broadest variety of necessary information. Such variety is also enhanced by multifunctional, cross-cultural, or interorganizational activities. Now we turn from enabling conditions, the receptive element, to the epistemological spiral, or active element, that is so central to Nonaka's and to Takeuchi's approach to knowledge creation.

Releasing the knowledge spiral

From tacit to explicit

The assumption that knowledge is created through the exchange of tacit and explicit knowledge allows Nonaka and Takeuchi to postulate four different modes of knowledge conversion.

1 From tacit to tacit knowledge – what we have termed a Southern humanist orientation.
2 From explicit to explicit knowledge – what we have called a Northern rationalist approach.

	Tacit knowledge	to	Explicit knowledge	
Tacit knowledge	SOCIALIZATION		EXTERNALIZATION	
from				
Explicit knowledge	INTERNALIZATION		COMBINATION	

Figure 10.2 The knowledge structure

3 From tacit to explicit knowledge – in our terms, an Eastern holistic orientation.
4 From explicit to tacit knowledge – our Western pragmatic approach.

Revealing the knowledge structure

Southern – Socialization   First then, there is a mode of knowledge conversion that enables knowledge officers, engineers or practitioners to convert *tacit* knowledge through interaction between themselves. Apprentices work with their mentors, for example, not through language but by observation, imitation and practice. The key to acquiring tacit knowledge, therefore, is through direct experience. The mere transfer of information will often make little sense if it is abstracted from embedded emotions and nuanced contexts. This process of creating tacit knowledge through shared experience is called, by Nonaka and Takeuchi, 'socialization'.

Northern – combination   The second mode of knowledge conversion involves the use of social processes to combine different bodies of *explicit* knowledge held by individuals, through such exchange mechanisms as formal meetings, office memos and codes of conduct. The reconfiguring of existing information through the sorting, adding, recategorizing and recontextualizing of such explicit knowledge can lead to new combinations of knowledge. Modern computer-based data processing systems, in fact, provide a graphic example of such knowledge 'combination'.

Eastern – externalization   The third and fourth modes, finally, relate to patterns of conversion involving both tacit and explicit knowledge, capturing the idea that each is complementary and can expand over time through mutual interaction. In the conversion of *tacit into explicit*, a metaphor or an image – portrayed orally or visually – plays an important role, alongside analogy and concept. For such 'externalization', in Nonaka's and Takeuchi's terms, requires knowledge practitioners, engineers or officers specifically to transform metaphor into analogy and then analogy into product or organizational concept.

Western – internalization   In the conversion of *explicit into tacit* knowledge, finally, that is 'internalization', action is important. Individuals internalize knowledge, tacitly, through direct, hands-on experience. Moreover, for explicit knowledge to become tacit it helps if the knowledge is verbalized or drawn into manuals, documents, or stories. The quality of that knowledge is influenced by both the variety of the experience and also the degree to which they are related. It is affected, moreover, by the degree to which the knowledge is embodied through deep personal commitment, thereby transcending the subject object divide, providing access to 'pure experience'.

Three of the four modes have partial analogues with organizational theory, that is corporate culture, and theories of group processes with socialization; information processing, total quality management and conventionally based business administration with combination; as well as action learning, team briefings and benchmarking practices with internalization. Yet, amongst the four modes, it is the least familiar one, 'externalization', which for Nonaka and Takeuchi holds the key to knowledge creation. It creates new, explicit concepts from tacit knowledge in a sequential use of metaphor, analogy and model building.

Finally, each of the four knowledge creating modes produces different outputs. Socialization yields what the two Japanese term 'sympathized knowledge' such as shared values and technical skills. Combination gives rise to so called 'systematic knowledge' such as computer programmes, financial accounts and management information systems. Internalization yields 'operational knowledge', encompassing project management, production processes, and action planning. Finally externalization produces conceptual knowledge, resulting in new product or organizational designs.

Unleashing the knowledge dynamics

While each of these four modes can create new knowledge independently, the central theme of the model proposed by Nonaka and Takeuchi is that organizational knowledge creation hinges on a dynamic interaction between the different modes of knowledge conversion. That is to say, knowledge creation is centred upon the building of both tacit and explicit knowledge as well as, more importantly, on the interchange between these two modes through internalization and externalization.

There are various 'triggers', moreover, that induce shifts between different modes of knowledge creation. First, the socialization mode usually starts with the building of a team or 'field' of interaction. This field facilitates the sharing of members' experiences and perspectives. Second, the externalization mode is triggered by successive rounds of meaningful 'dialogue'. In such authentic dialogue the use of metaphor or deep story-telling can be used to enable team members to articulate their own perspectives, and thereby reveal hidden tacit knowledge that is otherwise hard to communicate.

Thereafter, concepts formed by teams can be combined with existing data and external knowledge in a search for more concrete and shareable specifications. This combination mode is facilitated by such triggers as co-ordination between members of the organization, and by documentation of existing knowledge. Through an iterative process of trial and error, concepts are then articulated and developed until they emerge in a concrete form. This experimentation can trigger internalization through a process of learning by doing. Participants in a field of action share explicit knowledge that is thereby gradually translated, through interaction and such a process of trial and error, into different aspects of tacit knowledge.

In specifically developing products and identifying markets, moreover, Japanese firms encourage the use of judgement and knowledge formed through interaction with customers, and by personal hands-on experience rather than scientific conceptualization. Such 'knowledge of experience', though, needs to be counterbalanced by the rationally based data-processing that is dominant in the West, which is effective in creating digital, discrete knowledge. Individual knowledge is thereby enlarged through this interaction between experience and rationality, and crystallized into an original perspective unique to the individual.

In the final analysis, while tacit knowledge held by individuals may lie at the heart of the knowledge-creating process, realization of the practical benefits of that knowledge is dependent upon its externalization and amplification through dynamic interaction between all four modes. Tacit knowledge is thus mobilized through a dynamic 'entangling' of the different modes in a spiral. Thus organizational knowledge-creation can be viewed as an upward moving spiral process, starting at the individual level moving up to the collective (group) level, and then to the organizational level, sometimes reaching out beyond the organization.

Creating a knowledge field

More specifically for Nonaka and Takeuchi, the dynamics of the knowledge-creating process are enfolded within self-organizing, experience sharing, conceptualizing, crystallizing, justifying and networking activities.

Building a self-organizing team   The interaction between knowledge of experience and rationality enables individuals to build their own perspectives on the world. Yet these perspectives remain personal, as Nonaka and Takeuchi emphasize, unless they are articulated and amplified through social interaction, that is by a 'field' or self-organizing team in which individual members collaborate to create a new concept. By contrast with conceptions of groups as bounded entities within an organization, such evolving 'communities of practice' are more fluid and interpenetrative than bounded.

Such self-organizing teams trigger organizational knowledge-creation in two ways. Firstly, there is sharing of experience among members. Second, such shared implicit perspectives are conceptualized through continuous dialogue, and appropriate 'interaction rhythms'. Within the teams, therefore, rhythms of different speed are both generated and also amplified up to a certain point of time and level, and then are given momentum for convergence towards a concept. The crucial role of the team leader becomes that of balancing the process of divergence and convergence in the process of dialogue and sharing.

Sharing experience   In order for the self-organizing team to start the process of concept creation, it first needs to build up mutual trust amongst its members. Concept creation thereby involves the difficult process of externalization, that is converting tacit knowledge into an explicit concept. A key way to build mutual trust is to share one's original experience, which is the fundamental source of tacit knowledge. Direct understanding of other individuals relies on shared experience that enables members to 'indwell' into others and to grasp their world from 'inside'. Shared experience also facilitates the creation of 'common perspectives'. Forms of tacit knowledge brought into the field are converted through co-experience into a common base. In other words communication is like a wave that passes through people's bodies and culminates when everyone is synchronized with the wave. Such sharing of mental and physical rhythms among members of a field may drive socialization towards conceptualization.

Conceptualization   Once mutual trust and a common implicit perspective have been formed through shared experience, the team needs to articulate the perspective through continuous dialogue. This process activates externalization, whereby participants engage in the mutual co-development of ideas. Through the use of contradiction and paradox, a dialectical approach, in fact, can serve to stimulate creative thinking. Such dialogue, moreover, should not be single-faceted and deterministic but multifaceted, providing room for revision or negation. This dialectical thinking, finally, is a spiral process whereby affirmation and negation are synthesized to form knowledge. While deduction and induction are vertically oriented reasoning processes, what Nonaka and Takeuchi term 'abduction' is the lateral extension of the reasoning process based upon the use of metaphors, extending onto analogies and concepts. Concepts provide a basis of crystallization.

Crystallization   The knowledge created in an interactive field has to to be crystallized into some concrete 'form' such as a product or a system. The central mode of knowledge conversion at this stage is internalization. Crystallization

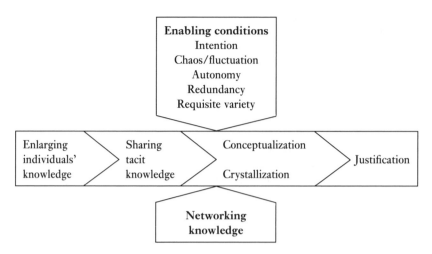

Figure 10.3 Organizational knowledge dynamics

may then be seen as the process through which the various departments within the organization test the reality and applicability of the concept created by the self-organizing team. These internalization processes are facilitated by encouraging experimentation, which needs to be followed by justification.

Justification Justification is the process of final convergence and screening, whereby it is judged whether the knowledge created is truly worth while for the organization and the society. Justification determines the 'quality' of the knowledge. Standards arising may include cost and profit, a product's contribution to a firm's development, as well a such criteria as adventure, romance and aesthetics. However, such a verification process is not the end of the knowledge-creating story.

Networking knowledge During knowledge creation the concept that has been created, crystallized and justified in the organization is ultimately integrated into a whole network of organizational knowledge. The organizational knowledge base is then reorganized through a mutually inducing process of interaction between the established organizational vision and the newly created concept. At the same time the environment is a continual source of stimulation to knowledge creation. For example, a product acts as a trigger to articulate tacit knowledge. Customers and other market participants give meaning to the product by their bodily actions of purchasing, adapting, using, or not purchasing. This mobilization of tacit knowledge of customers and markets, Nonaka and Takeuchi maintain, will be related to the organization, and a new process of knowledge creation is again initiated.

Having now identified the structure and dynamics of organizational knowledge creation, we need now to consider the overall management of the process, within the accordingly and newly conceived knowledge-based enterprise.

Managing the Process of Knowledge Creation

Introducing the guidelines

Guidelines for adopting and implementing a knowledge-creating organization, according to Nonaka and Takeuchi, include:

- creating a knowledge vision
- developing a knowledge crew
- building high-density interaction at the frontline
- piggy-backing on new product development
- adopting middle-up-down-management
- switching to a so-called 'hypertext' organization, and
- constructing a knowledge network with the outside world.

We shall now consider each of these in turn, placing heaviest emphasis upon the 'knowledge vision', the so called 'knowledge crew', the 'middle-up-down' approach to management, and the 'hypertext' approach to organization, each of which is central to the knowledge creating company. We start, though, with the knowledge vision.

Creating a knowledge vision

Top management, Nonaka and Takeuchi maintain, should create a knowledge vision and communicate it within the organization. Such a vision should define the 'field' or 'domain' that gives corporate members a mental map of the world they live in. It thereby provides a general direction regarding what kind of knowledge they ought to seek and create. The essence of strategy for the knowledge-creating company, in consequence, lies in developing the organizational capability to acquire, build up, and exploit the envisioned knowledge domain (see an example in figure 10.4). But at the present time, most companies only have have products and services in mind when formulating strategy. The preoccupation can be somewhat limiting, since products and, to a lesser extent, services have clear boundaries.. In contrast boundaries for knowledge are much more obscure, which helps to expand the competitive scope as well as the technological horizon of the company.

For example, in the spring of 1990 Japan's mighty Matsushita officially announced to the outside world its corporate vision of becoming a 'possibility searching company'. Under this vision, the global corporation set forth the following four sub-domains of business in the areas of business, technology, people and globalization:

1   *'Human innovation business'* – business that creates new lifestyles based on creativity, comfort and joy in addition to efficiency and convenience.
2   *'Humanware technology'* – technology based on human studies such as artificial intelligence, fuzzy logic, and neuro-computers as well as chips systems and networking, all necessary for the 'human innovation' business.
3   *'Active heterogeneous group'* – a corporate culture based on individuality and diversity.
4   *'Multi-local and global networking management'* – a corporate structure that enables both localization and global synergy.

For Kao, by way of a second example, explicit knowledge is captured and recontextualized under the 'five scientific areas' which provide the company with a sense of direction regarding which new markets it should enter for the future. Kao – Japan's equivalent to Europe's Unilever and America's Procter & Gamble – believes that there are five key scientific areas vital to their current technology. These comprise fat and oil science, surface science, polymer science, biological science and applied physics. These five fields are closely related to Kao's historical development. Moreover, they allow Kao to move into markets that may at first seem distant from its core business. Moreover, CEO Yoshio Maruta has been very conspicuous as the 'philosopher executive', and devout student of Buddhism. Maruta's philosophy can be seen to accord with three principles: (1) contribution to the consumer; (2) absolute equality of humans, and (3) the search for truth and the unity of wisdom. These philosophical principles, in turn, form Kao's tacit knowledge base. They provide the knowledge context under which Kao's corporate culture is defined, and the knowledge content which the company's officers, engineers and practitioners need to work. In the same way (see figure 10.4) Anglian Water in the UK has conceived its knowledge grounds.

Developing a knowledge crew

Engineers, practitioners, officers   Organizational knowledge-creation, as we have seen, starts from an individual's efforts to validate or justify his or her belief or commitment to the job or to the company. Highly subjective insights and intuitions are at the root of knowledge creation. To nurture these, a knowledge-creating company needs diversity in the pool of talent available. At the same time, and first of all, so called 'knowledge engineers', typically middle managers,

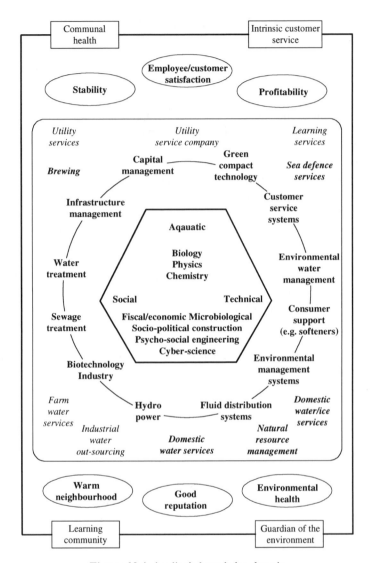

Figure 10.4 Anglian's knowledge domain

need to take the lead in converting knowledge. In the process they will be
creating a vertically directed spiral through socialization, externalization, combination and interalization, while facilitating another, horizontally directed
spiral across different organizational levels. In this respect these knowledge
engineers become the project leaders of the organizational knowledge-creating
process. Secondly knowledge practitioners (front-line employees and line man-

agers) become responsible for accumulating and generating both tacit and explicit knowledge. They consist of 'knowledge operators' who interface with tacit knowledge for the most part, and 'knowledge specialists', who deal primarily with explicit knowledge. Finally while knowledge engineers are responsible for converting tacit knowledge into explicit and vice versa – thereby facilitating the four modes of knowledge creation – knowledge officers are responsible for managing the total knowledge creation process at the corporate level. Moreover, they are required to create the knowledge vision. We can now describe the three roles more specifically.

Knowledge practitioners Knowledge practitioners, the organization's knowledgeable front-line, can be divided into tacit operators and explicit specialists. 'Hands-on' operators generally use their heads and hearts in close co-operation with their hands. As such they constantly accumulate tacit knowledge in the form of experience-based, tacit skills. Knowledge specialists mobilize explicit knowledge in the form of technical, scientific and other quantitative data. Ideally, knowledge practitioners should have the following qualifications:

- A high degree of skill-based competence
- A strong sense of commitment to recreate the world according to their own perspective
- A variety of experiences inside and outside the company
- Skill in carrying on dialogue with colleagues and customers
- Openness to discussion and debate.

Knowledge engineers Knowledge engineers synthesize the tacit knowledge of both front-line employees and senior executives, making it explicit, and incorporating it into new technologies, products or systems. As such they facilitate the creation of the knowledge spiral across epistemological and ontological dimensions. According to Nonaka and Takeuchi, for such middle managers to become effective knowledge engineers, they need to be:

- Equipped with top notch capabilties of project management and co-ordination
- Skilled at coming up with hypotheses to create new concepts
- Able to integrate various methodologies for knowledge creation
- Skilled in communication to encourage dialogue and trust amongst team members
- Proficient in employing metaphors to help others imagine, and subsequently conceptualize, creatively.

Knowledge officers If the job of the knowledge practitioners is to know 'what is', then the job of the knowledge officers is to know 'what ought to be'. Knowledge officers, therefore, are expected to give a company's knowledge-creating activities a sense of direction by articulating grand concepts on what the company might be; establishing a knowledge vision in the form of a policy statement; and setting the standards for justifying the value of the knowledge that is being created. In other words, knowledge officers are responsible for articulating the company's conceptual umbrella, the grand concepts that in highly universal and abstract terms identify the common features linking disprate business activities ito a coherent whole. Another key role of the knowledge officers is the establishment of the knowledge vision that defines the value system of the company. It is this value system that forms the crieria for evaluating, and for justifying the nature and scope of the knowledge the company creates.

A senior manager should, then, should have the following attributes to qualify as a knowledge officer:

- The ability to articulate a knowledge vision in order to give a company's knowledge creating activities a sense of direction
- The capability to communicate the vision, as well as the corporate culture on which it is based, to project team members
- The capability to justify the quality of the created knowledge, based on organizational criteria or standards
- The ability to select the right project leaders, or knowledge engineers
- A willingness to create chaos within the project team, for example, by setting challenging goals
- Skill in interacting with team members on a hands-on basis and soliciting commitment from them, and
- The capabilty to direct and manage the total process of organizational knowledge creation.

We now turn from the knowledge crew to the 'high-density field' in which they need to operate.

Building a high-density field

To nurture the highly subjective and personal mindsets of individuals within the company, a knowledge-creating organization should provide a place where a rich source of original experience can be gained, Within such a place, what Nonaka and Takeuchi call a 'high-density field', frequent and intensive interactions between crew members can take place. In other words, within such a field, typically, tacit knowledge is converted into explicit knowledge. More specifically, our hunches, perceptions, mental models, beliefs and experiences are converted into something that can be communicated and transferred in formal and systematic language. A high-density field is a place, then, where such knowledge conversion is triggered through some form of authentic dialogue. It is within such a context that crew members begin constructing a common language and synchronizing their mental and physical rhythms. It is also within such a force-field that product development takes place.

Piggy-backing on new product development

Organizational knowledge-creation is like a derivative of new product development. How well a company manages the process of new product development, therefore, becomes the critical determinant of how successfully organizational knowledge-creation can be carried out.

First, companies must maintain a highly adaptive and flexible approach to such new product development, which seldom proceeds in a linear manner. In fact such development involves continuous, dynamic and iterative trial and error. Second, knowledge-creating companies must ensure that a self-organizing team is overseeing new product development. Left to itself, the process begins to create its own dynamic order, beginning like a start-up company, and at some point developing its own concept. Moreover, such companies must allow the team to operate autonomously, and tolerate chaos and fluctuation. Third, knowledge-creating companies need to encourage the participation of non-experts who are willing to challenge the status quo.

New product development, in effect, is as critical to 'middle-up-down' management as efficiency and effectiveness is to the more conventional 'top-down' variety.

Adopting middle-up-down management

Top-down Such a 'middle-up-down' approach stands in distinct contrast to both the 'top-down' and the ' bottom-up' varieties. For the essence of a bureaucratic machine is top-down information processing using a division of labour and an hierarchy structure of organization. Top management thereby create basic managerial concepts (the premises of decision making) and break them down hierarchically – in terms of objectives, and means – so that they can be interpreted by subordinates. These senior managers' concepts thereby become operational conditions, according to Nonaka and Takeuchi, for middle managers who then decide how to realize such concepts. Thereafter, middle managers' concepts become operational conditions for lower managers who implement their decisions. To clearly break down the ends–means relationship, it is necessary to get rid of any equivocality or ambiguity in the concepts held by top management. In sum, the concepts anchor on the premise that they have only one meaning. By implication, such concepts are also strictly functional, definitive and pragmatic. An implicit assumption of this traditional model of organization is that information and knowledge are processed most efficiently in a 'family tree' structure. Moving from the bottom to the top of the organization information is processed selectively so that people at the peak would get only simple, processed information. Moving in the reverse direction, on the other hand, information is processed and transformed from the general to the particular. It is this deductive transformation which enables human beings with limited information processing capacity to deal with a mass of information.

Bottom-up   A bottom-up organization, conversely, has a flat and horizontal shape. Few orders and instructions are given by top managers who serve as sponsors of entrepreneurially minded front-line employees. Knowledge is created by these employees, who operate as independent and separate actors, preferring to work on their own. Autonomy, not interaction, is the key operating principle. In the bottom-up model, those who create information are middle and lower managers, or 'intrapreneurs'.

Top-down/bottom-up   These two traditional models may seem like alternatives to each other, but neither is adequate as a process for managing knowledge creation. The top-down model is suitable for dealing with explicit knowledge, but in controlling knowledge creation from the top, it neglects the development of tacit knowledge that can take place on the front-line of an organization. Bottom-up, on the other hand, is good at dealing with tacit knowledge. But its very emphasis on autonomy means that such knowledge is extremely difficult to disseminate and share within the organization.

Middle-up-down management   Unlike the above two models, the middle-up-down model takes all members as important actors who work together horizontally and vertically. A major characteristic of the model is the wide scope for cooperation. No one major department or group of experts has the exclusive responsibility for creating new knowledge. In other words, while top managers articulate the dreams of the firm, lower managers deal with the reality. The gap between these two is narrowed by and through middle management. In this sense it is a leadership style that facilitates the parallel knowledge-creation process taking place simultaneously at top, middle and lower management levels respectively. Front-line employees and lower managers are immersed in the everyday details of particular technologies, products and markets. No one is more expert in the realities of a company's business than they are. But while these managers and employees are deluged with highly specific information, they often find it extremely difficult to turn that information into useful knowledge. For one thing, signals from the marketplace can be vague and ambiguous. For another, employees and lower managers can become so caught up in their narrow perspective that they lose sight of the wider view.

The main job of top and middle managers in the model of middle-up-down management, according to Nonaka and Takeuchi then, is to orient a chaotic situation towards purposeful knowledge creation. These managers do this by

	Top-down	Middle-up-down	Bottom-up
Agent of knowledge creation	Top management	Self-organizing team	Intrapreneur
Management processes	Leaders as commanders	Leaders as catalysts	Leaders as sponsors
Accumulated knowledge	Explicit: documented/ computerized	Explicit and tacit: shared diversely	Tacit: embodied in individuals

Figure 10.5 Comparative management

providing their subordinates with a conceptual framework for making sense of their own experience. In both top–down and bottom–up management a high emphasis is given to charismatic leadership. By contrast middle–up–down management views managers as catalysts. Top management gives voice to a company's future by articulating metaphors, symbols and concepts that orient the knowledge-creating activities of employees, thereby giving form to organizational intention:

- What are we trying to learn?
- What do we need to know?
- Where should we be going?
- Who are we?

In addition to the umbrella concepts and qualitative criteria for justification, top management articulates concepts in the form of committed, equivocal visions, which are open ended and subject to a variety of even conflicting interpretations. A more equivocal vision gives employees and self-organizing teams the freedom and autonomy to set their own goals. The final role of top management is to clear away the obstacles and prepare the ground for self-organizing teams headed by middle managers, who serve as team leaders at the intersection of vertical and horizontal flows of information. They work as a bridge between the visionary ideals of the top and the often chaotic reality of the frontline. They mediate between what is and what ought to be, even remaking reality according to the company vision. Figure 10.5 summarizes the relationship between knowledge and roles within these 'management styles'.

In summary, middle managers synthesize the tacit knowledge of both frontline employees and top management, make it explicit, and incorporate it into new technologies and products. They are the true organizational engineers of the knowledge – creating organizations. Moreover, to function effectively, they need to be contextualized within a so called 'hypertext' organization.

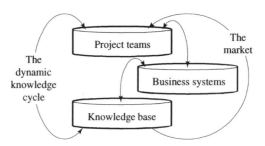

Figure 10.6 The hypertext organization

Switching to the 'hypertext' organization

For a company to qualify as a knowledge-creating company, as Nonaka and Takeuchi have said, it must have the organizational ability to acquire accumulate, exploit and create knowledge continuously and dynamically. It must, therefore, be able to recategorize and recontextualize knowledge strategically for use by others in the organization or by future generations. Unfortunately, conventional organizations are not flexible enough to perform all of the these functions. A hierarchy is the most efficient structure for the acquisition, accumulation, and exploitation of knowledge, while a task force is the most effective for the creation of new knowledge. Recategorizing and recontextualizing the knowledge generated in these two layers necessitates the establishment of a third layer that our two Japanese researchers call the 'knowledge base' (see figure 10.6).

The top layer, as we can see above, is the 'project team' layer, where multiple project teams engage in knowledge-creating activities such as new product development. The team members are brought together from many different units across the business system, and are assigned exclusively to a project team until the project is completed. At the bottom is the 'knowledge base' layer, where organizational knowledge generated in the above two layers is re-categorized and recontextualized. This layer does not exist as an actual organizational entity, but is embedded in corporate vision, organizational culture, or technology. Corporate vision provides the direction in which the company should develop its technology or products, and clarifies the 'field' in which it wants to play. Organizational culture orients the mind-set and action of every employee. While corporate vision and organizational culture provide the knowledge base to tap tacit knowledge, technology taps the explicit knowledge generated in the other two layers.

Once the task of a team is completed they move 'down' to the knowledge base layer at the bottom and make an 'inventory' of the knowledge acquired and created in the project. After categorizing, documenting and indexing the new knowledge they come back to the upper business system layer and engage in routine operations until they are called again for another project. A key design requirement is to form such a circular movement of organizational members who are the fundamental source and subject of organizational knowledge creation. The ability to switch among the different contexts of knowledge swiftly and flexibly, so as to from a dynamic cycle of knowledge, ultimately determines the organizational capability for knowledge creation. The knowledge base serves as a 'clearing-house' for the new knowledge generated in the business system and the project team layers. Bureaucracy is more adept at accumulating operational knowledge (via internalization) and systemic knowledge (via combination), while the project team generates conceptual knowledge (via externalization) and sympathized knowledge (via socialization), both within and without.

Constructing a knowledge network   Creating knowledge, finally, is not simply a process of processing objective information about customers, suppliers, competitors, the local community or government. Crew members also have to mobilize the tacit knowledge held by these outside stakeholders through tacit interactions. Tapping the mental maps of customers is a typical example. Moreover, the knowledge creating company is inevitably strongly networked into an outside world, which is only tenuously divided from the inside one. Knowledge, as we have seen, unlike more specific products and services, flows like water, resembling more of a free-flowing river course rather than a circumscribed channel. In summary then, the management and organization of knowledge creation is vision-centred, knowledge engineered, field dependent; product development oriented, middle-up-down in character, hypertext in form, and heavily networked both within and without the fuzzily bounded organization.

Conclusion

Individual and organization

In the final analysis, Nonaka's and Takeuchi's theory explains how knowledge held by individuals, organizations and societies can be simultaneously enlarged and enriched. Through the spiral, interactive amplification of tacit and explicit knowledge takes place through individuals, organizations and societies. The key for this synergetic expansion is joint creation of knowledge by individuals and organizations. In this sense, the theory of organizational knowledge creation is a basic theory for building not only a pragmatic and rational but also a holistic and indeed humanistic knowledge society beyond the limits of mere economic rationality. For organizations play a critical role in mobilizing tacit knowledge held by individuals and providing the form for a 'spiral' of knowledge created through socialization, externalization, combination and internalization.

Whereas the first two modes come naturally to the West, the second two are more natural to the East.

East and West

The interaction between tacit and explicit knowledge in the West tends to take place at the individual level, accompanied by internalization. Concepts tend to be externalized through the efforts of top leaders or product champions, and then are combined organizationally into archetypes of new products, services or management systems. In Japan, on the other hand, the interaction between tacit and explicit knowledge tends to take place at the group level, as a result of socialization. Middle managers lead knowledge-creating project teams, which play a key role in sharing tacit knowledge amongst team members. This tacit knowledge interacts with explicit knowledge, such as a grand concept advanced by top management and information sent from the business front line. This intensive human interaction produces mid-range concepts as well as concepts for target products, services, or business systems. In terms of the knowledge-conversion modes, the Western strength lies in internalization and combination. Japanese business people tend to rely heavily on tacit knowledge, and use intuition. They are relatively weak in analytical skills for which they compensate through frequent interaction.

Western style knowledge creation is more receptive to certain enabling conditions, such as clear organizational intention, low redundancy of information and tasks, high autonomy at the individual level, and requisite variety through natural differences. In contrast, Japanese style knowledge creation is characterized by relatively ambiguous organizational intention, high redundancy of information and tasks, high autonomy at the group level, and requisite variety through cross-functional project teams.

We will now turn from the knowledge-creating organization, in general, to how individuals can access each particular knowledge-base.

Bibliography

Nonaka, I. (1994) 'A Dynamic Theory of Organizational Knowledge Creation', *Organizational Science*, Vol. 5, No. 1, February.

Nonaka, I. and Takeuchi, H. (1995) *The Knowledge Creating Company: How Japanese companies create the dynamics of innovation*. Oxford: Oxford University Press.

11

Strategist to Symbolic Analyst

Strategy: the science or art of military command exercised to meet the enemy in combat; employing plans towards a goal.

Ecology: the study of the interrelationships between organisms and their environments, especially as manifested by natural cycles and rhythms.

Introduction

In the 1960s, 'long-range planning', as it was called, represented the intellectual pinnacle in management theory. Thirty years later the more conventionally termed business strategy represents the capstone of any MBA programme. In business schools around the world, whether in Cambridge or in Kuala Lumpur, students of management are learning how to SWOT. This ability to analyse the Strengths and Weaknesses, Opportunities and Threats facing a business, in relation to its competition, remains sacrosanct. Such a SWOT, moreover, is undertaken within a commercial environment that is intensely competitive, from a micro point of view, and is economically oriented, from a macro perspective. Not surprisingly, the most revered of today's strategy 'gurus', Harvard's Michael Porter, is both an economist and is also strongly focused upon what he refers to as 'competitive strategy'.

From the vantage point in this book, Michael Porter's *Competetive Strategy*, set exclusively within a commercial and economic context, is incomplete if taken by itself. In a global perspective, SWOT represents the Western dimension of strategy. Three other dimensions are necessary, one from each of the remaining three worlds, to complete the picture. As we shall see in this chapter, from the Northern world emerges *competent strategy*, from the East comes *strategic dynamics*, and finally from the Southern world we have *co-creative strategy*. When taken together, the four worlds of strategy constitute a *corporate ecology*.

The Four Worlds of Corporate Ecology

1 Competitive Strategy – Pragamatism and Natural Selection

Porter's world of strategy duly embodies the wisdom of the 'survival of the fittest'. He draws most specifically on the conventional Darwinian wisdom, subsequently reinforced by Richard Dawkins in his now famous, or indeed infamous, work *The Selfish Gene*. For Porter, then, competitive rivalry lies at the heart of strategy formulation, which is thereby underpinned by aggressive/defensive routines. In that context it is archetypically 'Western'.

2   Competent Strategy – Rationalism and Inner Variation

The second strategic approach, which is becoming increasingly popular in the 1990s, is that of Anglo-American Gary Hamel and his Indian colleague C.K. Prahalad. They focus on a company's core competence and also its strategic intent. Whereas Porter is oriented towards the outer-directed process of natural selection, whereby the fittest survive, Hamel and Prahalad place more emphasis on the inner-directed process of natural variation, to which Darwin alluded less emphatically. Thereby, companies as a corporate species recognize and harness their innately varied capabilities. Hamel's *competence-centred* approach to corporate strategy, set within an organizational and *technological* context, is more rational, systematic and – in terms of this book – 'Northern' in approach than Porter's pragmatic and structural orientation. As we move into the twenty-first century, though, it is likely that both Porter's 'Competitive Strategy' and Hamel and Prahalad's 'Core Competence' will be superseded, in relative though not in absolute terms, by the dynamic perspective of Ralph Stacey.

3   Co-operative Strategy – Holism and Evolution

Ralph Stacey, a Southern African based in the UK, has recently come to prominence through his work on strategic dynamics. Stacey, while having been educated as an economist, has based his strategic approach on the emerging physical sciences of 'chaos' and of 'complexity', and upon psycho-dynamic and cognitive psychological theories. His relatively *co-operative* approach to 'Strategic Management and Organizational Dynamics', set within a socio-political and *psychological* context, is more holistically and in fact 'Eastern' in orientation than those of either Michael Porter or Gary Hamel. Instead of focusing on 'the survival of the fittest' Stacey is oriented towards the interdependent nature of the 'chaotic' business world. As such he draws upon the evolving family relationships of all of life identified by Stacey's illustrious predecessor and fellow countryman, Jan Christian Smuts, in his pioneering work on 'Holism and Evolution'.

4   Co-creative Strategy – Humanism and Transformation

For Reich, finally, who adopts a humanistic and value-based perspective, business needs to reconnect with society at large and with government. Each nation's primary assets, according to Reich, are its citizens' skills and insights. The co-creative strategy is built upon the *cultural* and social grounds, and is more 'Southern' in its context. Reich's world of strategy is based on the interconnections that link business to the world. The transformation of one must simultaneously lead to the transformation of the other.

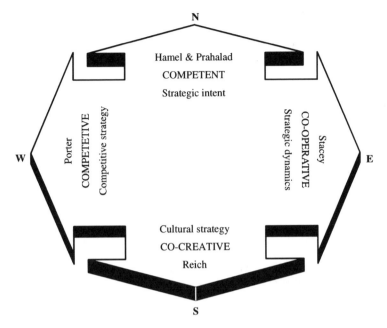

Figure 11.1 Comparative approaches to strategy

From an ecological perspective, the four strategies of *natural selection*, *inner variation*, *evolution* and *transformation* encompass the totality of 'Gaia', the planetary organism named after the Greek Earth Goddess Gaia. We now review, in turn, each of these strategic approaches, forming as a whole our interdependent corporate ecology, as summarized in figure 11.1.

We begin, then, by reviewing Porter's competitive strategy.

Pragmatism: Competitive Strategy

The commitment to compete

Michael Porter rose to prominence in the 1980s, alongside Ronald Reagan and Margaret Thatcher. For Porter, in effect, the goal of corporate strategy is to find a position in an industry where the company can best defend itself against external forces, or influence them in its favour. Without an instinctive drive to compete to win, a firm will have no business strategy to rightfully call its own. Porter describes three types of strategic commitment, each one designed to achieve a particular kind of deterrence.

1   The commitment to unequivocally stick to a move that it is making.

2   The commitment to retaliate, and to continue to do so, if a competitive firm makes certain moves. Such a commitment can guarantee the likelihood, speed, and vigour of retaliation to such offensive moves, and can be the cornerstone of defensive strategy.

3   The commitment to undertake no action, or forego an action.

The forces that drive industrial competition

Porter is best known in strategic circles, however, for his identification of the forces that drive industrial competition (see figure 11.2). An effective competitive strategy, for him, is one that takes offensive or defensive action to create a defendable position against five competitive forces.

Such a strategy for Porter broadly involves three alternative points of emphasis, that is a respective emphasis upon positioning, influencing and anticipating:

• Positioning the firm so that its capabilities provide the best defense against the exising array of five competitive forces
• Influencing the balance of the five forces through strategic moves, thereby improving the firm's relative position
• Anticipating shifts in the factors underlying the five forces and responding to them, thereby exploiting change by choosing a strategy appropriate to the new competitive balance before the competitors realize it.

Generic competitive strategies

In the final analysis, then, Porter cites three so-called 'generic' strategies, and only three, for ultimately attaining competitive advantage:

1   Overall *cost leadership*, requiring the aggressive construction of cost-efficient, usually large-scale facilities; the vigorous pursuit of the cost reductions arising; tight cost and overhead control; and cost minimization in areas like research and development, after sales service, and so on.

2   Aggressive product or service *differentiation*, thus providing insulation against competitive rivalry because of the brand loyalty of customers, and a resulting lower sensitivity to price. It also leads to an increase of profit margins, because the customer is willing to pay a price premium. This avoids the necessity of adopting a low cost position. Finally, the resulting customer loyalty, and the need for a competitor to provide uniqueness, creates significant entry barriers.

3   The final generic strategy involves *focus*. This competitive strategy, for Porter, rests on the premise that the firm is thus able to serve its narrow market more effectively or efficiently than competitors who are competing more broadly. This form of strategy has also been termed nichemanship.

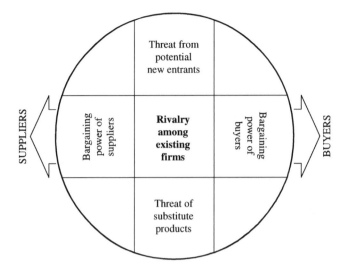

Figure 11.2 Competitive forces

As we can see, Michael Porter accurately reflects the attitudes and perceptions of many a business strategist in the eighties, particularly of the Anglo-Saxon variety who saw the international business arena as a global battlefield. For Hamel and Prahalad in the 1990s, with their focus on core competence and strategic intent, the emphasis is less primal and more rational.

Rationalism: Competent Strategy

Competence is integral

Hamel and Prahalad are relatively more oriented towards the 'inner variation' contained within the corporate species than is the outer-directed Porter. Such variation is contained within so called 'core competencies'. These are reflected in a bundle of skills and technologies rather than in a single discrete skill or technique. The core competence Federal Express possesses in package routing and delivery, for example, rests on the integration of bar-code technology, wireless communications, network management and linear programming. It is this integration that is the hallmark of a core competence. Such a competence thereby represents the sum of learning across individual skill sets and organizational units. The orientation of such a learning process is towards developing a wide and deep understanding of the skills that currently underpin the firm's success. The strategic intent is to thereby escape the myopia of the served market, to highlight the 'shared property' of the firm, to point the way to new business, to raise sensitivity to the reality of competition for competence, and to provide the basis for actively managing the firm's most valuable resources.

Competence is unique

Such a core competence, then, makes a distinct contribution to customer-perceived value. Very few customers, for example, choose Honda over competing marques merely because of some particular capability on the part of Honda's dealers. It is rather the fact that Honda is able to produce some of the world's best engines and power-trains that provides customers with highly valued benefits in the form of superior fuel economy, fast acceleration, easy revving, and less noise and vibration. To qualify as a core competence, moreover, a capability for Hamel and Prahalad must be competitively unique.

In short there is a difference between 'necessary' competencies and 'differentiating' ones. Moreover, a core competence must be extendable in the sense that it is possible to imagine an array of new products and services issuing from it. Unlike physical assets, core competencies do not 'wearout', although they may lose their value over time. In fact, the more a competence is used, the more refined it gets and the more valuable it becomes. As Honda has extended its engines competence across motorcycles, cars, generators, and the like, its overall understanding of combustion engineering has multiplied. The breadth of applications allows Honda, Hamel and Prahalad point out, to take a competence element developed in one product market and extend it to another.

For Hamel and Prahalad in fact, there is a hierarchy of competencies – from metacompetencies (logistics) to core competencies (package trading) to constituent skills (bar coding). Competition for competence, therefore, takes place at a three such levels. Firstly, a company has to acquire or develop a skill or technology that makes up a particular core competence. This competition takes place in the market for technology, talent, alliance partners and intellectual property rights. Secondly, competence represents the synthesis of a variety of skills, technologies and knowledge streams. A core competence is a tapestry, woven from the threads of distinct skills and technologies. Thirdly, a core product or service platform is most typically an intermediate product somewhere between the core competence and the end-product. For example, Canon sells laser printer engines to Apple, HP and others. How then are these competencies built and deployed?

Deploying core competencies

Given that it may take five, ten or more years to build world leadership in a core competence area, for Hamel and Prahalad consistency of effort is key. Consistency depends first on a deep consensus about which competence to build and support and, second, on the stability of the management teams charged with competence development. To leverage a core competence across multiple businesses, and into new markets, often requires redeploying that competence internally, from one division or Small Business Unit to another. Some companies are better at this than others. The goal is to establish a group of people who see themselves as corporate resources, and whose first loyalty is to the integrity of the company's core competences rather than to any single business unit. The aim, for Hamel and Prahalad then, is not to 'hardwire' the core competences into the organization through structural changes, but to 'softwire' the perspective into the heads of every manager and employee, building a community of people who view themselves as carriers of corporate core competencies.

Clearly the competencies that are most valuable are those that represent a gateway to a wide variety of potential product markets. To take a financial analogy, investing in core competence leadership for Hamel and Prahalad is like investing in options. A core competence leader possesses an option on participation in the range of end-product markets that rely on that core competence. Sony's unrelenting pursuit of leadership in miniaturization, for example, has given it access to a broad array of personal audio products.

Core competencies, then, are the wellspring of future product development. They are the 'roots' of competitiveness, and individual products and services are the 'fruits'. Every strategist is competing not only to protect the firm's position within existing markets, but to position the firm to succeed in new markets. Hence for Hamel and Prahalad, any top team that fails to take responsibility for building and nurturing core competence is inadvertantly mortgaging the company's future.

CORE COMPETENCE	**New**	What new core competences will we need to build to protect and extend our franchise in current markets?	What new core competences would we need to build to participate in the most exciting markets of the future?
	Existing	What is the opportunity to improve our position in existing markets by better leveraging our existing core competences?	What new products or services could we create by creatively redeploying or recombining our current core competences?

Figure 11.3 Establishing the core competence agenda

The competence imperative

In the final analysis, for Hamel and Prahalad, a multitude of dangers await a company that cannot conceive of itself and its competitors in core competence terms. First there is the risk that opportunties for growth will be needlessly truncated. Second, in very few companies are there any explicit mechanisms for ensuring that the best talent gets aligned behind the most attractive opportunities. Third, as a company divisionalizes and fractures into ever smaller business units, competencies may become fragmented and weakened. Fourth, the lack of core competence perspective can also desensitize a company to its growing dependence on outside suppliers of core products. Fifth, a company focused only on end products may fail to invest adequately in new core competencies that can propel growth in the future. Sixthly, a company that fails to understand the core competence basis for competition in its industry may be surprised by new entrants who rely on competencies developed in other end markets. And seventh, companies insensitive to the issue of core competence may unwittingly relinqush valuable skills when they divest an underperforming business.

So much for a competence as opposed to a competitively based approach to corporate strategy. As we can see the two different orientations are not polar opposites. In fact Hamel and Prahalad's seminal work is entitled *Competing for the Future*, but they are certainly very different in flavour. Relatively speaking, where Porter is extraverted, Hamel is introverted; where Porter's approach is nested within the outer-directed economic environment, Hamel's is lodged within the inner-directed socio-technical one. Where Porter is structurally oriented Hamel is systematic. With Ralph Stacey, though, we enter even more wholeheartedly into systemic thinking, as a process.

Holism: Co-operative Strategy

The need for complex learning

The essence of mastering systems thinking, as a strategic orientation, lies in seeing whole patterns where others see only part events and forces to which to react. This gives rise, for Stacey, to the need for complex learning which involves, not only adjusting our actions in the light of consequences, but also in the sense of questioning and adjusting the unconscious mental models we are using to design these actions. Complex learning is therefore essentially holistic, destabilizing and revolutionary, but vitally necessary for creativity and innovation. In that sense Stacey moves a step beyond Hamel and Prahalad, in identifying the psychological processes required if we are to partake in complex learning.

Closed, contained, and open-ended change

Strategists in any organization, for Stacey moreover, face a spectrum of change situations in every time frame, from the past to the present to the future. At each point the spectrum stretches from predictable 'closed' change, through statistically predictable 'contained' change, into unknowable 'open-ended' change. In open ended change situations the prime difficulty is not that of finding answers but identifying what questions to ask. New mental models have to be developed and shared. People in a group facing change, at the same time, typically become anxious, and the dynamic of their interaction becomes complex.

Closed change involves clear objectives, repetitive actions, measurable and known outcomes. Similar and yet different is contained change. It occurs when there are clear objectives and repetitive actions, but imperfectly measurable and largely unknown outcomes. Finally, and conversely, open ended change means that there are ambiguous and conflicting objectives, unique actions, non-measurable and unknowable outcomes. In conditions near to closed change, therefore, control consists of routine based monitoring and control. In conditions near contained change, control can take the form of shared culture, political processes and trial and error actions. In conditions that are open-ended control, however, will be possible only in its intuitive, political and judgemental forms. Whereas, finally, closed and contained change lend themselves to linear thinking, open ended change is holistically based and intrinsically non-linear.

Linear and non-linear systems

The dominant way of thinking about the relationship between cause and effect in Western (and Northern) culture, for Stacey, is what might be called linear and unidirectional. The key point about all forms of such 'equlilibrium' behaviour is that they are regular, orderly and predictable. Most theories of management have been developed within a similarly mechanistic framework. When we think of organisms and organizations as systems, however, we then become aware of more complex forms of causality involving interconnection and interdependence, where everything affects everything else. Such so called mathematically 'nonlinear' feedback systems can involve very complex and 'dynamic' connections between cause and effect.

Equilibrium, then, takes a stable form when the behaviour of a system regularly repeats its past. It takes an unstable form when behaviour diverges from the past, but in a perfectly regular way. The key point about all forms of equilibrium behaviour, Stacey emphasizes, is that they are regular, orderly and predictable. Most theories of business management and strategy, the majority of which have originated from North America and a select minority from France, have been developed within such an equilibrium framework. Dynamics, conversely, is the study of how a system evolves over time.

It is concerned with the effects of tension in a system, with the manner in which contradictions or variations cause tension and so create energy which drives behaviour. Whereas such an approach is characteristic of psychodynamic psychology and also of the new physics, it has been singularly absent from business management and corporate strategy.

Static and dynamic strategy

Central to the static and conventional wisdom, according to Stacey, is the belief that successful organizations conform to one of a limited number of configurations covering mission, strategy, structure, and style. This strategic orientation in fact characterizes the approaches of both Porter and also Hamel and Prahalad. The static 'posture' of an organization, in effect, is what you see when you stand at the organizational boundary and look inwards at its products and markets, technologies and competencies, organizational structure and controls, and its shared culture. The organization's 'position', moreover, is what you see when you stand at the organizational boundary and look outwards at market shares in particular segments, customer image, and core competence in relation to competitors. It is clearly reflected in the above mentioned SWOT – strengths and weaknesses, opportunities and threats – so characteristic of our conventional strategic wisdom. A successful dynamic strategy, conversely, is determined by an organization's ability, and the ability of the people within it, to survive by innovating and transforming themselves. Everything managers and strategists do, for Stacey therefore, depends fundamentally on the mental models through which they understand their world, particularly the models they share.

Companies that succeed in effect sustain contradictions which generate tension; tension creates energy; with such energy organizations transform themselves. Systems therefore can only be creative through experiencing instability; there is a fundamental relationship therefore between chaos and innovation. Such holistic and evolutionary thinking, moreover, is a distinct attitude of mind. Whereas Smuts in the 1920s, however, talked about holism and evolution, Stacey in the 1990s draws holistically upon chaos theory and developmentally upon the far-from-equilibrium organization.

The far-from-equlibrium organization

All organizations, for Stacey, are webs of nonlinear feedback loops connected to other people and organizations (its environments) by similar webs. Such non-linear feedback systems are capable of operating in states of stable and unstable equilibrium, or in the borders between these states, that is far-from-equilibrium. All organizations, moreover, operate paradoxically, in that they are pulled both towards stability by the forces of integration, and also towards the other extreme of unstable equilibrium by innovation.

If the organization gives into the pull of stability or instability it ossifies or disintegrates. Success lies in between, as a difficult-to-maintain 'dissipative structure'. The dynamics of the successful organization are therefore those of irregular cycles and discontinuous trends, falling within qualitative patterns, or wholes. Through unravelling these holistic patterns strategists discover and create the long term futures of their organizations.

Successful long-term planning therefore is a creative, innovative process that requires exposure to and management of contradiction. Effective strategy formulation in fact requires management to maintain a position away from equilibrium, in a state of contradiction between stability and instability, between tight and flexible controls. Creativity is thereby closely related to destruction, and instability is actually required to shatter existing paradigms so making way for the new. Such a dialectic generates tension that will eventually force a 'chaotic' rearrangement of conflicting forces.

Self-organization

Such 'chaos' in its scientific sense is not utter confusion but a combination of qualitative patterns and specific randomness; a combination of fuzzy categories accompanied by endless variability. Stable and explosively unstable equilibria are not the only attractors of systemic behaviour. Nonlinear systems can operate at a level of bounded instability far from equilibrium, a state between differented and integrated extremes. This is a complex state of orderly behaviour which requires continual inputs of attention, time and resource to sustain the organization as a dissipative structure. Strongly shared cultures push an organization back to stability, while countercultures are required to sustain the dissipative structure far from equlibrium.

Those who succeed, therefore, in the borders between stability and instability will be strategic managers who see patterns where others search for specific links between causes and events. Since, for Stacey, little can be said about the future of complex systems, it makes sense to identify meaning retrospectively with a view to designing future action. Trained incapacity needs to be supplanted by a continual questioning of existing mental models, and the development of new ones to cope with the unfolding future. Moreover, it must be accepted that unconscious defence mechanisms against anxiety will be touched off when uncertainty and ambiguity levels rise, and when the nature of power is changed. These need to be accommodated as integral to change. Change cannot therefore be comprehensively anticipated; creative development depends, in effect, on some form of spontaneous self-organization, with management providing favourable conditions.

Politics and learning

Holistic strategists, therefore, do not drive and control new strategic directions. Instead, they create favourable conditions for, and participate in, complex learning and effective politics. Instead of mission statements and plans, such managers and strategists focus on ever managing agendas of strategic issues, challenges and aspirations. Multiple, contradictory cultures should therefore be developed to foster different perspectives and provoke the complex learning that is necessary to handle changing strategic agendas. Learning groups that work in spontaneously self-organizing networks that encourage open conflict, engage in dialogue, and publicly test assertions, become vital. Self-organizing political networks, according to Stacey, function to undermine the hierachically based status quo. Without the consequent tension between control and freedom there could be no change.

The most important learning that individuals and organizations undergo, moreover, flows from the trial-and-error action they take in real time, arising especially from the way they reflect on these actions as they take them. How well people learn under these circumstances depends on the way they interact with each other in groups. Continuing success flows from creative interaction with the market environment, not simply building on existing strengths but intentionally steering away from equilibrium. The result is organizational tension, paradox and never-ending contradiction, and this provokes conflict and learning, the source of creativity. The only route to long term success, for Stacey then, is through innovation and accelerated organizational learning, because no competitive advantage is inherently sustainable. This view of organizational development is a dialectical one in which contradictory forces produce, through learning, a new synthesis of more complex strategies and structures. Adapting to the environment is thereby replaced by creative interaction with other actors in the environment. Comprehensive control systems and culture change programmes are replaced by organizations as complex, evolving systems where managers and strategists can only intervene at sensitive leverage points.

Corrective action will usually be experimental at first, so as to provide a vehicle for further learning. As unclear open-ended issues proceed through experimentation to emerge as potentially successful new strategies, the formal bodies play a more prominent role. Managers come to share memories of what has worked and not worked in the past. In this way they build up a business philosophy for the company. Activity is spontaneous and self-organizing in that no central authority can direct anyone to detect and select an open-ended issue for attention. The political activity of building support for attention to some detected issue is also self-organizing. It requires continuing inputs of energy and attention to sustain consensus within a far-from-equilibrium organization, conceived as a dissipative structure.

Dissipative structures

The border area between equilibrium and non-equilibrium is a state of paradox in which stability and instability pull the system in different directions. Scientists, as Stacey has already indicated, have called this combination of specific unpredictability and qualitative pattern a chaos, fractal or change state. Only when a system operates in this chaotic, far-from-equilibrium state is it continually creative. Chaotic behaviour has an overall pattern within which specific random outcomes occur.

Such 'chaos' is not utter confusion but bounded – rather than explosive – instability. A combination of order and disorder continually unfolds in irregular but similar forms. 'Chaotic' managers seize on small differences in customer requirements and perceptions, and build these into significant differentiators for their products, through amplifying feedback. Then they establish quality and cost targets against which they control production of the product to satisfy the demand they have created, through dampening feedback.

When non-linear feedback systems are pushed far from equilibrium, both Stacey and Smuts maintain, they follow a common sequence of steps in which they move from one state, through chaos, to unpredictable states of new order. These 'dissipative structures' are difficult to sustain because they require continual inputs of energy if they are to survive. Functional politics then involves continual dialogue around contentious issues. It is the means of attracting organizational attention to open-ended issues. Its function is to spread instability, within boundaries. Such instability is necessary to shatter existing patterns of behaviour and perceptions so that the new may emerge. At each point of transition systems driven far from equilibrium move through patterns of instability in which symmetry is broken, confronting the system with choices at critical points. Through a process of spontaneous self-organization, involving a form of communication and co-operation among the components of the system, new order may be produced.

Strategy and learning

The strategic management process, then, as far as the holistic strategist is concerned, goes something like this:

1 *Detecting and selecting issues* Open-ended change is typically the result of many accumulated small events and actions.
2 *Gaining attention and building support* The birth of strategy involves some individual, at some level of the hierarchy, detecting some potential issue and beginning to push for organizational attention to be paid to it.

3   *Interpreting and handling the emerging agenda*   That issue becomes part of the organization's strategic issue agenda – the focus of the organizational learning through which a business develops new strategic agendas.
4   *Clarifying preferences*   At some critical point, pressure arising from power, personality or group interaction forces a choice, whose outcome is unpredictable depending on the power play and group dynamics.
5   *Taking experimental action*   Action will usually be experimental at first, thus providing a vehicle for further learning – task forces may be set up to carry out experimental actions such as with new product development.
6   *Gaining legitimacy and backing*   Before such informal action is built into a strategy, formal bodies and procedures are required to legitimize choices being made and to allocate resources.
7   *Incorporating outcomes into organizational memory*   In sharing memories of what has worked or failed to work in the past managers build up a business philosophy; these recipes, taken together, become the company culture; they provide another boundary around the instability of the political and learning processes through which strategic issues are handled.

Anticipation and participation

Because trying to predict the future, for Stacey then, is a pointless exercise for an innovative company, corporate strategy requires anticipation and participation. It must be based firmly on the qualitative nature of what is happening now and what has happened in the past, focusing particularly on the anomalies in the current situation. It means generating new perspectives on what has been going on. It means framing problems and opportunities. It means noticing potential and possibility. It means creating group dynamics that encourage participation in complex learning activities, making explicit and also exploring not only issues themselves but also the group's learning behaviours. It involves trying to identify the mental models that have led to the way problems and opportunities are being framed, with a view to developing a different learning model and changing mind-sets.

Complex group learning occurs far from equilibrium when individuals are in conflict and confusion, and incorporating a newly shared meaning, and a willingness to engage in dialogue and listen.

Steps towards managing an unknowable future

When the future is unknowable, Stacey concludes, managers cannot mechanistically install techniques, procedures, structures and technologies to control long term outcomes. They can holistically manage boundary conditions, thereby pushing the organization far from equilibrium in which spontaneous self-organization may occur and new strategic directions may emerge. The key question strategists face, in that case, is not how to maintain stable equilibrium but how to establish sufficient sustained instability to provoke complex learning. It is through political interaction and complex learning that businesses create and manage their unknowable futures.

The heart of Stacey's strategic dynamics, therefore, is a flexible, ever changing agenda of open-ended issues that is identied, clarified, and progressed by the self-organizing networks of the organization. Group members should be chosen on the basis of personality rather than their position in the formal hierarchy, drawing membership from a number of different functions, units and levels. A team can only be self-organizing if it discovers its own goals and objectives. This means that top management must limit themselves to presenting the group with ambiguous challenges.

Cross-cultural learning is finally promoted by rotating people between functions, companies, and countries. New perspectives seldom appear when the same culture and unconscious mental models are shared. Their learning is complex because it is not simply the absorption of existing knowledge, techniques, or recipes, but the continual questioning of deeply held and usually unconscious beliefs. The creative work needed to deal with open-ended issues ultimately takes time and resources, but without this investment new strategic directions will never emerge.

Humanism: Co-creative Strategy

The emergent wisdom – we win or lose together

To enter into the fourth world of humanism, we now turn to Reich. Life on this planet, argues Reich, has become less a set of contracts in which one party can be victorious, and more an intricate game which we win or we lose together. Britain's economy is both independent of, but also interdependent with, Germany's. America or Britain or a Tory party, then, cannot withdraw in fear and distaste from the mob at the gates. Its interests are too intimately bound up with theirs. Nor can the Anglo-Saxon world, or the Japanese for that matter, boldly assert its will. Either's control over the rest of the world, according to Reich, is too contingent and tenuous. 'Rather, we must seek our possibilities for mutual gain. *The world has evolved beyond the point at which either assertion or isolation is a tenable option.*'

So by 1986, by way of example, almost every American industry, with a history of bitter conflict with Japan was seemingly showing signs of 'born again co-operation'. Similarly Anglo-Japanese co-operation had gained apace. Therefore, Reich argues, for example, trade names were becoming irrelevant for distinguishing Japanese from American products. General Motors was buying diesel engines from Isuzu, Ford was buying key parts from Mazda, and Kodak's copiers were being made by Canon. As an overall pattern, though, Americans took charge of the two ends of the production process, the major research innovations and the final assembly and sales, while the Japanese concentrated on the complex production in-between. This division of cultural labour has emerged out of the individual ingenuity in America, and group effectiveness in Japan.

Beyond the triumphant individual – collective entrepreneurism

The Horatio Alger cosmology presented America, as Samuels Smiles' *Self help* might have done in Britain, with a noble ideal, a society in which imagination and effort summoned their individual reward. The key virtue was self-reliance. The goal was to be your own boss. Such a myth, of the triumphant individual, may have been appropriate, Reich maintains, to a simpler and more insular economy. But within a complex economic system, with so many potential bottlenecks and critical levers, so many transactions to be co-ordinated amongst so many people, opportunistic individualism more often than not short circuits progress rather than advances it. Each party is led to limit his own responsibility and commitment, and to take refuge in explicit contracts, rules, and other guarantees. Thus the current version of the myth of the triumphant individual may have outlasted its time.

Managers have sought stability by resorting to intricate, economically sterile legal and financial dodges that dump risk on employees, suppliers or investors. Investors, meanwhile, have rewarded managers who cut short run labour costs. Workers have absconded with valuable training and experience. The frequent result has been gridlock. The resulting loss is largely invisible, Reich claims, because we cannot see the potential in an economy that remains unfulfilled. What is required, in effect, is mutual investment for long term gain, through what Reich terms 'collective entrepreneurship'. While owners continuously invest in workers by giving them training and experience in new technologies, workers invest in one another by sharing ideas and insights. Suppliers of materials and parts invest by committing to produce specialized components. Creditors supply capital without requiring a rigid projection of how the funds will be used. What distinguishes these investments from the standard form is that they rest primarily on trust.

Each party trusts that its contributions will eventually be reciprocated. In this case of collective entrepreneurism, for Reich, all those associated with the firm become partners in its future. Each member of the enterprise participates in its evolution. Business becomes part of a benevolent community.

Business as a benevolent community

Compassion and generosity, according to Reich, are still sentiments that America can endorse and act upon when it is a matter of charity concerts, cake sales, and other such voluntary activities. But when it comes to government welfare programmes the consensus has dissolved. It is widely accepted that welfare does not work, but there is no alternative vision of public action that might. The Benevolent Community is bereft of any guiding philosophy for demarcating public and private responsibilities. As private individuals, Americans understand their obligations towards the poor; as citizens they are frequently baffled, disappointed, and suspicious.

A society premised soley upon the principle of selfish interest, for Reich then, even of the enlightened variety, cannot summon the shared responsibility upon which any scheme of social insurance or social investment can depend. But it is equally true that a society premised upon altruism and compassion toward others cannot sustain those noble sentiments when the going gets tough. The former arrangment asks too little of its citizens; the latter too much. A truly benevolent community must both inculcate mutual responsibility and simultaneously celebrate the resulting mutual gain. To be motivated, in the final analysis, to contribute rather than to exploit, a person needs more than good health and a solid education. He must feel that he is a member of a society that respects him, and whose respect is worth retaining. For this to occur both business and government have their part to play.

Beyond the rot at the top – reconnecting business and government

For Reich the liberal version of 'rot at the top' typically concerns itself with the business exploitation of the wider community; the conservatives are similarly alarmed by the meddling of government. The common error of both variants, for Reich, is the rigid delineation of 'us' and 'them'. The conservative morality tales speaks of 'their' strength and deviousness; the liberal morality of 'our' weakness and need. Neither feature stories of mutually rewarding encounters, or common efforts to overcome perils. It is here, in the premise of generally opposed interests, that the prevailing myths seemingly serve worst as guides to reality. For the reality involves an overlap of interests, in commmon cause that transcends each side of the public-private divide.

'The key to Japan's successful industrial policy,' says Reich, 'has lain not in any elaborate plans emanating from MIT, but in an industrial structure that has been designed and redesigned for the express purpose of pushing Japanese industry (and Japanese workers) into ever more complex and efficient production, thereby extending their experience and extending outward the frontier of their production capacities as quickly as possible. Their rules of the game – taxes, public procurement, the organization of banks and labour – are tilted in favour of the rapid accumulation of new knowledge and skills.' The current version of rot at the top, then, and the sharp division between business and government, undercuts any rational assignment of their responsibilities. Business has no clear mandate for the development and deployment of workers; government alone lacks the competence to take on the task. It is this conundrum that led Robert Reich, five years after writing his tales of a new America, to publish his treatise on *The Work of Nations*, taking on perhaps from where Adam Smith left off. Reich also leads us, at this point, right into the learning society, via the 'work', if not directly the 'wealth' of nations.

The Work of Nations

Citizens' skills as primary assets

For Reich then, as he sees things in the 1990s, 'there will be no national products or technologies, no national corporations, no national industries. All that will remain rooted within national borders are the people who comprise the nation. *Each nation's primary assets will be its citizens' skills and insights.*' As borders become ever more meaningless in economic terms, those citizens best positioned to thrive in the world market are tempted to slip the bonds of national allegiance, and by so doing disengage themselves from their less favoured fellows. The future standard of living of Americans, therefore, like that of any other nation's citizens, depends upon their capacity to moderate their overall consumption (both public and private) while simulatenously making investments in their unique resources – people and infrastructure – and thereby attract global investors to do the same.

The real economic challenge facing the US in the years ahead, according to Reich, is to increase the potential value of what its citizens can add to the global economy, by enhancing their skills and capacities (human capital), and by linking those to the world market. The standard of living of all citizens is coming to depend less on the success of a nation's core corporations and industries, or even on something called the 'national economy', than it is on the worldwide demand for people's skills and insights. At the same time, economic success lies in adding such value to enterprise webs.

The high value web of enterprise

The new barrier to entry, for Reich, is not volume or price; it is skill in finding the right fit between particular technologies and particular markets. In the high value enterprise, profits derive not from scale and volume but from continuous discovery of new linkages between solutions and needs. Thus the key assets of what he terms 'high value enterprise' are not tangible things, but the skills involved in linking solutions to particular needs, and the reputations that come from having done so successfully in the past. Power is diffused, depending not on formal authority or rank but on the capacity to add value to enterprise webs. Points at the periphery where a few threads once intersected, evolve into new webs. Such webs centre on groups of people who create the most value and attract the most talented followers.

These new organizational webs of high-value enterprise, Reich claims, which are replacing the old core pyramids of high volume enterprise, are reaching across the globe. Thus there is coming to be no such organization as an 'American' (or British or French or Japanese or German) corporation, nor any finished good called an 'American' product. In such global webs products are international composites. What is traded between nations is less often finished products than specialized problem solving (research, product design, fabrication), problem identifying (marketing, advertising, customer consulting) and brokerage (financing, searching, contracting) services, as well as routine components and services, all combined to create value. Such value, in effect, arises out of learning.

Because Reich's high value enterprise is based on skills and insights, the highest returns and the greatest leverage belong to skilled people within the web (including the lisencees, partners or subcontractors) rather than to shareholders or executives occupying formal positions of authority. No longer should other countries, Reich argues, be seen to be taking over America's assets; instead they should more accurately be perceived as helping the country to become more productive, and its people to increase their personal worth.

Increasing personal worth

The transformation of work   As corporations of all nations are transformed into global webs, the important question – from the standpoint of national wealth – is not which nation's citizens own what, but which citizens learn what to do what. As such, Reich maintains, they are capable of adding more value to the world economy and therefore increasing their own potential worth. Today no more than 3 per cent of the price of a semiconductor chip goes to the owners of raw material and energy, 5 per cent to those who own the equipment and facilities, and 6 per cent to routine labour. More than 85 per cent, according to Reich, is for specialized design and engineering services and for patents and copyrights on past discoveries made in the course of providing such services. Unlike machinery that gradually wears out, raw materials that become depleted, patents and copyrights that grow obsolete, and trademarks that lose their ability to comfort, the skills and insights that come from discovering new linkages between technologies and needs increase with practise.

By 1990 routine production work comprised about one quarter of the jobs performed by Americans, and the number was declining. In-person services accounted for about 30 per cent. Symbolic-analytical services formed the third category. These services do not enter world commerce as standardized things, but as symbols, data, words, and visuals.

The sinking boat of routine producers   The boat containing routine producers, for Reich, is sinking rapidly. Twelve thousand people are added to the world's population every hour. Most of them will eventually happily work for a small fraction of the wages of routine producers in America. For example by 1990, American Airlines were employing over 1000 data processers in Barbados and the Dominican Republic to enter names and flight numbers from used airline tickets.

Also vanishing are lower and middle level management jobs involving routine production. Between 1981 and 1986 more than 780,000 foremen, supervisors and section chiefs lost their jobs. As America's core pyramids were transformed into global webs, many middle level routine producers were as obsolete as routine workers on the line.

The gradual demise of 'in-person service'   The second of the three boats, carrying what Reich terms 'in-person servers', is sinking as well, but somewhat more slowly and unevenly. The fiercest competition comes from labour saving machinery, such as automated tellers, robotized vending machines, self-service gasoline pumps.

Unlike the boats of routine producers and in-person servers, however, the vessel containing what Reich calls 'symbolic analysts' is rising. Worldwide demand for their insights is growing as the ease and speed of communicating with them steadily increases. The formal education of an incipient symbolic analyst, moreover, entails refining Reich's four basic skills: *abstraction, systems thinking, experimentation* and *collaboration*. According to Reich: 'The fortunate student gains from formal education the techniques and habits of abstraction, system thinking, experimention and collaboration – all of which are prerequisites for a lifetime of creative problem solving, identifying and brokering. From then on, learning comes from doing. The struggle over complex problems yields new insights and approaches relevant to even more complex problems, and so on, as learning builds on itself. Abstraction becomes more sophisticated; system thinking expands and deepens; the repertoire of *experimental techniques widens*; collaborative skills improve.'

The rise of the symbolic analyst

The habits and methods of '*experimentation*', firstly then, are critical for Reich in the new economy, where technologies, tastes, and markets are in constant flux. So the cinematographer tries out a new technique for shooting scenes; the design engineer tries out a new material for fabricating engine parts. Such experimentally based 'action learning' is pre-eminently Western. Secondly, Reich's capacity for '*abstraction*', for discovering patterns and meanings – pre-eminent in the Northern world – is the very essence of symbolic analysis, in which reality must be simplified so that it can be understood and manipulated in new ways. The symbolic analyst therefore wields equations, formulae, analogies, models, contrasts, categories and metaphors in order to create possibilities for reinterpreting and then rearranging the chaos of data swirling around us.

Thirdly '*systems thinking*' for Reich, strongly engrained within the East, carries abstraction a step further. To discover new opportunities one must be capable of seeing the whole, and of understanding the processes by which parts of reality are linked together. In the real world, issues rarely emerge predefined and neatly separable. The symbolic analyst must constantly try to discern larger causes, consequences, relationships. Such a systemic approach is represented in Peter Senge's so called 'fifth discipline'.

Finally, there is Reich's Southern communal capacity to '*collaborate*'. Symbolic analysts typically work in teams, spend much of their time communicating concepts and then seeking a consensus to go foreward with the plan. In the best classrooms, students learn to articulate, clarify and then restate for one another how they identify and find answers. They also learn to work together.

Paths to the Future

In conclusion, and for Reich, we are now presented with a rare historical moment. Although localized conflicts are sadly proliferating, the threat of worldwide conflict has become remote. Moreover, the transformations of economy and technology are blurring the lines between the industrialized nations. As Reich says in *The Work of Nations*: 'The modern nation state, some 200 years old, is no longer what it was. Vanishing is a nationalism founded upon the practical necessities of economic independence within borders, and security against foreigners outside. There is thus an opportunity for us, as for every society, to redefine who we are, why we have joined together, and what we owe each other, and the other inhabitants of the world. The choice is ours to make. We are no more slaves to present trends than to vestiges of the past. We can, if we choose, assert that our mutual obligations as citizens extend beyond our economic usefulness to each other.'

Reich sees 'positive economic nationalism' as an orientation whereby each nation's citizens take primary responsibility for enhancing the capacities of their countrymen for full and productive lives. At the same time they work with other nations to ensure that these empowerments do not come at the other's expense. This form of nationalism seeks to encourage new learning within the society, to smooth the transition of the labour force from older industries, to educate and train the nation's workers. It seeks to improve the nation's infrastructure, and to create international rules of fair play for accomplishing all these things.

Conclusion

It is also important to emphasize that the managerial and strategic world is a reflection of not only the cultural environment but also of the ecological, physical and the psychological. In the final analysis, moreover, it will be reflected in the theory and practice of the knowledge creating company.

As far as the ecological environment, in which this book is particularly strongly rooted, is concerned, it is worth reminding ourselves of the different orientations of the different strategic approaches, before we move on. For Michael Porter's work on 'competitive strategy' is lodged pragmatically within Darwin's world of natural selection, whereby only the fittest survive. Hamel and Prahalad's strategic intent, duly focused on core competencies, places much more emphasis on the inner variation of our species, and is therefore more purposefully rational in its orientation. Ralph Stacey's strategic dynamics, draws upon Jan Smuts' seminal concept of 'holism and evolution', which makes this dynamic approach, by definition, more holistic than the other two. Finally, Reich's approach to strategy draws, on the one hand, upon notions of ecological succession, and, on the other, upon the diverse humanities of the globe.

Bibliography

Porter, M. (1980) *Competitive Strategy: Techniques for Analyzing Industries and Competitors*. New York: Free Press.

Dawkins, R. (1989) *The Selfish Gene*. Oxford: Oxford University Press.

Hamel, G. and Prahalad, C.K. (1994) *Competing for the Future*. Cambridge, MA: Harvard University Press.

Stacey, R. (1996) *Complexity and Creativity in Organizations*. San Francisco: Berrett Koehler.

Reich, R. (1984) *The Next American Frontier*. London: Penguin.

Lovelock, James (1979) *Gaia: A new look at life on Earth*. New York: Oxford University Press.

Reich, R. (1987) *Tales of a New America*. Times Books.

Reich, R. (1991) *The Work of Nations*. Simon & Schuster.

WORK

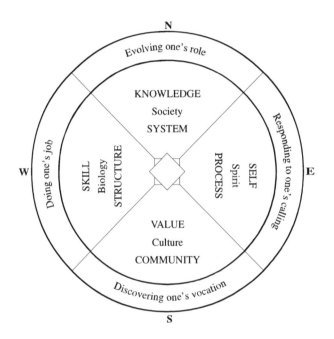

For we are the men who get the job done

Cowboy Song

The first task in remodelling education is to understand it as education for work and not merely for jobs

Mathew Fox

Practice not doing, and everything will fall into place

Tao Te Ching

In our culture, every one works four hours a day and the rest of the day we make things

Australian Aborigine

Your Work

From the four worlds of philosophy, environment and knowledge, we now turn to the four worlds of work, at the personal and the organizational level. As individuals, our sphere of work is centred within the four worlds of *job*, *role*, *calling* and *vocation*. Similarly, our organizations are centred in the four worlds of *structure*, *system*, *process* and *value*. You will find that each of these four dimensions correspond respectively to the four generic philosophies and the four domains of knowledge creation.

By the end of this section you will have learnt to:

• Visualize your work in terms of four worlds
• Chart your own developmental journey across the four worlds
• Take the first steps to managing your organization in the four worlds of *structure*, *process*, *system* and *value*
• Manage the developmental journey of your organization.

12

From Job to Vocation

Introduction: The Need for Redefining Work

Our present definition of work goes back to an era when the function of work was perceived purely in terms of the production of goods. Moreover, productivity itself was seen as a limitless frontier; the belief was that with advancing technology, production by the individual laborer could only keep increasing. This basic assumption on which was founded a modern edifice of work is now clearly obsolete. For productivity to keep increasing, the economic product must increase to maintain the same number of jobs. The assumption that the economic product must consequently grow prevailed until as recently as the Reagan-Thatcher era of world politics. However, this assumption tends to (and has) run into a simple problem: economic growth is constrained by limits of environmental resources, and political, social and ethical factors. What we have ended up doing as a global phenomenon, is trying to circumvent this fundamental issue without seeing the inherent incoherence that is built into it. There have been two major consequences of this incoherence:

1 In physical terms, the creation of a group of 'superfluous people' – the unemployed.
2 In psychological terms, the perpetuation of a disempowering industrial culture.

John Maynard Keynes, writing amidst growing worries of chronic unemployement just before the Second World War ended, said that governments could promote full employment ony by promoting mass consumption and economic growth. Around 1950, the first mass-consumption society of the world was born in the United States. Putting aside old habits of frugality and self-denial, Americans learnt to waste. The 'consumer' was born and a whole new world of 'planned obsolescence' came into being. Work was by now little more than a 'job to be done', a trivial element in the new economic equation of production equals consumption equals waste. This soon led to growing unemployment and rise of the social and psychological costs of being out of work. Today there are close to one billion human beings out of work. At the same time, a large number of people, especially in organizations, see work as a necessary evil. Life in organizations is seen as intrinsically devoid of meaning, leading to a sharp dichotomy of 'professional values' and 'personal values'. It is taken for granted by countless humans that the organizations they work for cannot provide values of self-fulfilment or actualization; they are purely a source of income. When work gets degraded, it is human dignity that suffers in the long run, leading to the disempowering of vast groups of people. Through that we create conditions in our society where meaningful work becomes increasingly replaced by drudgery and millions engage themselves in the endless churning out of so many meaningless products of no quality and value. Consequently, we create a global context which defines economics in terms of the employed and unemployed.

The place to begin the change, we feel, is from within ourselves. If as employees, as managers or as CEOs we can see the new organization as a place where we create meaning both, for ourselves as individuals and for our societies, we have the influence to change the larger social issues of unemployment and worthlessness. We feel that this can be achieved through a simple redefinition of the notion of work itself.

Work as the Joy of Life

One of the great incoherencies in our societies is that at a time when the need for 'meaningful work' in rebuilding society and the environment is at its greatest, so many of us are out of work. Added to that a vast majority of us continue to be locked into fuelling the 'production-consumption-waste' cycle when the consequences of this in economic, social, psychological and environmental terms is obvious.

Unfortunately in terms of our traditional world view, which as we have seen is based on outdated concepts of science and economics, the growing unemployment becomes a problem to be solved. What we hope to outline in this chapter is that it is merely a symptom of a deeper problem of an outdated paradigm that defines work solely in terms of production and consumption.

Writing in *Small is Beautiful*, the economist E. F. Schumacher makes a distinction between what he calls 'good work' and 'bad work'. 'How do we prepare young people for the future world of work? . . . We should prepare

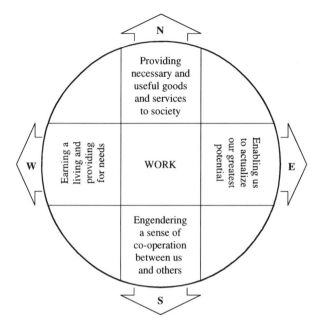

Figure 12.1

them to be able to distinguish between good work and bad work and encourage them not to accept the latter. This is to say, they should be encouraged to reject meaningless, boring, stultifying, or nerve-racking work in which a (person) is made the servant of a machine or a system. They should be taught that work is the *joy of life* and is needed for our development, but that meaningless work is an abomination.'

Building on Schumacher's work, we spell out the four functions of human work as follows:

- To *earn a living* and provide for one's (and for the group's) needs.
- To *provide* necessary and useful *goods and services* to society.
- To *enable* every one of us to *actualize* our deepest selves.
- To *discover* the deep interdependence that binds people together.

We can now weave this into our four-world model to give figure 12.1.

The first world of providing for one's own and the group's need is the *pragmatic* world of *doing one's job*. Its rightful philosophical base is the West, although as we have seen this several times in the book already, the model is such that each world intrinsically enfolds the other three worlds in it.

The second world of providing necessary goods and services to society is the *rational* world. At this stage, you are no longer defining your work purely in

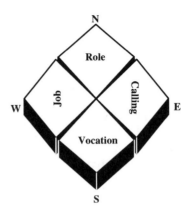

Figure 12.2

terms of doing a job, but in terms of your *role* in the larger system of the organization and society. The home of such a role evolution is the North.

The third world is that of actualizing your 'self' through work. This is the *holistic* world of transforming your life's patterns through your *calling*. The philosophical base of this dimension is East.

Finally, the fourth world of co-operation with our fellow human beings and our communities is the *humanistic* world of discovering one's life's *vocation*. The rightful home of this is in the South. (See figure 12.2.)

Once again, we would like to emphasize that the four worlds are inextricably interconnected and form a cohesive whole. The wholeness of 'job', 'role', 'calling' and 'vocation' defines a *personal ecology* that identifies our meaningful place in organizations. Consequently, it provides the organization an agenda with which each employee can be encouraged to live and work in all four worlds.

The Western World of Skill: Doing One's Job

The word, 'job' is derived from an old English work 'jobbe', which meant a piece or 'piecework'. In the pragmatic, Western world of 'identity', your job is defined on the basis of territory. This therefore provides the *structural* dimension to work. Your job therefore brings into focus a specific area that relates to the use of specific skills and techniques. If you have a job in the Production area of an organization, you need to specialize in the skills necessary to run and manage the production work of the organization. The important thing in the world of skill-based knowledge is to be able to perceive the organization in terms of its component parts and the functions and tasks that are necessary to keep the organization running. As we have seen, this world is isomorphic with the first stage of resource-accumulation in which individual emphasis is largely on survival and physical growth. As a result, the mental model used in this world is clearly an *analytical* one. From a pragmatic perspective, skill-based management is closely linked to *problem solving*. We are of course referring to linear problems here, which are based on the assumption that every effect is preceded by one cause which can be realized through 'trouble-shooting'. Obviously, this approach is possible only if the organization is regarded mechanically.

This skill-and-technique world of the pragmatic West is facilitated by the classic *training* programmes that organizations value so much, in which employees pick up specific skills in a short term period. The premise is that specific situations at work require specific skills and techniques; marketing skills in the marketing department, sales skills in the sales department, etc. The interconnections between sales and marketing for instance are either deliberately ignored or not understood at all.

The Northern World of Knowledge: Evolving One's Role

The second, rational world of the North provides precisely what is missing in the pragmatic, Western world: a *systematic* dimension to your work in which the seemingly separate functions in the organization become interconnected to each other. To evolve a role in the organization, requires that you add on – to your pragmatic world – a lateral perception of your organization, and a *rational* knowledge-base that links the categories together. To go back to the example mentioned before, while the job of a marketing person is all about marketing and nothing else, a role evolution involves a shift in perception to seeing marketing being cross-functionally interlinked to all the other departments in the organization. From a mechanical model of the organization which is the hallmark of the job dimension, role evolution is about the organization becoming more of a *lattice structure* or an *electronic network*.

From just doing a job, you now begin to actively play a role that links you to many other functions in the organization. From a skill-based specialist, you now evolve to becoming a knowledge-based generalist, capable of multi-task functions and networking along many departments. Role evolution therefore is no longer about short-term training programs but of developing methodologies for *knowledge creation*. Unlike the problem-solving stage in the first world, this stage is about *problem conceptualizing*. Unlike the trouble-shooting approach of the first world, this stage takes into account the multiferous factors that have resulted in the problem. The approach is thus divergent unlike the convergent approach used in the first world.

The Eastern World of the Self:
Transformation through Calling

The Western job dimension is about perceiving and acting out one's part in a machine, thereby bringing into focus a specific skill necessary to perform a specific function. The Northern role dimension is about perceiving and acting out one's role in a lattice network, with the knowledge that the organization is not just a structure composed of autonomous units, but a system of interconnected parts. In both cases, the person continues to regard the organization as an objective reality. There is thus a sharp disctinction between the organization as being 'out there' in contrast to the person's self being 'in here'.

The Eastern *calling* dimension seeks to undermine and destroy precisely this dichotomy between yourself and the organization. Transforming your work into a calling is about questioning and ultimately destroying the notion that the ego is the center and the source of all the work you do in the organization and otherwise. In the Eastern world, and in sharp contrast to the North, neither you nor your organization can be perceived in terms of hard delineating boundaries that provide a sense of identity. On the contrary, both your 'self' and the organization are dynamic and fluid 'non-entities'. The metaphor that best describes this Eastern fluidity of perception is *holographic*. In a hologram, every single part of, say, a picture, contains the whole picture enfolded in it. In other words, it becomes meaningless to talk in terms of organizational categories like marketing and production and sales. None of these categories have any existence by themselves, for their individual identity is merely an abstraction. When you look deeper into any function in the organization – from the work of a manager to routine clerical work – it enfolds the whole organization and its links to the world outside. Your job may be that of a finance manager; your role may interlink you to product development, but from a holographic perspective, these are only conveneient abstractions. The reality in the world of calling is of an organization in flow, manifesting itself in different guises in what we abstract out to be parts. Unlike in the first two worlds where the organization was seen as a material entity, in the Eastern world, the organization is energy itself.

When the holographic view is applied to yourself, your position and title turn out to be equally abstract categories. Your identity turns out to be a convenient notion, for who are you if not just another manifestation of the same energy that makes up the organization? Given this situation, you and the organization become parts of an unbroken whole. What you do therefore transforms the organization, and the organization in turn, transforms you and your work now begins to embody the subtle connections between yourself and the organization. You no longer just look for categories to 'fit into', the way you did in the West. Neither do you just evolve a role in the organization, the way you did in the North. You now perceive the organization to be an extension of yourself, and in the work you do, you seek to discover your innermost self. For this reason, unlike in the Western and Nothern worlds, the Eastern world of calling is deeply subjective. In the *objective* worlds of the West and the North, your work is defined by external criteria, and so is the route along which you may evolve your role; after all you are dealing with a static entity that is defined in terms of its parts. Now, you have the opportunity to perceive your work from inside-out thereby destroying all the external categories because they do not make sense any more. Instead your work becomes a deeply subjective matter and is therefore possible only if you put 'all of yourself' into it. This is different from overworking, which is in fact an escape from your self; rather pouring 'all of yourself' is allowing your self to unfold out through your work.

From an Eastern, calling perspective, your approach to problems – both organizational and otherwise – is fundamentally different from the Western and Northern approaches. You no longer look for answers to problems, because you have realized that all answers are relative and are either based on *ad hoc* assumptions about the organization or on a theory that has worked before. Because you see every situation as unique, any answer that comes from an analytical or rational source is bound to be limited and short-termed in its applicability. The Eastern way is to respond to this situation by not seeking the answer at all, to *ask the right question*. When self and work are fused together, which is what constitutes the calling, the right question is the answer.

The Southern World of Community:
Discovering Your Vocation

Finally, your work must be grounded in the shared *value* that links your organization to your community and the world outside. Your vocation is rooted in a deeply *humanistic* dimension: the desire to work with others, to feel responsible for the larger good of humanity and the urge to create value.

As in the Southern homeostatic dimension of our ecological environment, where the resources of the ecosystem spread out over the widest area possible, the stage of vocation is one in which your own resources become available, not just for yourself and your organization, but for all society. The assumption we are making here is that each one of us is capable of creating and adding value to the society in which we live and the world at large. Each one of us is uniquely gifted and the ultimate purpose of the organization is to gve us the possibility to become aware of what that uniqueness is. This is the reason why vocation is always 'discovered' and not given to you. Once found, it is of benefit to more than just you and the organization.

Your vocation earns you more than just a place in the organization. It gives you a deep feeling rootedness in the culture and society you are in. It gives you a place in the world. For this reason, the Southern world of vocation is characterized by an *ecological* model. Each and every detail in our planet's ecology has a niche, a place from where it adds value. Nothing is superfluous and moreover, all things exist in a state of mutuality.

In the Southern world, you are profoundly aware of these interdependencies and as a result, any action you take must reflect both, this knowledge and a concern for all the consequences of the action. The Southern approach to problems is characterized by a *problem-sharing* mode rather than anything else. Since the vocational stage is about discovering the sense of interdependence that binds your work to that of the community you are in, the emphasis here is on consensus-building. Your aim to is create an organizational culture which is based on shared values and a common vision. These, rather than needs of career and external rewards, become the driving force of your work.

Inner and Outer Work

Mathew Fox, writing in *The Reinvention of Work*, talks of there being essentially two kinds of work: inner and outer. 'The inner work refers to that large world within . . . ourselves, the outer is what we give birth to or interact with outside ourselves.' Rather than being two distinct categories, the world of outer work is a manifestation of the inner world. While the inner work is the implicit, outer work is explicit. The implicit unfolds into the explicit and the explicit in turn, creates conditions for deepening our inner work. 'In bringing together inner work and outer work,' according to Fox, 'we contribute to a cosmology, a making whole, a putting of order into our lives and that of our species.'

In our own cosmology of the four worlds, while the Western and Northern worlds provide for meaningful outer work, the Eastern and Southern worlds provide for inner work. While job and role are characterized by external referencing, calling and vocation are internally referenced. Of course, the 'making whole' that Fox refers to is seeing the inner and outer world as two sides to the same coin. But too often, we find ourselves working solely in the external world where our point of reference is provided by somebody else or by a faceless system. When this is the case, work is done either for a pay check, for external rewards or because of a situation of external threat. Fox forcefully points out that 'In work that is motivated [only] from the outside – through either rewards or punishment – lies the death, literally, of work.' When inner and outer work come together, humans work 'primarily for their self-respect and not for others or for profit'. In this scenario, profit – although important to most organization – is incidental and can never be the prime mover. 'For the person who is working for the sake of his own satisfaction, the money he gets in return serves merely as fuel, that is, as a symbol of reward and recognition, in the last analysis, of acceptance by one's fellow men.'

In societies that are chiefly characterized by the production–consumption–waste equation, the Western and Northern worlds are familiar enough to organizations and managers. The Eastern and Southern worlds are elusive precisely because they tend to question and undermine the power of the above equation. According to Fox, the one lesson we need to learn from the industrial revolution is that work is not primarily about factories and industries. The 'new work' is, 'work on the human being itself'. How then does one move from outer to inner work? In other words, if the explicit level of jobs and roles is all the we have been conditioned to believe in, how do we journey to the implicit world of calling and vocation? Fox lists three ways of doing so.

1   The first way is to enter into *work as a process* – as the way – not as a product. This teaches us that our work itself is a holy journey and that it is not the pot of gold at the end of the work that justifies the journey.
2   The other way is to enter into our depths, our ground, our mystery, our hiddenness, and work from there. *Nothingness* as applied to work means no outside goals; the work must be its own reward, its own grace.
3   The third way is to understand that work, like life, arises out of itself from its own foundation. Working without a why means *letting go* of all superficial enticements to our labor and working out of our innermost selves.

The Developmental Journey

As we have already explored, what matters is not so much what you are, or what you have been, but what you are in the process of becoming. We called this the very essence of the 'individuation process'. Jung saw the issues of the first and second quarters of life – the Western and Northern worlds – as essentially biological and social respectively. On the other hand, the third and fourth quarters – the Eastern and Southern worlds – are respectively spiritual and cultural. The developmental journey from job to vocation is then a journey through the four worlds of *biology*, *society*, *spirit* and *culture*.

The Western world of 'doing one's job' is synchronous with your 'youthful', biological stage. In terms of our ecological metaphor, this is the realm of the manager as the 'hunter/gatherer', whose purpose – as we have discussed – is to maximize gains in as short a time as possible. This world is externally referenced, through salary, security, status and other physical criteria. Like the youthful adult, the Western world of jobs is about a search for *identity* through work. The notion here is that it is the job you do that defines your identity.

The Northern world of 'role evolution' is part of the adult stage of your life, marked by a need to become an *entity* that then provides a meaningful position for you in the organization. In ecological terms, this is the stage of the 'herder' manager, whose main purpose is to conserve as much of the resources as possible. This world is also externally referenced although the criteria are broader than those in the Western world. No longer searching for identity, the stage of role evolution moves is a movement from the biological to the social stage. The adult person is not just looking for personal security; now he or she has to form part of a network of relationships, which could be filial, as part of the organization, or those that link the person to the society.

The Eastern world of *calling* is the spiritual stage of development in which the search is no longer for either identity or security, but for the *self*. Paradoxically, this involves a 'letting-go' of the self, which is what we earlier referred to as becoming the '*non-entity*'. This is the stage of 'renewal' in your life, and you become more engaged with the dissolution of your ego. You attempt to creatively destroy the traditional dichotomy of self and organization by beginning to destroy your dependence on external references. Your 'inner voice' becomes more important than external criteria. This is also a period of struggle in which you begin to question previous aspects of your life and work.

In the Southern world of 'vocation', the emphasis now shifts to unravelling your sense of belonging to a *community*. You are by now completely free from any external references in your work and your work is its own reason. This is the legacy stage of your development in which you give far more than what you take. In ecospheric terms this is the stage of homeostasis, in which you spread your resources out. In your work, you no longer think of the organization as a separte entity; rather your organization is an inextricable part of society and so any change you initiate in the organization is synonymous with a change in society.

Conclusion

The four worlds of 'identity', 'entity', 'non-entity' and 'community' that we introduced in the introduction to this book prevail simultaneously in the world outside and within the development path that our life takes. While the notion of having a job provides identity, the evolution of a role actualizes the entity who we are. Likewise, transformation through a calling creates the non-entity while the discovery of a vocation gives us the sense of a community.

Bibliography

Schumacher, E.F. (1973) *Small is Beautiful*. London: Abacus.
Fox, M. (1994) *The Reinvention of Work: A new vision of livelihood for our time*. New York: HarperCollins.

13

From Structure to Value

Introduction

In chapter 6, we referred to the four generic worlds of ecology, namely *competition, conservation, catalysation* and *co-creation*. Whereas the first world of competetion is about establishing territories, the second world is about conserving resources through internal networks. And whereas the third world of catalysation is about creative destruction and destabilization, the fourth world of co-creation is about transformation through a distribution of resources and gains over as wide an area as possible. We had linked these four worlds to the four respective generic philosophies of pragmatism, rationalism, holism and humanism. We implied that the pragmatic Western manager is at once the territorial hunter manager; the rational, Northern manager is the herder manager; the holistic, Eastern manager is the gardener manager and the humanistic, Southern manager is the steward manager.

Having said this – and we have referred to this before – the true benefit of using this model is not to perceive the four worlds as mutually exclusive. On the contrary, the four worlds are complementary wholes that have to be taken together. In other words, although a typically western manager is more likely to be a hunter manager than anything else, the same manager has to tap into the other three worlds that are latent in him or her. We shall explore this theme more concretely in the next chapter. For the time being, we would like to focus on the four worlds of an organization. These four worlds are four force fields that create the totality of the organizational form. Management then becomes the art of creating a resonance at the centre of the four organizational worlds.

The Four Worlds of an Organization

The four fields that we referred to are regions of activity that apply to any organization. Interestingly, not all of them are equally present in all organizations. A cultural bias results in one field of activity predominating over the other three. What we shall see in this chapter is that each of the four worlds are vitally necessary for the proper functioning of any organization. As in ecology, where the four worlds are characterized by alternating stability and instability, the four worlds of an organization have a similar tension between them. Moreover, each of the four worlds is a replica of the four levels of perception of Jung, namely *sensing, thinking, intuiting* and *feeling*. What we are in effect saying is that there is a common form, a 'morphology', that manifests itself at all levels of organization: the organization of human perception, the organization of the ecosystem, the organization of the four cultural forms and finally, of the organization itself. This morphology of the four worlds provides a holistic picture of the world we live in, of who we are and the work we do. Not surprisingly, it also provides a powerful key to managing organizations creatively.

Before we go on to the four worlds of the organization, let us summarize the four worlds of ecology, human perception and culture, as shown in figure 13.1. We now consider each of the four morphologies.

The Western World of Structure:
Security through Survival

The two catchwords for traditional Western business organizations have always been, 'size' and 'profit'. As we saw before, this is typical of the 'youthful' pioneering organizational form, seeking to carve out expanding territories, and maximizing gain. The pioneering era of Western businesses was made possible by a variety of factors: firstly, through a transition from craft-based activity to mass-production systems using technology as the medium; secondly, through a strong underpinning of science whose mechanistic principles paved the way for territorial growth; and thirdly, because of a generic, tendency in which the individual rather than the collective dominates the Western cultural psyche.

The Western organization is a highly *instinctive* organization, relying on the senses more than rational thought and is characterized by the 'hunting' management mode. Since the main emphasis of this pioneering mode is the search for *security*, this organizational world is designed for maximizing security through structures that can *react* to the environment. Since the identity of the structural organization is largely derived from the environment it is in – vis-à-vis its reactive character – this creates an essentially unstable organizational form. The

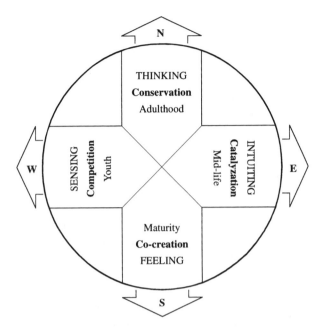

Figure 13.1 The Four Worlds of Ecology

structural organization therefore relinquishes integrity for keeping an ear to the ground. However, this quality does run into trouble as the organization grows, tending to ossify into rigid structures that eventually break. The examples of IBM and TI are appropriate here. Both companies kept following old maps, strayed away from the generically, Western instinctive mode and in the bargain ossified into brittle structures.

At a primal stage in an organization's life cycle, the structural world is a highly successful one. Comparable to the initial growth phase in organisms and eco systems, and the youthful stage of the human being, this Western world thrives on individuality, quick gains and short time-frames. The hallmark of the structural organization is autonomy. It functions by demarcating territories within and without. It is therefore a disconnected organization composed of and managed through distinct areas reducing it into autonomous, disconnected structures. The structural organization is best managed through analysis and fragmentation: the assumption that work is best managed by breaking it down into smaller routines and tasks. The following points characterize this world.

The Western World of Anglo-Saxons – 'doing well'

- Structure-building (competition) requires you to perceive your organization as a conglomerate of *parts*, like in a machine.
- The structural world is highly *differential*. Categories are created instinc-

tively inside the structure giving a preliminary sense of order to the organization.

- Clearly laid-out categories make trouble-shooting easy.
- Structures are built on *convergent* logic: for every problem, there is one solution; every cause has one effect.
- At their best, structural organizations can be highly efficient. Clearly defined department structures, neatly delegated functions, supervision and monitoring of all routine tasks make for youthful efficiency. As a result, structural organizations can '*do well*'.
- At their worst, these organizations can become heavily *top-down*. A lack of communication networks within the organization is usually the result.

Structures by themselves serve an important need in the first phase of the organization. However, to develop further, the Western organization must soon weave these structures into integrated systems. This is the Northern world of *adulthood* and *conservation*.

The Northern Systematic World: Meaning through Intention

Whereas the structural organization has been compared to the turbulent, pioneering stage, the Northern organizational form is one of order and stability. No longer instinct and reaction, the Northern organization is highly *intentional* and is based on the ecological principle of herding as against territorial hunting for resources.

Unlike the instinctive Western World, the Northern world is more *responsive*, relying on a conditioned, logical system of control through procedure. As a result, it is highly 'systematic', resembling an electronic network more than a machine. The Northern world is not about searching for security; its identity in place, the quest is for internal coherence and meaning. As a result, the Systematic world of Northern organizations is highly stable. If the Structural organization relies on autonomous structures to maintain control and order, the Systematic organization does precisely the opposite. Because it is inherently secure and does not depend for its identity on the external environment, control is maintained through information sharing networks. As in the Danish company Oticon, information-access is regarded as a fundamental prerequisite to management. The case of the SBN bank is another case-in-point: the very notion of Ethical begins with the assumption that ethics is born out of free discussion and free access to information by the stakeholders of the organization.

Organizations like Oticon and SBN in the Northern, systematic world are purpose-driven organizations, in which there is commitment in word and action to a higher ethical purpose. According to James O'Toole in his book *Vanguard Management*, '. . . these corporations exist to provide society with the goods and services it needs, to provide employment, and to create a surplus of wealth with which to improve the nation's general standard of living and quality of life. In this view, profit is the means, not the end of corporate activity.' Two organizations, Patagonia of northern California and Body Shop of the UK, are examples of such purposeful, ethical organizations with a distinct sense of overall purpose and vision. Patagonia gives profit money to about 250 organizations. It has a goal of recycling 70 per cent of all the waste produced by the company as well as in the homes of employees.

Taking a leaf out of the Northern world, Levi Strauss CEO, Walter Haas proposes that business 'make alliances with many sectors of the public and deal ethically and openly with employees, shareholders, customers, and not least, the general public. The social responsibility of business requires establishing standards of excellence in all phases of operation-such as truth in advertising, quality of products, accuracy of labelling, appropriate disclosure, job content, working conditions, and upward mobility for women and minorities.' It must be remembered that for the Northern organization, territory is no longer at stake; rather it is the conservation and recycling of resources for the collective good. The ethical bias of the systematic organization is apparent when Haas says: 'A corporation must stand, steadfastly, for something worthy of the efforts of its many constituencies. A prime function of top management is to articulate with consistency and clarity a central governing idea, one that appeals to a noble or high human aspiration or purpose. In effect, great corporations must be governed by great ideas.'

The Northern World of Scandinavians – 'doing right'

- System-forming (conservation) requires you to perceive your organization as a *network* of activities.
- Systems enhance the notion of *order* by restricting structural deviance. Systems conserve resources within the organization by linking up one territory with the other. This linkage is what constitutes a system.
- Without a System, structures remain disconnected and lacking in intrinsic meaning. The system links up one category to another and gives a sense of *direction* to structure.
- A clearly laid out system is *information-intensive*. As a result, resources are preserved and distributed evenly across the system.
- Setting up a common code to prevent deviance from the norm and to mainatin a high level of *homogeneity*.
- Systems use deductive logic in which the general is deduced from the particular. Problems are tackled through attempts at *consensus*.
- At their best, systematic organizations like Oticon are highly *ethical* work

places, which 'do right', with a collective benefit to all. At their worst, the
organizations turn *bureaucratic* and *impersonal.*

Because of their high dependence on information technology, resource-sharing
and procedure, systematic organizations soon become homogeneous. Like in the
ecospheric world of morphosis, this stage of development is marked by high
stability. Not surprisingly, the next world is one of instability and turbulence.
This is the Eastern world of *process.*

The Eastern World of Process:
Insight through Awareness

Whereas structures in the Western organization serve to differentiate the organization into categories, processes do precisely the opposite. They destroy the
categories and as a result, create a sense of flowing wholeness. A tree, for
instance, is a structural entity. It has a trunk, branches, leaves, roots, etc. that
can be perceived as differentiated 'parts' of the tree. However, the structure of
the tree is simultaneous with a processial 'unfoldment' in which processes such
as photosynthesis, nitrogen cycles, oxygen cycles, etc destroy notions of the tree
as an individual entity. It is not as if in the Eastern world, there are no parts.
There are, except that parts are perceived as sub-wholes, in unbroken flow with
the whole. The sales department in a company, from a processial perspective, is
a sub-whole in unfoldment, inextricably woven into the flow of the totality of the
company and the world outside.

In other words, a structure is a process made explicit, while a process is an
implicit structure. From this perspective then, the 'sales department' is a process – the relationship between the company and the customer – made explicit. It
is when the process unfolds out, that it is perceived as structure! In effect, the
relationship gives form to the structure of the department. If the relationship is
managed well, then that very process engenders a pliable, dynamic structure of
the sales department. If it is not, the structure becomes predominantly vertical
and fragmentary.

As a result of this processial bias, the Eastern world relies on an intuitive
mode of management. Like in the structural organization and unlike the systematic organization, the processial organization derives its identity from the environment it is in. However, while the identity of the structural organization is
based on reacting to the environment, the Eastern non-entity is based on harmony. Taken as a flowing whole, the processial organization is characterized by
an unfolding movement. It unfolds out, into the world and simultaneously,
with the world. The only way this can happen is through a relationship of
harmony between the organization and its environment. Harmony, in the Eastern sense is not a derivative; it is not something that can be put together, from

the outside. Rather, harmony precedes anything else. Harmony happens by itself, and creates order. The gardener manager of the East does not seek territorial structures or systematic organizations. His or her forte is to play a part in the harmony of the whole, the music of the spheres. As Shyam Ahuja displays clearly, the Eastern organization works by the minimum of explicit effort. What is at work is more implicit than explicit, the attempt to harmonize details into a cohesive whole.

The Eastern World of Japan – 'undoing'

• Processes for the Eastern organization provide the underlying principle to structures and systems by creating a sense of the whole organization. Processes can be defined as a *flowing wholeness*.
• Processes serve to integrate and through the use of *harmony*, weave together all the threads of an organization. In doing so, they destroy static concepts of structures and systems.
• Processes are therefore *destabilizing*; they creatively 'undo' the structures of the West and the systems of the North.
• A process is not what happens between structures. On the contrary, processes work around and through structures, making them *porous* and *permeable*.
• Without processes, the organization remains disconnected and abstract. Processes *undo* predetermined notions of order and procedure.
• At their best, processial organizations are dynamic, highly *innovative* work places. At their worst, the organization may turn *autocratic* and *whimsical*.

The Southern World of Value: Wisdom through Discrimination

In the four worlds of ecology, the Southern world is one of homeostasis, a dynamic balance between the various components of the system and between the system and the universe. Homeostasis has been defined by James Lovelock, the ecologist renowned for the Gaia theory of the Earth, as 'the wisdom . . . whereby a state of constancy is kept in spite of external or internal change.' However, unlike the Northern world, the world of homeostasis is not homogeneous, but teems with diversity as a necessary precondition to this state.

In the four organizational worlds, the Southern world is the one that provides a sense of purpose to the three worlds of Structure, System and Process. If the Northern world is based on rational ethics, the Southern world forms the moral basis for organizations, taking their functions and activities far beyond their four walls. As in the ecological world of homeostasis, the purpose of this world is to distribute resources over a wide area. In the discriminating wisdom of the Southern world, real profitability is not just about making profits for the company or the shareholders, but about creating a standard of sustainability. Unless the world in which we do business is sustainable, our organizations are bound to be themselves rendered unsustainable in the long run. The emphasis of course is on the long time-frames in the Southern world. To paraphrase an ancient African statement on sustainability, your organization belongs to the dead, living and the unborn. Within this expanded scale, the Southern manager – as we saw in the chapter on the ecosphere – is more of a steward than anything else, one who envisions and implements, keeping the past and the future in mind. From a global perspective, the organization is an indelible part of the nation, its culture, the economic and political system and the planet itself. From this viewpoint, the purpose of the organization is not simply decided by its managers, but is naturally preceded by its being an inextricable part of the world.

A genuinely extended world that goes beyond the walls of the organization can exist only when there is a deep sense of vision and a new culture of homeostasis. From these two elements, comes the one Southern element that is crucial to the value-based organization: genuine empowerment of the individual through a deep sense of shared destiny. Empowerment is your 'psychological contract' with the organization that encourages and nurtures the notion that work is an instrument for self-realization and personal growth. Promon International in Brazil is a professional services organization in the field of geophysics, engineering and electronics. It is totally owned by its 3000 employees. According to the chairman, Tamas Makray, this participation in the capital of the company is synchronous with a participation in the 'life of the organization – in a creative, living, dynamic community'.

With the workplace becoming the central interface between the individual and society, it becomes the focus of value for both. In the Southern world, the individual and society are interchangeable terms, one naturally leading into the other. Value being intrinsically integral, the delineation between the two is at best a convenient abstraction. In an article called 'Purpose and Spirit', Sabina Spencer writes: '. . . of making a difference, of creating meaningful work, of being fully alive, of living with integrity, of developing sacredness in their relationships, and of turning the organizational environment into a community where everyone can learn and grow . . . Meeting bottom line objectives and making sure the numbers are right is not enough. We are seeing greater attention focused on personal and organizational vision, quality of life, personal empowerment, a sense of organizational community, and an increasing desire to influence the future health and well-being of our home planet Earth.' 'A key management issue of the year 2000,' according to Marsha Sinetar writing in an article entitled 'The Actualized Worker', 'will be the workers need for self-actualization. By actualization, I mean a healthy personality, wholeness, a full-functioning being and psychological completion.'

Yvon Chouinard of Patagonia invented the '5–15 Report', which is so named because it requires no more than fifteen minutes to write and 5 minutes to read. It is submitted each Friday by most employees of the company, and has three sections in it. The first one is a simple description of what each person did during the week. The articulation involved in writing this serves as a good feedback system for the persons writing it: if the reports become repetitive, that may be a signal for a role change for the person. The second part of the report is an honest note on the person's morale, and an assessment of morale in his or her department. The third part requires each employee to present one idea that will improve the company, or the department or his or her job. That is 52 ideas a year from each person and a whole lot of empowerment along the way.

As we shall see in the case study on South Africa's Cashbuild, the essentially Southern organization becomes the place where the divine will of its employees fully manifests itself. As Koopman asks, 'How do we bring together the rights of people, their spiritually based humanity and the economic process as represented in the workplace?' In the feeling quadrant that represents the Southern world, fellow employees are regarded primarily in terms of morals and emotions than in terms of their roles or functions. 'Indaba', as we saw, is the removal of all dissent by engaging interactively with the morality of the issue.

The Southern World of South Africa – 'doing good'

- Value in an organization provides the *ground* and the purpose, the *raison d'être* for everything that is done.
- Value gives a sense of *purpose* to the structures, systems and processes.
- Value is the creation of *meaning* in the organization.
- Value builds and *preserves* the organizational culture through consensus.
- At their best, value-based organizations are *visionary* workplaces, characterized by a powerful contribution to society. At their worst, they can turn highly *impractical* and *static*.

The Limitations of Structure and System

Seeking territorial control is intrinsic to the pioneering stage of organizational development. The emphasis is on maintaining a youthful looseness and a vibrant flow of resources in the organization through a high level of individuality and autonomy. The Western organization is especially good at maintaing this looseness and individuality by demarcating itself, firstly as structure, separate from the environment and secondly, through internal substructures. Structure building requires the organization to be perceived in mechanical terms, as a conglomerate of parts. Structures serve to differentiate, slot things into boxes, and give an apparent sense of order to chaos. Moreover, clearly laid out structures make trouble-shooting easy. Cause-and-effect mechanisms play a quintessential role in company policies, market strategies and other management functions.

The pioneering stage of organizations is followed by the conservation stage of morphosis in which the individualistic structures of the Western organization are now integrated into systems. These systems enhance the notion of order by restricting structural deviance. Without a system, structures remain disconnected, too highly 'individualistic' and therefore do not contribute to the total well-being of the organizational whole. Systems link up one category with another, giving a sense of direction to structure. System forming requires the organization to be perceived in networking terms: more like an electronic circuit board than a mechanical model. Although cause-and-effect remains the predominant logical form, the systematic organization is more complex than the structural one and is composed of vertical as well as lateral networks.

What is of crucial importance at this stage is the understanding that structures and systems by themselves can no longer be relied upon to provide a business edge. The world in which we do business today is not the same world in which the structural and the systematic forms worked, agreeably with much success. There have occurred major transformations in the social, technological, economic and the cultural spheres, particularly in the last three decades, that have indelibly altered the whole context in which business is done and managed. However we in the Western and Northern worlds are still locked up in the same mind-set that worked at a time when the world was simple enough to be run on the basis of effective structures and systems. This scenario is now obsolete. The model that best describes traditional Western organizations are those of vast plumbing systems or a line of organ pipes or simply, large mechanical systems. When people were employed, they were 'fitted vertically' into this mechanical model, by formatting a structure of routine tasks and functions. Likewise, the work that these people did was vertically stacked by structuring it in a way that broke it down into smaller and simpler units. As a result, from this structural perspective, processes were perceived as what took place between the structural pillars holding up the organizational edifice, comparable to air or water flowing within the fixed structure of pipes. A process typically began with a structural constraint and ended with one. A simple process of providing service to a customer, when it is fragmented by vertical structures, becomes a cumbersome and time consuming process. Likewise with all decision making 'processes' in structural organizations. Broken down by vertical channels, these processes, which in their true nature must move fluidly around and through structures, become structured themselves within fixed management policies. Decisions taken seldom reflect the need of the customer or the external environment, but the very structural constraints of the organisation. Vertical structures are like blinkers. When you have them 'on' for a long length of time, you forget about their existence and believe that this is how the organization really is.

From a traditional perspective then, process is what takes place in between structures. It is that 'which happens' after structures are erected. The logic is that it is the purchase department that makes purchasing happen, not the other way around. Likewise, all traditional trouble-shooting is geared towards the structure, assuming that a change in structure will automatically make a change in process happen. In reality however, processes are the spirit of the organization. They are the invisible meridians through which flows, the very energy of the organization. Structures are essential, but when they start impeding the flow of process, something is going wrong. In a mechanical organization, processes are always given second place, the belief being that unless they are controlled by structure, they create disorder. Hence the supervisor, the controls, the checks, the hierarchy, the expert, the specialist, the structured decisions, the structured communication systems, the structured customer contact and all the rest.

Whereas the structural approach to managing organizations is to manage them from 'outside in', the processial approach is to manage them 'inside out'. Structures that arise in complement to process are unlike the static, vertical structures that we have traditionally erected in our organisations. While process carries the momentum of energy through and out of the organization, structure permits the focusing and acting out of the energy. Interestingly, this balance between structure and process abounds all around us. The contrast between structure and process breaks down in the atom as well as in the living organism whose structure is at the same time the expression and the bearer of a continuous flow of matter and energy. As interacting processes define temporary structures, so structures define new processes, which in turn give rise to new temporary structures.

A structural organization, like the territorial world of the ecosystems has no significance in itself. It has to be complemented by the other three worlds of conservation, catalysation and renewal. Pioneering expansion of territory in itself, in the emergent business context, has no meaning. For one thing, this kind of growth implies the existence of a steady, stable environment in which change is predictable and forecastable. Secondly, it implies a state of never-ending resources in terms of raw material, labor and markets that comply with the old rules of predictability and control. But as resources start wearing thin, as a new intelligent work force takes charge, and as new competetitors who are able to provide cheaper, higher quality products arrive on the scene, the limitations of the exclusively Western or Northern worlds become starkly clear. In this state of turbulence, where the structural and systematic poles reach the threshold of their applicability, the imperative thing to do is to re-enter the worlds of intuition and feeling and so to speak, turn Eastwards and Southwards.

Conclusion: Journeying to the East and the South

At one time, the craft-based industries were characterized by the involvement of the whole person in the four worlds of *sensing, thinking, intuiting* and *feeling*. Over time, craft-based activities were replaced by mass-production which brought in the age of the so-called objective manager who assumed that he or she could effectively run a business by detaching himself or herself emotionally and spiritually from his or her work. Any involvement with the non-quantitative sides of business were seen as impediments to growth and thus had to be curtailed. Because craft-based activity involved the whole person, the knowledge that was necessary for the craft manager was more responsive and interactive. Like in Charles Chaplin's classic parody of the mass-production age, *Modern Times*, production-line work in the twentieth century embraced rational and empirical knowledge exclusively and was stripped of the more intuitive and feeling forms of knowledge. Whereas intuition is our ability to look deeper into the underlying, invisible and sometimes chaotic processes that weave the organization together, the feeling dimension is characterized by our ability to seek out and broaden a sense of shared value between people.

For organizations, the disappearance of intuition and feeling – at least on an official level – meant a loss of access to the Eastern and Southern worlds of management. The West–North bias thus created the quantitative organisational form, best characterized by a scientific approach to management. This scientific form was helped by the fact that in the heady days of big business, whatever was manufactured was sold. The consumer was a stable, manipulable entity who would buy what was served. The market was easily forecastable and growing bigger was the order of the day. Competetion was predictable and there was plenty of room for most players. In such a paradigm of seemingly unending growth, managing organizations became increasingly restricted to the first two worlds. Whereas the former emphasized the actual physical territory that structured the organization, the latter devised systems that put the fragmented blocks of territory together in a framework. American, British and European organizations reached into the collective consciousness of Europe, dominated by the likes of Adam Smith, René Descartes, Samuel Smiles and Keynes, creating highly structured and systematic companies. The Western stronghold was the inherent capacity to create youthful, energetic organizations that were based on instinct for marking territorial structures. Northern strength lay in providing internal form to organizations with systems that interconnected the organization.

As we move towards the close of this century, we stand once again at the gateways to the South and the East. This time, however, the choice will have to be a conscious one.

Bibliography

O'Toole, J. (1985) *Vanguard Management*. New York: Doubleday & Co.

Lovelock, J. (1979) *Gaia: A New Look at Life on Earth*. New York: Oxford University Press.

Harman, W. (1990) *Creative Work: The constructive role of business in transforming society*. Indianapolis: Knowledge Systems Inc.

Spencer, S. (1989) 'Purpose and Spirit', *Organizational Development Practitioner*, June. pp. 18–20

Sinetar, M. (1987) 'The Actualized Worker', *Futurist*, March/April. pp. 21–25

BUSINESS

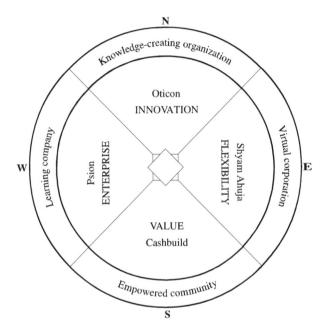

It's all about learning. Organizations fail when they begin to stop questioning
David Potter, Psion

My ideas are created out of dialogue, not through a process of formal analysis
Lars Kolind, Oticon

Business is all about people. We rely on people with their hearts in the right place
Shyam Ahuja, S. Ahuja

Key questions went through my mind. Why do workers actually work? What is their social or divine will?
Albert Koopman, Cashbuild

Business

This section brings you four business vignettes from the four worlds: Psion from the West, Oticon from the North, Shyam Ahuja from the East and Cashbuild from the South. These are also stories of four individuals who have created business successes by anchoring their companies in the generic strengths of their worlds and simultaneously incorporating the other three worlds. As you will see, each case study reflects one of the four cultural philosophies and one of the four knowledge worlds. Interestingly, the four individuals, Englishman David Potter, Dane Lars Kolind, Indian Shyam Ahuja and South African Albert Koopman, are similar in that each of them embodies the two forces of *harmony* and *creativity*. As you may recall, we have earlier called them *centripetal* and *centrifugal*, forces that oppose yet complement each other.

While reading through this section, try to make the following connections:

- Identify what is *structural* about Psion, *systematic* about Oticon, *processial* about Ahuja and *value-based* about Cashbuild
- Where do these four worlds overlap? Do these companies exist in more than one world?
- How is knowledge created in each of these companies?
- What kind of business leaders are Potter, Kolind, Ahuja and Koopman? Can you identify the personality type?

14

Psion Computers

Introduction

Psion, a company with some 500 employees based in north London, is Europe's leading producer of hand-held computers, after having existed for less than 15 years. As we shall be uncovering, in each of our case studies of successful business enterprises across the globe, it has strong roots in its own culture, while also reaching across, albeit less markedly, to parts of the businessphere. Our first, Western case in point then, is both typical and atypical. It is typical in that its founder, David Potter, is a southern African, who emigrated from colonial Rhodesia to Britain as a young man. In that respect he represents one of innumerable would-be entrepreneurs who have left their original abode to set up business in the UK, or indeed in America. Potter is also typical of the West in so far as he has that streak of individualism, and of self-reliance that is so characteristic of the Anglo–Saxon world. Finally and as we shall see, Psion as a company is markedly disconnected from the sociopolitical fabric of English society, something that distinguishes it, most particularly, from a 'Southern' Cashbuild.

At the same time, Psion is atypical in several distinctive respects, again largely attributable to its founder. Firstly, as an African, Potter has a strongly romantic streak that cuts across the pragmatic Anglo–Saxon grain. Secondly, perhaps influenced by his Jewish connections, he is a strange amalgam of intellectual and entrepreneur, scientist and engineer that cuts across many a divide in British society. Thirdly, and born out of his romantic nature, he has a depth of intuition which distinguishes him from most of his British colleagues. Finally, and perhaps most importantly for Psion, Potter transcends the personality ridden brand of individualism that inhibits so many Western enterprises from progressing into larger scale organizations.

Business Start-up – The Early Years

Psion was founded by David Potter with £50,000 start-up capital. It was started in a small room with no clear business plan. Potter knew the technology and was in touch with the way the market was moving. People were still playing with the newly emerging electronic devices. Apple II and the Commodore PET had both just come out and the technology was still terribly primitive. Potter didn't have the capital to become involved with hardware, but he had the knowledge and experience to know what he was doing in software terms. By 1981 David had also got to know both Sinclair and Acorn, the major British players in the personal computing fields.

While he was negotiating a sales agreement with Sinclair, in 1980, he was also developing a business on the software side. He probed his personal contacts and combed the magazines for computer games software, sorting out the good from the bad. He finally found a chess game that had been produced by an engineer from British Airways. Soon, Potter was convincing him that he could sell many more of his product by a more professional marketing approach, if he was willing to operate on a licensing basis. David packaged the product in an upmarket way and found a manufacturer to multiply the volume. He did it all cost-effectively, sending samples to to distributors all over Europe. With this particular product, and with subsequent others, Potter began to ship significant quantities. With the income generated he brought in Charles Davies, a former PhD student of his, who was ultimately to become Psion's head of research and development.

So there were now two of them sitting in an office in London's Edgware Road. They began to develop their own games software, working first with the Acorn machine and started selling products on an even larger scale than they had done before. By this stage Psion had become far more sophisticated than its competetitors in the leisure software field. Soon, Psion recruited people with flair and originality who were willing to accept a pretty unconventional job.

Standing Out from the Crowd

By 1982 Psion had been approached by both Sinclair and Acorn to produce software under licence. At this stage the big retailers were just beginning to get interested. The company was moving out of the embryonic stage. With its high level software team and good facilities, Psion was beginning to stand out from the games software crowd. Potter decided to do a deal with Sinclair, because of the wider potential market. The company's turnover in 1981 had been £120,000, with a net profit of £12,000. A year later it had gone up to £1.5 million, with a net profit of £625,000. Psion's return on sales was 40 per cent, and on capital it was astronomic.

Getting Organized

By 1983, David Potter had already begun to question the longevity and durability of the games software market. He really couldn't see the useful applications coming from their current products. Psion by now had a team of outstanding quality. So Psion decided to diversify into two areas. On the one hand, it wanted to develop integrated application software for business use. This was already on the cards in 1982, before *Lotus 1, 2, 3* and *Symphony* had even appeared on the scene. On the other hand, Psion wanted to develop a handheld database machine. At this stage it was a development company, adding value through software and had no marketing people to speak of. Its products sold through original equipment manufacturers and David Potter ran the whole of the business side, together with an assistant. It was in the early part of 1983 that a sales director was brought in as Psion's first business executive, with a second one to look after suppliers.

Towards the end of 1982, IBM and Victor (Sirus) came out with their first 16-bit machines. Potter was impressed with their superb graphics and the large memory capacity. Moreover, they were purpose-built for the office environment. The trouble was, though, that people were using the machine for arcane purposes, like storing suppliers' lists. 'I can vividly remember Charles Davies and I,' Potter reminisced, 'having lunch together and saying to one another, "if we could produce such a machine for simple databases more cheaply and simply there would have to be a huge market". And that was exactly what happened.'

With the subsequent development of Psion's handheld database machine, which had since evolved into a small computer, the company had to create a sales force. It needed to gear up for the production, marketing and launch not only of its applications software but also of its handheld 'Organizer'. 1984 was a seminal year for Psion. Its future was laid in two particular ways. Firstly it succeeded in starting up a crucial second side to its business, that is the marketing – image and communications – facet. In fact Potter sketched out the bare bones of his company's image. For the first time some of the values of Psion were articulated. Secondly, the company brought both of its new developments, the application software and the handheld computer, into volume production.

It's an interesting facet of Psion that, as a smaller company, it has been able to work extremely well with large ones. 'I suppose we have that element of seriousness, of quality, and of organization,' Potter maintains, 'that attracts them to us.' As a result of the technical and market experience Psion had gained, coupled with the onward march of the silicon industry, the company's handheld machine underwent a major development from September 1985 to the end of April 1986. It evolved radically in terms of capability and adaptability. Above all, through the development of Psion's software systems, the company was able, in the spring of 1986, to launch *Organizer II*. Like Apple II, it was an enormously successful product. In 1988 Psion became the largest supplier in the world of handheld machines, shipping some 200,000 units per annum and creating a whole new market area. In May of 1986 it had been producing 200 units per month; by the summer of 1988, 20,000.

Learning and Development

Like its product, Psion's organization developed in stages. The way the company was originally structured, as five people, was totally different from the way it became organized as 125. For Potter, 'its all about learning. If there's growth there is flux. Organizations fail when they begin to stop questioning.' Through 1982 and 1983 Psion was led from the top. It was leadership by example. In 1983 and 1984 a first attempt was made to introduce some form of management structure. Until that time the structure was informal and implicit. Now Psion brought in executives with titles. Formal structures were introduced in the face of increasing complexity. David Potter no longer made all the business decisions. Psion introduced groups and departments into the organization. In 1985 and 1986, as the company grew even bigger, it began to develop a wide range of formal controls, both computer-based and manual. In a way, it began to articulate its nervous system. Psion introduced sophisticated budgeting systems, though it built in ample scope for discussion around them. It didn't believe in hierarchy for hierarchy's sake. 'Everyone here calls me David. But we do believe firmly in planning and control, and in clear communication.'

The first thing Psion did, then, with *Organizer II*, was to produce a booklet on its features and benefits. Potter himself produced it three months prior to launch, covering the what, where and why of the product. When the product was launched Psion focused on a restricted set of people. It concentrated on the computer cogniscenti, that is the opinion leaders in the data processing world. The company produced large, and very detailed brochures. Psion pumped out hundreds and thousands of them, directed at the computer literati. It knew that they were its prospective ambassadors. They, in turn, would communicate with a wider group. It was only a year thereafter that Psion began to advertise in the lay press. The company repeated the same process in France, creating progressively wider ripples. At the same time Psion introduced financial and administrative systems to ensure that there was proper control.

Entering into Turbulence

At the same time as Psion was reconstituting its organization, it was extending its product line. The company embarked, in 1986, on a massive programme of research and development, working on what it called its SIBO technology, that is a range of products from lapheld computers to voice recognition. In 1989 Psion had had a turnover of £19 million, and by the following year it had climbed dramatically to £31 million. Then in 1991 company performance dipped markedly. In 1992 Britain was in the midst of recession. The communications subsidiary that Psion had acquired was in financial trouble. Something had been going pretty wrong.

In 1991 Psion had experienced a major trauma when introducing a new technology. The quality problems that arose were enormous. When Psion went into production itself, the company actually had no choice. Psion had developed and promoted its most recent innovation, the Series III, and there was high demand for it. This was in 1992, with recession all around. The company, in its turn, had developed a 'gap product' in portables, that straddled Organizer II and Series III. This gap product had not sold well. The communications subsidiary that it had acquired at the time, DACOM, was in financial trouble. The banks wouldn't lend the company the money Psion required for working capital. Psion, in fact, had a huge chunk of such capital tied up in inventories. For the company had until then bought in the components, and handed them onto subcontractors. So it had to bear the inventory costs. The only way to liberate working capital, therefore, was to reduce inventories, by bringing production in-house. In that way Psion could co-ordinate procurement and production itself and thereby closely control stock levels. It was able, thereafter, to finance 70 per cent of increased turnover itself. The company couldn't have done all of this, of course, without the close involvement of senior executives and staff. They talked to their suppliers extensively. They wrote up the technical specifications. They consulted with their partner Motorola in the US: 'We live in a world of continuing turmoil and flux,' Potter stresses. 'Controlled chaos. You have to undergo flux to survive.' Psion had been changing from 8-bit to 16-bit to now 32-bit computing over a period of some ten years. Everything has had to be re-engineered. 'It's been like – if we use and aircraft analogy – moving from piston to jet engines.'

Yet, ironically enough, out of these ashes arose Series III, the epicentre of Psion's success today. Series III was envisaged as a successor to the Organizer. The Organizer had mainly been developed for the industrial market. The company had originally planned for the Series III to precede the notebook computer, but it turned out the other way around. In fact Psion never lost faith in its technical ability, for it had achieved the project from a technical standpoint. It still perceived itself as an elite band in the world. It was now, moreover, battle hardened. People had been coming in week after week, working all night. 'We became, interestingly enough, a high performance team. And the company survived commercially. We had more to do. A lot of what had been accomplished, technically, provided the basis for Series III.'

By 1994 sales had risen to £64 million. 'The nineties,' Potter maintains, 'has been a period of considerable transition. Two themes predominate. One is technology driven. Since 1988 we have been developing a new set of software and hardware architectures for portable computing in the nineties. As a consequence we were in a position to produce a swathe of new products. The second theme is organizational. We have grown substantively in the last five years, employing now 500 people, as compared with 200 in 1989. As a result the company has become more sophisticated and complex. In essence we have moved away from a prior emphasis on developing products and markets to our current emphasis on enabling people and processes to develop. The shift in orientation, in fact, is quite profound.'

Total Quality Management

As a company gets bigger, it has to rely on more and more people. So in 1991 Psion introduced a major quality inititiative. 'Within a large organization,' Potter says, 'you need different people to perform different, though overlapping, functions. Unless one group is aligned with the other you get chaos. You have to write things down. You need to be systematic. The kind of products we're shipping out, today, are a thousand-fold more sophisticated than the ones we delivered yesterday. They also cost far more to develop than the original Organizer.' In the process of implementing total quality management Psion learnt both from its suppliers – particularly the Japanese – and from its customers, as well as from its own reflections. The first people to get on the learning curve were indeed the executive directors.

In that way the quality programme sprang into life, that is after Psion had gone into manufacturing. The company then had to ensure that it had a quality system at least in development, engineering and production. So it hired Colin Heaven, who had been a quality consultant to the firm before he joined Psion full time. Heaven made a tremendous difference. What he instigated involved not only a change in specific processes but in the whole way that development was managed. Charles Davies, in development, soon came to strongly espouse the quality message himself. All processes and procedures were systematically documented. Development became so stuctured that a group of 100 people could be motivated and managed, altogether. When Colin Heaven first got involved with Psion in 1991, in fact, there had been reliability problems with Series III. Psion, as we saw, had hit the Laptop market at the wrong time, and the software wasn't quite up to scratch. As a result of that experience Charles Davies and Colie Myers had felt there must be a better way to approach development. 'When I joined the company full time,' Heaven recollects, 'it was tremendously free-spirited. There was little formality, no written procedures, and a lack of awareness of techniques in reliability testing, or project management. There were just clever people, who were terribly enthusiastic. There were also problems in the recently established factory which was engaged in state-of-the-art production, rare in this country. So they had to start more or less from scratch.'

These were the early days of Series III. Most of the assembly work had previously been subcontracted. The subcontractors didn't have a vested interest in getting things right, particularly as they were freely issued with components. 'When I first joined, Psion needed to improve its general organization. Customers were being charged the wrong prices, we were failing to credit people for returns, there were technical deficiencies, and so on. We had a major problem with a component that we had adopted on our Series III, because of its low price. In the end we had to go to a Japanese supplier who charged three times as much, but at least the component was reliable. I started off then with engineering, by slowing them down a bit, encouraging them to take their time. We began to conduct design reviews, to look for potential problems. We installed a lot more testing and evaluation.' David Potter, according to Heaven, was relatively relaxed about doing the job properly, despite the commercial pressures. Psion designed new equipment for accelerated as well as for temperature and static testing. The company put in a radio frequency chamber. Heaven started up a formal approval system. The production people pre-built production samples, made one, tested it, and then made a couple of hundred, tested them, before Psion went on to manufacturing a few thousand. 'Every other organization I have worked with supposedly espoused quality, but when the chips were down they were not prepared to carry the thing through. Here they're not kidding. There's no management by fear here. No shouting. Little politics. However, it was not a planning culture, at least in any detail.' So Heaven started people thinking, got them to debate quality. He provoked ideas by sending them out articles to read. He began to set up cross-functional teams to break down barriers between electronics and engineering, manufacturing and marketing. The company did not know what a project was, as opposed to getting on and doing something. Psion's greatest difficulties had been experienced not within departments but at the interfaces between them. So Heaven set up cross-functional teams with a project leader, recruited from the technical side.

At the outset alot of work was done to tighten up on component sourcing, and to validate new suppliers. The company had to develop a consistent stand rather than rely on a wing and a prayer. Colin Heaven also started to run courses in project management, and brought in John Adair, one of Britain's best known – albeit traditional – management thinkers, renowned for his work on action-centred leadership. To do all of this really well, particularly on the manufacturing side, required highly skilled direction and management. Adair seemed right for Psion because he was very pragmatic. He provided a simple framework, almost a procedure. People could buy into it, and Adair himself had the gravitas to carry weight with David Potter. At the same time Charles Davies had recently been turning from a software guru into a management one.

'Historically we had subcontracted manufacturing. We did our own packaging. So we had thought to ourselves, when we decided to take the manufacturing on ourselves, what's the difference between a cardboard box and a plastic one? I can remember when we set out the tales in the factory and hired in new people. We didn't have anyone with a manufacturing background. We just hire bright people at Psion. The ethic was "just do it". It's my job here to change that ethic. By golly you learn from experience. We're in the process of seriously empowering our middle management. We're getting disciplined and scaleable. We allow people to have their heads. They make their own mark. I've always read a lot technically. Now I'm shifting my focus to management.'

According to Heaven, moreover, 'Psions's management as a whole, hitherto, had tended to be a bit autocratic in many areas. There were a lot of male egos about the place (no women) in the company. People needed to learn, therefore, about team building and delegation. The company as a whole needed to grow its people; we needed a lot more passing down of authority. Charles Davies, on the other hand, is a superbly balanced manager, in terms of combining task and people skills. We have doubled our development staff over the last year. They work funny hours. There's a large amount of trust. There are no rules on timekeeping. They're determined to keep it that way.'

Managing Across Cultures

Today Psion runs its engineering and maufacturing, from the UK, while a series of trading companies have been set up in the US, as well as in France, Germany and Holland. Moreover, Psion has some 40 partner-distributors around the world. Sixty per cent of its customers are based outside Britain, that is predominantly in continental European and in North America. In the UK its biggest customer today is British Telecom's service engineers, Barclays and Natwest Banks and Prudential Insurance. Then there other major corporate clients, namely BMW in Germany and Motorola in the United States. The company's supply chain extends across the globe but more particularly is plugged into America and Japan. Individuals at Psion know the companies and the people there. The company's next step is to develop significantly in Asia. Psion buys alot from Japan, Korea and Taiwan but is has not yet developed a market for its products in these countries. It recognizes that it needs to become increasingly sensitized to different cultures.

'One has to say that the Americans,' says Potter, 'embrace change as something intrinsic to their persona. Their very *raison d'être* appears to be that of bringing about change, especially within their newer businesses, such as in computers, telecommunications, biotechnology and also in retailing. Europe, by comparison, is very diverse. The data shows that the UK is most innovative in new product and market areas. Then follow the Italians and the French with the more Teutonic – German, Dutch and Scandinavian – following behind. The latter are of course careful planning cultures, as are the Japanese. But unlike the

Germans, the Japanese are dynamic. They know about re-learning; they've set their culture in a global context. They're innovative in an organizational sense.' For Potter in fact, as far as development is concerned, Psion is quite American. 'I believe I bring to our organization a sympathy with a world of flux.' Psion's development people come to work in jeans and tee-shirts, and they read Dr Dobbs' Calisthenetics, published in California. They feel that they're rather special in the UK, operating at the frontiers. At the same time, 'we are otherwise,' Potter argues, 'very European. We're not confrontational and contractual, like the Americans; rather we sit around a table and come to an agreement, with customers or suppliers. It's a co-operative way of doing business, a way of balancing freedom with order.'

Psion and the Four Worlds

The secret of Psion's success, as an innovative company operating around the world, while based in the UK, is its:

- Strongly internalized (Western) commitment to commercial as well as to technical growth and development. 'Psion never lost faith in its technical ability; for, having achieved the project from a technical standpoint, it still perceived itself as an elite, now battle-hardened, band.'
- Due moderation by its intellectual capacity to combine knowledge (Northern) into unique products. 'Good engineering results in quality and value, which has been creatively developed and meticulously implemented.'
- Underpinning through an ability to visualize (Eastern), and thereby externalize, the development of products and markets. 'It had become clear to me by the late seventies that something as profoundly important as the invention of the lathe was going on. In the 1800s the lathe had generated steam engines, motor cars, and petrol engine aeroplanes for a generation to follow. Now the silicon chip was about to move us radically on.'

This distinctive interrelation of sensing, thinking and intuiting has much to do with David Potter's own cross-cultural background, albeit ultimately grounded in Anglo-Saxon soils.

At the same time, limits to the company's growth and innovativeness have been set in two major ways:

1 The relative lack of (Southern) socialization, when compared with a company like Bennetton or Body Shop, has meant that the expression of Psion's collective imagination has been restricted, both internally and externally. While, internally, emotional inhibitions – 'if I'd have gone public on my negative feelings I'd have jeapordized my career' – are likely to have re-

stricted creativity, externally, the corporate image has been low key – 'we
used to apologize to people, because of the appearance of the thing, saying if
only you could see the engine underneath!'

2   The restricted scope of (Eastern) externalization, when compared with a
    company like Canon, or Sony – until recently – has meant that, while Potter
    himself is deeply intuitive, his search for beauty and truth has not pervaded
    throughout Psion as a whole. As a result there is a lack of harmony between
    the developmental dynamics underlying product (thing and information
    related) and organization (person and community related) development,
    which may have been one major factor responsible for some of the traumatic
    events that have characterized Psion's growth and development.

Conclusion

Reflecting on what Potter had been saying, we recognize some profound truths
there. At the same time it had to be recognized that Psion itself had been
struggling to achieve the right balance between creativity and planning, ever
since it had started. Moreover there were other balances to be struck, most
particularly those between masculinity and feminity, individuality and
teamwork.

In fact, we might ask Potter what sort of business and cultural lessons could
be learnt. Was Psion more 'Western', that is American in style and culture, or in
fact more 'Northern', or European? Was David Potter's 'southern' influence at
all evident, or had it been eclipsed over the course of time? In terms of the
knowledge-creating organization to which Ikijiro Nonaka had referred, had
Southern 'socialization' and Eastern 'externalization' fallen somewhat behind
Western 'internalization' and Northern 'combination'? In other words, had the
pragmatic and rational sides of Psion overtaken its humanistic and holistic
orientations? More importantly, and in the final analysis, would the company
become more successfully innovative if it became more wholly global?

*This case study was substantively drawn up under the auspices of the Berger Founda-
tion, based in Munich, as part of a research project into European-ness and Innovation, conducted over the period 1994/7.*

15

Oticon Hearing Care

Introduction

Unlike the Western organization which is more pragmatic than rational, as we saw in the case of Psion, the Northern organization is a highly systematized one. Likewise, unlike the more individualistic Western manager, the Northern manager is typically a team-person. Moreover, the Northerner perceives the organization more as a networked system to be managed as a whole. As a result, the chief characteristic of a Northern company is information-sharing. Without an extensive network of communication, the system is apt to run down. This is one reason why most Northern companies are quick to go in for advanced information technologies that are able to tie up the system through its networks. In this chapter, we shall be looking at a Danish company, Oticon which has established itself as a world leader in hearing care, through a complete restructuring of its hard and soft sides. The former has been accomplished through the use of information technology and lateral networks of people and concepts, while the soft side is grounded in rational ethics.

Innovation through Dialogue

Oticon is a characteristic Northern company with its emphasis on systematization of procedures and principles. However, there is a very strong Southern element prevalent in the company through a clear orientation towards what Lars Kolind, the CEO, calls the human dimension. And although Lars himself operates through a strong Eastern, intuitive side to himself, the organization as a whole is orientated on the North–South axis.

At Oticon, although everything else is computerized, including the vistors' register, and where paperless desks are the norm, fostering direct communication between people is uppermost on the management agenda. 'This place was created for dialogue,' says Lars and it is absolutely true. When the company moved into its present headquaters in 1991, an entirely different kind of architecture was brought into significance. Walls were pulled down and the new office began to resemble a huge open space whose monotony was broken only by plants and indoor trees. There are no literally no walls at the Oticon office. Each floor is centred by a central coffee bar, where the spokes of the open space converge and meet. Kolind believes that learning takes place only among equals and given the opportunity, people learn instinctively. Inspired by an old Danish adage from the father of Danish education, Grundtvig, 'Not for School, but for Life', Kolind translated this inscription from his elementary school in Aarhus into a cutting-edge strategy at Oticon.

According to Kolind, an atmosphere of openness and dialogue lies at the heart of innovation and creativity. This is precisely the Southern element of the 'social field' that Nonaka uses as the starting point in his knowledge-creation model. Without the socialization process, tacit knowledge does not get converted to explicit knowledge.

Unlike in traditional offices, the atmosphere at Oticon is refreshingly relaxed, and communication involves strolling across and talking to one's colleagues. Or perhaps, converging at the coffee bar. Dialogue-time is strongly perceived as part of so-called 'productive time'. The traditional fragmentation between work and leisure is gone; the dialogue heals the divide between the two.

With openness goes unequivocal trust. Helle Thorup-Uuitt an employee, recalled Lars Kolind once saying that as adults, people know how to drive cars, raise children, deal with their banks, surely they also know when to come to work and when to leave. There are no set working hours and as befits a truly knowledge-creating company, employees often work flexible hours depending on the nature of work. There is no fear of authority. Inger Kristofferson who has seen the trasition of Oticon from the old to the new, spoke of the supportive culture that prevailed at Oticon, adding that employees are 'proud to work at Oticon'. The status of women has undergone a profound change since the transition from the old to the new. In the new atmosphere of openness, Inger thinks there is more mutual respect because people get to see what each other is doing. Whenever there is an urgent problem, whoever is at hand is quick to solve it. Co-operation and helpfulness are the foundations of working life at Oticon.

Cogitate Incognita: Think the Unthinkable

Dismantling the bureaucratic structure also meant abandoning all titles and departments. With the belief that all individuals are capable of 'multiple intelligences', Kolind introduced the principle of a *multi-task job profile*. All Oticon employees are expected to expand their work area beyond their formal job description. This principle is successfully borne out by Lars Aegerlin, an electro-mechanical engineer who specializes in micro-electronics. Today he spends part of his working time in marketing and the other part in his previous engineering function, moving between the two effortlessly. Kolind takes this notion of multiple intelligences back to his scouting days. He speaks of a co-ordinator of scout activities he knew, who also happened to be the village blacksmith. She was also the chairperson of the board of directors of the local folk high school, raised four children by herself and played the organ in the church on Sundays. Today, Oticon is a collection of multidisciplinary individuals who form cross-project teams, cutting across the traditional departments of finance, product development, marketing, sales and manufacturing. An employee may be a member of several different projects simultaneously, and in addition may be a project manager on one of them. Neither membership nor management of project teams is permanent. When the task is over, the project team is spontaneously dissolved, paving the way for a new team. Membership and management have to be earned through professional competence and social negotiation.

Preempting the work ethic at Oticon, *Harvard Business Review*'s Rosabeth Moss Kanter writes: 'As work units become more participative and team oriented, and as professionals and knowledge workers become more prominent, the distinction between manager and non-manager begins to erode . . . [managers] must learn to operate without the crutch of hierarchy. Position, title, and authority are no longer adequate tools, not in a world where subordinates are encouraged to think for themselves and where managers have to work synergestically with other departments and even other companies. Success depends increasingly on tapping into sources of good ideas, on figuring out whose collaboration is needed to act on those new ideas, on working with both to produce results. In short, the new managerial work implies very different ways of obtaining and using power.'

Such a change, says Kanter, will force managers to find new methods for motivating their people. She has identified five such sources of motivation:

1 *Mission*: Inspiring people to believe in the importance of their work
2 *Agenda control*: Giving people the opportunity to be in control of their own careers
3 *Share of value creation*: Rewarding employees for their contribution to the success of the company . . .
4 *Learning*: Providing people with a chance to learn new skills
5 *Reputation*: A chance to make a name for oneself in terms of public or professional reputation

Kanter concludes by saying: 'commitment to the organization still matters, but today's managers build commitment by offering project opportunities. The new loyalty is not to the boss or to the company, but to projects that actualize a mission and offer challenge, growth and credit for results.'

Unlike traditional teams that are at best a collection of indivuiduals working together, the team at Oticon is defined by a combination of high professional competence and a spirit of togetherness.

Allan Cox, writing in *Industry Week* in January 1991, said: 'An effective work team is a thinking organism where problems are named, assumptions are challenged, alternatives generated, missions validated, goals tested, hopes ventured, fears anticipated, successes expected, vulnerabilities expressed, contributions praised, absurdities tolerated, withdrawals noticed, victories celebrated, and defeats overcome.'

This extent of organizational flexibility is facilitated by Oticon's mobile office. As part of the imperative mobility, no manager or employee has a private desk. Everyone is equipped with 'drawers on wheels', which makes it easy to move around depending on where a specific project takes the individual. Lars Kolind himself has a similar table-on-wheels and changes his place regularly like everyone else. The other interesting aspect of the open-space organization is that there is no segregation of people on the basis of their work. For instance, customer service people share a work area with the engineers. As Inger Kristofferson indicated, this means that apart from the natural 'socialization field' that is set up, people begin to appreciate each others' problems and participate in multiple-solution modes. Apart from these mobile desks, the two other pieces of equipment that all employees have is a personal computer and a mobile telephone. There is a conspicuous absence of papers in Oticon's electronic office. All incoming mail is scanned into the computer networks making it open to all. All papers are shredded in large glass containers.

Last year, Oticon recorded a profit of £8 million. The success of the new Oticon can only be judged by comparing these figures to those of 1987, when it experienced its worst financial deficit, £4 million. Faced with closure, Lars Kolind was brought in to do a turnabout for Oticon. The story of Oticon's transformation in the last six years is in a way, the story of Lars Kolind.

The Spirit of Voluntary Work

One-time associate professor of planning theory at the University of Copenhagen, Lars Kolind was hired by the foundation that owns Oticon to take over as vice president. Before that he had also been an Operations Director at Risø, the foremost research laboratory in Denmark, started by the Nobel Laureate physicist, Neils Bohr in 1953. Much of his innovative leadership style is actually anchored in the boyscout tradition. Starting at age 9, Kolind became leader of his scout troupe at 17, then became national leader and then went on to international scouting. In the midst of a busy schedule even now he is working to set up a World Scout Network for nature and the environment on the Internet which would mobilize a million scouts wordwide. Being a boyscout for almost 40 years has been the major influence in Kolind's life. 'When you are put in situations where you have no formal training, there is only your self-confidence to rely upon. I believe in myself strongly . . . even in 1992, in the darkest periods of Oticon, when I had borrowed all that money and we were faced with huge deficits, at no point did I lose my confidence. There was not one single night that I did not sleep well.' Kolind believes in the power of voluntary work and the goodness of human beings that takes them beyond the lure of money and promotion.

The first problem that Kolind tackled after taking over the management of Oticon was that of bureaucracy. With the voluntary scouting instinct in him, Kolind was convinced that 'bureaucracy destroys the human dimension of things'. He had also seen at Risø the 'price paid for bureaucracy'. 'I was tired of bureaucracy. I was tired of people adding absolutely no positive value. I felt there was a need for a breakthrough in running an organization with less structure, rules and regulation and more vision and leadership.' Having seen the extent to which results are achieved through voluntary service and commitment with hardly any need for bureaucratic structures, Kolind's mission was to infuse Oticon with a simple set of values and vision. With the knowledge that to work together involved a set of values and vision, Kolind brought in a vision of fundamental trust and enthused the others at Oticon to believe that they were there together to 'create a better world'.

On New Year's day, 1990, Oticon's destiny was changed for ever. With an imperative to transform it from a functional bureaucracy to a knowledge-based enterprise, Lars Kolind, who had taken over as CEO in 1988 committed himself to fundamental change. This transformation was defined by Kolind in the following words: 'Instead of perceiving ourselves as a manufacturing company with a service to its customers, we want to see ourselves as a service company with a physical product'. Overnight, Oticon changed from a hearing-aid manufacturer to a hearing-care company.

The stumbling block was to discover a completely new way of perceiving the innovative process and the notion of a product. With a strong engineering tradition of eight decades, Oticon had a clearly defined 'hardware product' focus. Kolind's purpose was to change that to a knowledge-based service focus. Deeply committed to innovation at every conceivable level, Kolind needed a motto that would 'provoke' people to break through the barriers of their thinking. This is when he came up with his vision of 'Think the Unthinkable'.

Breaking with the Past

Established in 1904, Oticon had developed a reputation in Denmark as a well-known and respected hearing-aid manufacturer. The company coasted along on the basis of its sound engineering and good reputation for the next four decades. In 1950, the Danish government introduced a policy in line with its egalitarian welfare system, to provide all its citizens with reduced hearing with free hearing aids. The market boomed and in the 1950s and 1960s, Oticon not only captured the Danish market, but expanded worldwide, establishing an international distribution network. Thirteen foreign subsidiaries were set up and Oticon soon became a name associated with high quality at a high price. Run by a strong management team, Oticon's success reached an all-time high in 1979, with a world market share of 16 per cent, making it the world's largest producer of hearing aids. 'The products almost sold themselves,' as one manager recalled, was an apt way of describing the euphoric success of the 1970s.

The heroes of this success story were the development engineers. In 1979, it was decided to separate the engineering division from the rest of the team members including those at the headquarters and the sales people at the international division. The fragmentation grew over the years, with the engineering division developing its own culture of heirarchy and of a very limited relationship to the rest of the organization. The 1980s saw Oticon struggling against a rapidly changing market for which it was completely unprepared. Firstly, new players were introducing digital technology to the market which was an immediate threat to the traditional analogue technology on which Oticon had built its reputation. The competetion was all the more serious as the new players were also competeing on price. Secondly, a new market segment of younger people with moderate hearing disabilty were replacing Oticon's traditional target group of older severely impaired users. And thirdly there was a global shift from selling products to providing service that simply wasn't part of Oticon's traditional agenda.

The Knowledge-based Enterprise of Tomorrow: 'From Product to Solution'

According to Kolind, 'products which perform traditional and well-defined functions will be outperformed by solutions aimed at maximizing customer satisfaction'. He mentions that the knowledge-based organization of tomorrow will be more like a brain rather than a machine. Unlike the machine, the brain is flexible, it builds on a number of knowledge centres, and it comprises an almost chaotic network of relationships between those centres. Even today, he spends a good deal of his time talking to users, retailers, doctors and salespeople which, according to him, continually 'shapes my perception'. Kolind is convinced that tomorrow's organization will constitute learning at two levels: single loop, wherby learning occurs within a certain framework, and double loop in which the very framwork is open to change. Just like the shaping of one's perception.

Giving a strong 'Southern' foundation to a typically Northern systematic organization, Kolind believes that a knowledge-based organization is built on consensus and human values. He calls consensus essential because it is the only basis on which the individual employee can be liberated from the inflexibility and limitations of traditional management. True to Nonaka's model, the process of knowledge creation at Oticon begins with the creation of an open socialization field. This is facilitated by open networks of communication and dialogue. Through dialogue and the coming together of individuals from different fields, there is a convergence of differing mental maps that open the way to creative interaction. Although there is no direct evidence of the use of metaphor as a knowledge-creating mode, there is certainly a high level of product and process innovation, like the 'Oticon For Kids' programme which was developed in 1993, in co-operation with audiologists in childuren's clinics in the US. The purpose of this is to make it easier for children to accept their hearing aids, and to help them experience a hearing aid as a natural aid instead of a tool for the handi- capped. At the stage of what Nonaka terms combination, the knowledge-base of Oticon comes from a creative combination of technology, audiology and psy- chology and a close co-operation between the different professionals involved in the actual selling, fiting and fine-tuning of the hearing aid to individual needs. This is borne out by the fact that the development time for a product is now half of what it was before.

Kolind mentions that he has never believed that the concept of making maximum profit should be the purpose of any company. 'It just doesn't feel right. What really drives me is creating value and making about two thousand people happy every day . . .' Even today, Kolind spends a lot of time 'talking' to users, retailers, doctors, salespeople, engineers. 'My ideas are created out of dialogue, not through a process of formal analysis.' The transformation to a 'hearing care' company was effected through what Kolind refers to as 'personal intuition'. Going more by gut level feel than analysis, Kolind says, '. . . when I make decisions, small and large, the driving motive is what I feel is right, without knowing why'.

In 1993, Kolind arranged a seminar for Oticon's employees to discuss its fundamental human values. What emerged from that has become Oticon's mission statement and is summarized here.

• Oticon's objective is to help people with hearing deficiencies to live the life they would like to live, with the hearing they have.
• The core of Oticon's strategy is not to deliver the world's best hearing instruments but to provide a solution that gives each user the highest possi- ble quality of life.
• This solution is based on an in-depth knowledge of hearing and hearing deficiency; proficiency in a range of technologies; interaction between many different specialists; co-operation from the user, the dispenser and the manufactuer.

- Oticon concentrates on the whole process, which is the way to better hearing.
- Oticon sets high standards for the order and integrity that characterizes their way of doing business. We regard our suppliers and dispensers as partners instead of adversaries. We treat our competitors with respect, and we support fair and reasonable product comparisions. We will not speak negatively about competitors and their products. We will conduct business in such a way that we make a positive contribution to each country in which we have activities. We support the principle that industry shares the responsibility for maintaining the environment.

Conclusion

We quoted the Danish bard and philosopher, Nicolai Grundtvig in chapter 2 as saying, 'Man is nothing in himself, but encircled by and dependent on . . . an invisible reality'. At Kolind's Oticon, what emerges as the underlying ethos is this invisible reality comprising of a strong commitment to quality, a nearness to customers and a network created by sophisticated information technology. Oticon is the quintessential Northern and, in particular, Scandinavian organization with a strong global orientation. Although lodged in the North, it has a distinctly Southern, humanistic flavour, an Easternness that is apparent, although not overtly, in its product development processes and a Western spirit of adventure. From here, we now turn Eastwards and take up an organization with a difference, where intuition rather than any rational management mode rules the day.

Bibliography

Kanter, R.M. (1987) 'Attack on pay', *Harvard Business Review*, March/April, p. 60.
Cox, A. (1991) 'The Homework behind Teamwork', *Industry Week*, 7 January 1991, p. 23.
Oticon Mission Statement. Oticon, Denmark, 1993.

16

Ahuja Designs

Introduction: The harmonious manager

'Now a dragon, now a snake,
You transform together with the times,
And not willing to act unilaterally,
Now above, now below,
You take harmony as your measure.'
Tao Te Ching, Lao Tzu

The ultimate measure of the Eastern organizational form is harmony. The manager or the CEO who knows when to cross over from playing the dragon to the snake is the one who knows the value of 'appropriate action'. An intuitive rather than rational methodology is called for and the approach is one of active participation rather than observation.

In the Eastern management mode, there is no standardized procedure to be followed. The understanding is that events unfold while the company moves along on its destined path and the manager must respond to each event uniquely. Nothing is ever the same again and, like a river, the organization meanders through a maze of interlinking processes that link it to the world outside. The role of the manager and ideally, that of every employee is to participate in the river-like flow of the organization, guiding it to its prepared destiny. At most, the manager is a catalyst in the events of the organization's life.

The main characteristic of the Eastern company is relatedness, as contrasted with the drive to autonomy that characterizes Western organizations. Interestingly, a different kind of autonomy is present in the Eastern world, in a shadowy form unlike the explicit autonomy of the Western world. The fact that there is a lack of formal, standardized structures makes each organization, be it in Japan, Korea, China or India, uniquely different. So although on the outer level, Eastern organizations are marked by their lack of individuality vis-à-vis their flowing and merging aspects although, deeper within, they are marked by individual differences.

Working through Intuition

At Shyam Ahuja, the management emphasis is unabashedly on loyalty, a willingness to grow with the company, honesty and common sense. As Shyam, the founder of the company says, 'Business is all about people. We rely on people with their hearts in the right place.' It is often an enigma for non-Easterners that so little of managerial time in the East is directed towards preserving outer structures and management systems. At Shyam Ahuja, it is the inner processes that link the person to the organization that get top priority.

Drawing unconsciously on an age-old cultural form, Shyam has created an important niche in the prestigious international floor-covering market. His 50 million-dollar company is unique in that it employs only 254 people on its full-time staff. The other 18,000 are the weavers who create all the magnificent patterns and designs on wool and cotton. There is no management structure to speak of. Shyam himself is the visionary architect behind the organization. He has no fixed office or staff working directly 'under' him; rather he takes his office wherever he goes, whether it is Paris, New York, London or the remote villages of northern India. He is supported by his son Vikram who manages the financial and marketing sides and his daughter-in-law Meera who looks after the design production.

Every design, every new innovative pattern even today is still Shyam's. His unchanging emphasis is on 'quality, quality, quality'. 'I always tell my people to be first concerned with the quality of the product. Then you don't have to worry about distribution. That solves itself. A good product will always sell.' This is the philosophy of the man who in 15 years has built a multimillion-dollar business from scratch.

Much of the way in which Shyam Ahuja is managed is more by intuition rather than by pure rational reason. Having identified that business in the Eastern sense is all about people and relationships, Shyam Ahuja has been able to turn that into a highly sophisticated art form. Although he calls himself adaptive rather than creative, Shyam intuitively conjures up new designs and colours with a finely tuned aesthetic sense. More importantly, these intuitive inspirations are then translated into concrete motifs for the weavers to take on. Shyam Ahuja as a company is strongly located in the 'intra personal' and 'inter personal' worlds, which makes it decidedly South-Eastern in terms of our four-world model. However, the company is rounded off with a high visual-spatial intelligence that is distinctly Northern and a shrewd, innate, entrepreneurial business sense that is squarely Western.

Tapping Sentient Knowledge

The success of Shyam Ahuja is in having been able to convert a dying, tacit knowledge-form into an explicit, high-quality product. As Shyam says, 'Go to an area where weaving has been in existence for centuries. Draw some blood; you'll find the art dormant, somewhere out there, in their chromosomes'. Shoshana Zuboff, writing in *The Age of the Smart Machine*, calls this kind of knowledge '*action-centred*'. Zuboff describes four components of action-centred knowledge as follows:

1 *Sentience:* action-centred knowledge is based upon sentient information derived from physical cues.
2 *Action-dependence:* action-centred skill is developed in physical performance. Although in principle it may be made explicit in language, it typically remains unexplicated – implicit in action.
3 *Context-dependence:* action-centred skill only has meaning within the context in which its associated physical activities occur.
4 *Personalism:* there is a felt linkage between the knower and the known. The implicit quality of knowledge provides it with a sense of interiority, much like physical experience.

Action-centred knowledge is destroyed by mass-production. Mass-production, as the name goes, is about quantitative measures and not qualitative ones. The person behind the work is devalued and what occupies prominence is how much he or she has been able to produce. On the other hand, craft production is a dignified form of activity, one that does not distinguish between living and livelihood. The following list illustrates some of the contrasting differences between the two categories.

Craft production	*Mass-production*
Requires highly skilled workers	Uses narrowly skilled professionals
Customized production	Standardized production
Competes on quality	Competes on price
Creates a variety of products	Creates standard runs
Provides sense of worth for the worker	Diminishes the worth of workers

As Shyam says: 'Weaving is all about art and heart, unless there is heart out there and poetry, nothing that is handcrafted has soul.' The tradition of '*dhurrie*' weaving goes back to the fifteenth century. Once a coveted art-form, it began to decline and wither away with the coming of the mass-produced, cheap imitations in synthetic fibres. Skilled Indian craftspeople were giving up their looms for more lucrative factory jobs. So much so that just 15 years ago when Shyam went looking for a weaver who could translate his design on to wool, he just couldn't find any. Having just peddled an idea to a major American buyer in New York, Shyam was looking for a 'master' who could weave a *dhurrie* in the traditional way. 'Everywhere I went,' he recalls, 'I was told that a *dhurrie* just didn't exist anymore.' Finally by chance, he happened to run into a jobless master who had sold his land and home and was preparing to move back to his native vilage in Pakistan. Of course, from an Eastern perspective, there was nothing 'chancy' about this meeting; it was simply intended to be! Shyam managed to persuade the master to make him just one *dhurrie*. 'I gave him a very simple design and he made me a piece that Irwin Corey of New York's Rosecore was ecstatic about.' The first wool *dhurrie* was created and Shyam Ahuja had revived a dying craft. That first pattern is still stocked as Design No. 1. A new renaissance in floor-covering began. That was just ten years ago. Today, Shyam Ahuja *dhurries* are stocked in major company outlets in London, Stockholm, Paris, New York, Hong Kong and India and they also produce exclusive designs for Ralph Lauren Home Furnishings.

The Production Process

The production process at Shyam Ahuja goes through five stages.

1 Inspiration

The story of how each *dhurrie* is produced starts with Shyam himself. He travels the world over looking for inspiration in simple motifs and designs. Informed by an inner wisdom about what people want to have and what they are bored with, Shyam conjures up unique ideas and designs. At a time when reds and royal blues and greens marked the Persian carpets, Shyam entranced the world with pastels that seemed so much more harmonious with people's sorroundings; they were carpets to live with. However, Shyam never relies on market feedback and is critical of bending over to the dictates of the market. Operating more with intuition than market analysis, Shyam Ahuja's products have created a revolution in the world of floor coverings.

Combined with this intuitive sense is Shyam's knowledge of raw materials. He seeks the best in natural fibres from the world over, never compromising on quality. The wool mostly comes from New Zealand, Australia and India. The silks come from China, the cotton from Egypt while all the linen is purchased from Ireland. This uniquely multicultural aspect is prevalent also in Shyam's designs. Ecclectic to a fault, Shyam's designs are from all corners of the world.

2 Adaptation

At the Design Studio in Worli, Bombay, Shyam's new designs are plotted and coloured on graphs with utmost precision. Once approved, the design is traced on to tracing paper and then filled out with three to four colour combinations.

Each design takes about three months to conceive. Once approved, the design plate is sent to a traditional 'mapmaker'. About 60–70 designs emerge from here every year in addition to the 350 that already exist in the repertoire.

3 Communication
Once the designs and colours have been finalized at the Design Studio, four copies are made. One is sent to the mapmaker, one to the craftsperson or the artisan, one to the main warehouse where the finshed product will return to and one is stored on file. A unique process of information storage with the minimum of information technology ensures that each *dhurrie* can be traced from concept to product and the quality monitored. It also ensures that customers can order exact duplicates several decades later! The mapmaker lives more than 2000 miles away in Mirzapur, a little hamlet in North India. For 25 years the mapmaker and his family have been performing this function of receiving scaled-down designs, then enlarging them to the actual size of a prototype *dhurrie* for the weavers to follow. Real colours are now filled in before the design is sent to the weavers.

4 Experimentation
Before the weaving begins, the yarn is dyed at the dyeing centre through an age-old process in large burnished copper vats using coal driven furnaces. The chief dyer is another old hand, who works with 14 basic colours and can create anywhere up to a million shades of pales from that. The yarn is boiled for 90 minutes and then cleansed in cold running water. The yarn is finally hung up to dry in the hot sun.

The finished yarn is then taken to the disbursal centre at a rural centre, Badohi, where the 'master' gives out weaving contracts to weavers and all the instructions that go with that. The weavers arrive from the local villages on foot, bicycle, camel and donkey. Nearly 40,000 kg of yarn is disbursed from here flawlessly by the master who has been with Shyam Ahuja since 1969. He is also responsible for collecting the finished *dhurries* and doing the first quality test on them. The rejection rate here is approximately 10 per cent.

5 Distribution
The *dhurries* are finally finished in large sheds at the disbursal centre. Scissors snip off fluff, edges are bound by large needles and then with cord. The surface of the dhurrie is done over with a blade to de-fluff. Pincers and brushes are used to remove rubbish and grit that may have been caught in the rugs. Once again there are no systematic procedures involved that standardize the final finishing. Apparently, once the order was for a *dhurrie* so large that it needed to be carried to the local railway station where it was laid on the plaform to be measured and cleaned! This is only possible when there are no hard-and-fast procedures and rules to be obeyed. As we have seen, the Eastern, aesthetic form is characterized by an absence of pre-assigned first principles.

Once this is completed and everything has met with the approval of the master, and the regional office, the product is shifted to the main warehouse in Bombay. Once again it is ruthlessly checked for the tiniest of defects. If there is the slightest mismatch with the original colours the *dhurrie* is rejected. The rejection rate here is about 20 per cent. The approved *dhurries* are then shipped to all over the world.

The Virtual Corporation

A 'virtual product', according to Davidow and Malone includes the following characteristics:

- It provides customer satisfaction using cost-effective techniques
- It can be produced in diverse locations and offered in a great number of formats
- A virtual product exists before it is produced. Its concept, design and manufacture are stored in the minds of co-operating teams and in flexible processes of production.

A virtual product comes into existence when mass-production and bureaucratic structures lose their sharp edges, and seemingly permanent systems continuously adapt to the changing needs of the situation. By this definition, Shyam Ahuja is a virtual corporation chracterized as follows:

- It is marked by permeable structures
- It is founded on trust and loyalty
- It provides for employee empowerment
- It focuses on the customer as the driving force
- It is less middle-management intensive and more worker-competence intensive
- It involves close partnerships with suppliers
- It incorporates 'lean production'.

In the words of Wormack and Roos writing in *Machines that Changed the World*, 'Lean Production is lean because it uses less of everything compared with mass production: half the human effort . . . , half the manufacturing space, half the investment in tools . . . has fewer defects, and produces a greater and ever growing variety of products.' Lean production is much more an organizational innovation than a technological one. It depends not so much on computers and automatic machinery as it does on worker skills, organization on the factory floor, and relationships between manufacturers, suppliers and customers.'

The complex product markets that are emerging globally, are demanding varied, customized products. The ability of the customer to be involved in the design of the product necessitates radical organizational changes. While bureaucratic, top-heavy management structures are bound to fail, so will those companies that are not able to deliver quality in a sustained manner.

Eccles and Nohria's 'Beyond the Hype' mentions that the key strategies to managing in an uncertain future involve:

1 *Acting without certitude*
   - High tolerance for uncertainty, ambiguity
   - Willingness to act without fully knowing the consequences
   - Willingness to quickly act upon past errors.

2 *Constantly preserving flexibility*
   - Preserving/increasing degrees of freedom
   - Keeping more than one option open at any time.

3 *Maintaining a sense of relationship*
   - Interlocking one's actions with others
   - Staying informed about the actions of others
   - Ability to form and communicate stories.

4 *Having a feel for the whole*
   - Contextualizing one's action in the whole
   - Working through interdependent networks instead of through autonomous units.

5 *Having a sense of timing*
   - Intuition about rightness
   - Knowing exactly when to do what.

The whole management structure then moves away from the older, more traditional rigid ways of managing to the 'softer' processes that lie underneath the structures. In Shyam Ahuja's case, this is strongly supported by a holistic, corporate philosophy that clearly states that it is not in the business of manufacturing *dhurries*. Rather, it is in the business of changing the way people live.

Conclusion: Serving Society

The first real multinational company in India, Shyam Ahuja has been an object lesson in how successful businesses can sustainably develop societies. Vikram Ahuja, writing in a perspective on the *dhurries*, mentions: '. . . we'd like to spotlight the fact that (our success) has been a lesson on how the private sector and private initiative can create and sustain rural enterprise and employment.'

Keeping to cultural tradition, the 20,000 odd weavers, dyers, printers, tailors mapmakers and general workers who come from some of the poorest rural sections of India are part of the Shyam Ahuja extended family. Many of them have been with the company for twenty five years, and they have prospered along with the company. The company arranges loans for the artisans in times of need and other benefits are given. Shyam himself has a close rapport with several thousand weavers.

Secondly, every aspect of the production process is ecological. Natural dyes and environmentally friendly policies add to the high quality of the Shyam Ahuja product. In a social setting where carpets have come to be synonymous with child labour, Shyam Ahuja is different. As a recent advertisement states: 'Our philosophy is very clear: our carpets are for children to live on. Not to live by.'

Bibliography

Zuboff, S. (1988) *In the Age of the Smart Machine*. Oxford: Heinemann.

Davidow, W. and Malone, M. (1992) *The Virtual Corporation*. New York: Harper Business.

Wormack, J.P., Jones, D.T. and Roos, D. (1990) *Machines that Changed the World*. New York: Rawson Associates/Macmillan.

Eccles, R.G. and Nohria, N. (1992) *Beyond the Hype: rediscovering the essence of management*. Boston: Harvard University Press.

17

Constructing Cashbuild

Introduction: The Beginning

'Class distinction has rarely altered since 1831. Humans have remained humans. Basic human nature still remains intact, and this is precisely what makes dealing with people so fascinating.'

Albert Koopman

This chapter takes us to the Southern world of Cahsbuild and the unique case of Albert Koopman. One of those 'Davids', Albert Koopman set out in the eighties to fight the 'Goliath' of the South African business and political establishment. To be true to the Southern world which is profoundly rooted in story telling, the best way to convey what Koopman achieved, both philosophically and practically, is by enabling him to tell his story, in his own inimitable words.

'I entered life as a moral fighter'

I was raised as a street fighter. My mother died when I was 13 and my father lived in Mozambique, 1240 miles from me. Set free at a very early age I had to learn to survive. That meant dealing with people, including people who had hang-ups, and people who wanted to do me in for what I believed. The one thing that I learnt as a result was that I was going to enter my life as a clean, moral fighter, 'someone who sterilized his bicycle chains' before he entered the fight of interpersonal relationships. Unlike the animals with claws and teeth, God gave me his supreme gifts; choice and intellect. Making use of these two gifts I was able to observe my fellow man going about his daily activities and make his life more meaningful. From this I acquired my moral purpose.

The story you are about to hear is one of my personal experience in an African context, through my involvement as the Chief Executive of a Cash and Carry Building Material Merchant in South Africa. It is a story of success and many failures, a story of victories and sadnesses in my attempt to create an excellent company, to put it mildly, in a somewhat turbulent society. It is the story of how a white (Western) man in Africa became a White African. It is the story of how I combined the rationality of the First World with the spirit of the Third World.

First World and Third World Failed to Meet

Cashbuild was started as a wholesaler in 1978 and became a very successful business in a short space of time. Situated predominantly in the rural areas of South Africa and focusing on the black housing market, our staff complement consisted of 84 per cent black, 13 per cent white and 3 per cent Indian. However, by mid-1982 with 12 outlets, profits started sliding. Everything was in place – systems, procedures, technology, a booming market – but something was going wrong and I did not know where to start looking. We embraced our cardinal principles of giving value to our customers, being innovative, adaptable, and totally committed to the business as well as having efficient organizational structures, but obviously something was changing and we did not know what it was.

Our hierarchy was well displayed on the walls of all our outlets, everyone was placed in neat little boxes with prescribed job descriptions and functions, and no one was achieving our objectives as had been laid out! I came to the conclusion that we had a lot of trained men but no actual committed soldiers. It was clear that our organizational structure was autocratic, as was my own personal management style. We had to change, but how? What if people started seeing me as soft when I became more participative and democratic.

What about the chaos that might occur during the period of transition? Well there was no other way to do it at the time but by 'MBFA' – managing by fumbling around. There was no other way but to plunge in at the deep end and to risk my neck and possibly be forced to say 'I'm sorry' for my original way of doing things. I immediately commissioned an attitude survey and found that pro-company feelings, to the tune of 89 per cent in 1980, had slipped to 74 per cent in 1982. Typical remarks of the predominently white (Third World) management team about the majority of our Third World workforce were: 'There's no way one can train them; they're too badly educated'; 'They simply won't open up as people and talk about their aspirations, needs and fears because of cultural barriers'; 'None of them understands our business and the simply don't care'. Remarks about myself were even more demeaning: 'You're pompous, egocentric, and very distant from what's happening at the coalface.'

Uncovering the Divine Will of Africa

Key questions went through my mind. Why do the workers actually work? What is their social or Divine Will? What went wrong in Cashbuild with respect to capital and labour? What were we actually trying to achieve as a business organism? How do we bring together the rights of people, their spiritually based humanity and the economic process as represented in the workplace? Subsequently I conducted a succession of brainstorming sessions to uncover the purpose of Cashbuild's existence. It soon became clear to us that one purpose existed in management's head and another in the workers'. Management was pulling one way and the people another. There was no transcendent purpose linking one with the other.

Meanwhile, in the course of particpating in these workshops over six months, it became clear that active listening and intensive interaction between people made each aware of the other's spirit. Day in day out I was confronted with people's vitality, their reasons for being, and their creatvity. I became aware that there was a spirit or soul that lay deep within each person which needed awakening. However, our current Cashbuild organization was patently incapable of releasing it. Typically a chief executive, after fighting like hell to get to the top, goes into hybernation once he gets there and forgets his leadership role. In order to enrich his own existence he all too often forgets his responsibility to benefit his followers. Until this point I had become just such a self-centred person. Perhaps now, though, I had begun to see the light.

The Middle: Establishing Our Cardinal Principles

Arising out of 3000 issues that came to our attention through the brainstorming sessions, we drew up a set of cardinal principles emerging out of the interdependent relationships that existed between customer, employee, company, competitor and motivation (see figure 17.1).

We realized, at the same time, that the principles would have to embrace the social spirit of every employee, so they were spelled out as follows.

- We recognize that the marketing process of getting goods from supplier to customer is the concern of every employee and that we have to liberate him or her to achieve this.

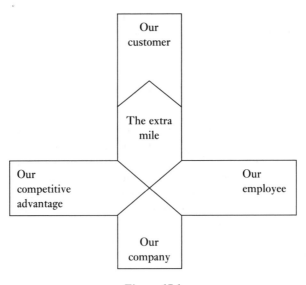

Figure 17.1

- We want to strive for quality service through people and keep our system as balanced as possible through on-the-job training, motivation through better supervision, self-measurement and statistical control rather than boss control, giving people a say over their workplace.
- We recognize that quality service and total productivity will only come if we rediscover the spirit of man within the workplace, providing job enrichment by changing the work people do.
- People need to belong to and identify with the company's cause; customers must be satisfied through committed people.

At every workshop session which subsequently followed we probed all the obstacles which stood in the way of our following our cardinal principles. No stone was left unturned and over a period of one year we listened to why people worked, with whom they preferred to work, and what they saw would be the design of the perfect workplace. After spending extended periods of time living amongst our black employees, experiencing life within their communities, and consulting with them directly, I found I had to review my whole understanding of the people I employed, as well as how they saw their relationship with our business and with its philosophy. The degree to which aspects of indigenous culture were to become 'spiritualized' in the workplace was to depend on the type of organization imposed upon the individual, including the degree to which the organization would allow expression of these elements.

The End: Turning our Thinking about People Upside Down

I was therefore forced to seek a way in which we could spell out and determine our objective common interest in the production of commodities – customer service – to replace capital's pure interest in increasing profits. Lots of meetings, small group activities, discussion groups and open two-way communications had to form as much of the way we ran our business as did the work itself. Everything had to be focused on the common interest of creating wealth and fostering an understanding amongst workers that the correct management of capital benefits the organization as a whole. This correct management, in turn, could only occur if the worker was democratically involved in contributing towards the overall success of the organization. I visualized that in this manner capitalist exploitation would no longer be able to exist.

We had to turn our thinking about people upside down and look at our business totally differently. The perception of capitalist exploitation at Cashbuild had to be changed, not merely through some superficial reform programme, but through an active restructuring of the hierarchy to liberate the work ethic. We had to design an organization that was truly free so that the co-operation between all individuals in fact became its own sustainable social form. We needed a social form that could accommodate the freedom to be enterprising, as well as harnessing to spirirtual consciousness of all our employees. Enter our '*care*' philosophy – Cashbuild's Aspirations with Regard to Excellence.

Care philosophy

In essence the *care* philosophy sought to bring about a balancing of power within the organization. At that stage, in 1982, authority was vested with management (but no power) and power with the unions (but no authority). Firstly we built in mechanisms for the protection of individual rights vis-à-vis the organization, through a code of conduct. Secondly *care* groups were formed to give expression to the spritual consciousness of individuals, serving as a vehicle for discussion of issues affecting their working life. Groups were formed at five levels – general labourers, semi-skilled personnel, junior, middle and senior managers – each with their own majority-elected president. Thirdly these groups were to engage with the economic process, sharing information about efficiency and productivity, and learning about as well as influencing the company's wealth creating process.

A *care* philosophy designed by the people for the people spelled out how our workplace should be regulated, and set out the rules of the business game. Some of the salient points were:

- Commitment to joint decision-making at all levels, with everyone playing their part in finding solutions to problems.
- An open and free culture with everyone in the organization having access to any line manager.
- A team consisting of different races, sexes and cultural creeds, none of which were to be discriminated against.
- A belief in the 'extra mile' concept both for the organization and for the individual.

After the philosophy was translated into seven languages and a little booklet given to each and every employee to read, we felt we could start moving into the future. Our view towards people changed dramatically as we recognized that:

- Each employee had his own rights, will to work, and wanted some control over his or her destiny.
- We needed to understand the cross-cultural complexities of our workplace through continuous interaction.
- The company would place no limits on human growth.

They told it like it was

Whilst our *care* horizon extended over five years I found, after only eighteen months, that resistance to change had become an inordinate obstacle. Indeed we started experiencing that people actually cared for their company, and began to find such meaning and purpose in their work that productivity was considerably enhanced. But the euphoria was short-lived. After many consultative workshops we decided to have a major get-together to assess our performance so far. As the management team, our ears fell off – they told it like it was!

'Mr Koopman, I would like to resign as President because my fellow men see me as siding with management; they're no longer carrying out my instructions.'

'I have no power. Although my people voted me in I cannot get my manager to act on their requests. He simply is not interested.'

'The company has cheated us for so long. Why is it suddenly changing? We don't believe in it.'

'My manager told me the other day that he sees me as a threat and will not co-operate with me.'

'We don't trust our manager. He is prejudiced against blacks.'

'What happens to my family if I die?'

Venturecom: A New Way of Communicating

It was time to look at the whole situation again. We were sure that our belief in raising spiritual consciousness was valid, but we could now see our employees expressing their social selves as apart from the economic process. While they were perceiving their labour power as intimately associated with themselves as human beings, they still saw the company as viewing their labour content as part of the production-distribution-consumption process. They were being treated as commodities. Our *care* structures, as representatively democratic, were still separating management and worker. What they were crying out for was for participatory democracy, thereby integrating their economic and social selves, relieving labour power of its commodity character.

It dawned upon me as a result that:

- no one can demand productivity from anyone, but one can create a climate within which social man is willingly productive;
- one cannot manage people, only things, but one can create a climate within which people take responsibility and manage themselves;
- one cannot demand quality from people, but one can create conditions at work through which quality work is a product of pride in workmanship.

So these new conditions we thought would help to create the human face which I had been looking for earlier. Exploitative capitalism demands quotas, productivity and quality, all as part of a commodity outlook on life. People remain part of the production-distribution-consumption process, without their spiritual work or social ethos being recognized. The protagonists of class consciousness, meanwhile, became a rallying point in the name of social justice, without actually giving expression to the human face. We promptly decided at Cashbuild to pursue our own course, dividing control of the business into soft variable (enterprise and labour) and hard ones (capital and land). A convention of some 200 workers was held and the ground rules were established:

- Respect human dignity and individual freedom of speech.
- Allow everyone to have access to company results and performance standards.
- Give everyone a role in developing company policy.
- Improve the quality of life of all employees outside the work sphere through active community involvement.

Views and feelings just poured out of the hearts of the workers for the first time. The basis for removing false marks ('isms') between capital and labour was still the *care* groups, but this time around we were talking *team* – total *team*, only *us* – this was *our* company. It was proposed that a governing body of five people be constituted to each outlet, with each person being democratically elected to hold a portfolio, save for the manager who was appointed to the Operations Portfolio, based on his or her expertise. This portfolio was concerned with the hard variables whereas the Safety, Labour, Merchandise and Quality of Work-Life portfolios were the soft ones. Moreover each of these managers was continually assessed by lower levels in the hierachy. The subsequent newspaper headlines – 'Cashbuild – the company where workers have the right to dismiss their managers' – frightened the hell out of the capitalist fraternity. Yet precisely because that right existed within the workforce we never needed to use it.

In fact the Cashbuild Venturecom system was socialistic in that it reinstated distributive justice and offered security against destitution. It was likewise capitalistic to the extent that self-expression was given its due reward. Our system thus gave expression both to the work ethic and also to the enterprising spirit of people.

Reviewing My Learning Curve

As managing director, in 1982, I had begun to realize that the internal workings of the organization were simply not matching up with external demands. Profits were going down. To me, power had been a thing, a toy. My nature was individualist and competitive. I was the only person existing in the world. I saw coercion as the way to get things done. So when I confronted the results of our attitude survey I was inevitably confused. At the end of a protracted period of soul searching I began to realize that I had been using power and the 'ism' through which it had to be executed in pursuit of the protection of my class. In a sense I was still a product of the industrial society, and had thereby forgotten that there was actually no such thing as the means of production. There were only people who actually work machines in order to produce. Without the people, the machines and the factories would stand still. Without the effort of human enterprise, there would be no progress in humanity. Here was my key to change. I could now see that if I restored the dignity and pride of the workforce I could achieve a new human spirit that would drive the enterprise for the better of all. I would therefore be able to change, not by losing my individual competitive value system but by finding solidarity as managing director with all the people in the organization.

This entailed, at a technical level:

- taking Cashbuild employees on a journey, strengthening their relationships with management;
- turning all employees into stakeholders of the organization;
- aggressively addressing the distributive aspect of the business, through

HAVING MODE
- Self-reliant/rational
- Individual
- Self-interest
- Reward/punishment base

Management oriented

Directive style

Production concern

Individual	Competitive
Individual control	Wealth and status
OWN	ACCUMULATE

Goals and deadlines
DEMANDING

*The more I have,
the more I am*

BEING MODE
- Co-operative/emotive
- Collective
- Community interest
- Recognition/rejection

Leadership Oriented

Participative style

People concern

Group	Co-operative
Sharing	Giving
TEAM CO-OPERATION	DIGNITY/ RESPECT

Sacrificing
VISION/FAITH

*I am, therefore
the more I give*

Figure 17.2 Modes of life

profit sharing, in the ultimate interest of the business, its workers and their families;
- promoting excellence of quality and productivity, within the organization, and fostering a communal climate for its achievement.

At the structural level I had to restore meaning into people's lives, by constructing a code of ethics around which people could be rallied for the common purpose. This entailed developing:

- a superordinate goal for the enterprise through the people themselves – bottom-up;
- a philosophy of social justice and equality;
- pride and dignity within every employee.

Individual Competitive	Group Communal
Profit for me is derived from self interest	Profit to me is a vote of confidence my society gives me for service rendered to that society
I am actually exclusive from my fellow man	I am mutually inclusive
I prefer to be a self actualized person	I prefer to be a social man
The more I have the more I am	I am, therefore the more I am prepared to share and give
I demand productivity from people	I prefer to create a climate in which people will be willingly more productive
I am actually an aggressive kind of a person	I am actually a receptive kind of a person
I look you in the eye and challenge you	I bow my head and show you respect
My concern is for production	My concern is for people

Figure 17.3 Competitive vs. Communal

I found later that this last point was in fact the spark for all endeavours, and took precedence over any of the other technical systems, rewards, or structures we introduced. It reflected, in fact, the 'divine will' of Cashbuild which in its turn reflected the 'divine will' of the communities which the company represented.

The African Work Group

In my ten years of experience at Cashbuild I observed that the African work group regarded their fellows primarily in terms of morals and emotions rather than in terms of their roles and functions. Traditionally blacks have emerged through the spoken word. Wisdoms were carried forward in the form of metaphors and stories as opposed to the written word which preserved information for Western cultures. So blacks will tend to think aurally and emotionally, which is why they would think aloud and use continuous discussion as the main part of their reasoning process. The traditional *indaba* (debating society) of black cultures had, at its base, the removal of all dissent before the group could proceed. The African work group therefore has to clear dissent by engaging interactively with the morality of an issue. Thus performance is valued less for its own sake than for the sake of the group.

Conclusion

The 'divine will' of Africa then, reflected in the work groups that I came across at Cashbuild, is hidden between the lines of the following passages:

- Africa shows a strong reverence for ancestors and other departed relatives who are believed to be able to affect the living
- Africa sees that the principle of age is an important source of wisdom
- Africa places a high value on ceremony and ritual in many aspects of social life
- Africa attaches great importance to group life and to social harmony, thereby placing a high premium on consensus in group endeavours
- Africa is extremely social through its spontaneity of self expression and ease of communication, thereby regarding correctness of speech as a prerequisite for social standing
- Africa can forgive and forget very readily because of its great capacity for reconciliation.

Bibliography

Koopman, A. (1991) *Transcultural Management*. Oxford: Blackwell Publishers.

Conclusion:
Creating a Learning Ecology

From Genesis to Metamorphosis

Returning to the centre of the four worlds, and drawing upon the ecological metaphor once again, where all natural systems are located – at once stable and unstable, individualistic and collective – the ecosystem is the epitome of our evolving organization.

Stephen Toulmin, an American social ecologist, tells us in *The Return to Cosmology: Postmodern Science and the Theology of Nature* (University of California Press, 1982) that 'our own natural science today is no longer "modern science". Rather, it is a "post-modern science" in which the old disciplinary boundaries that we took so much for granted turn out to be nothing else but "historical accidents".' What the new ecology and new physics teach us is that we cannot separate who we are from what our business environment is. Toulmin refers to such a 'transdisciplinary' development in ecology that has a direct relationship to changes in society. He asks a fundamental question: "How do living things, including human beings, exist in relation to one another in their common habitat?" You will remember that in chapter 10 we defined four aspects of nature that are common to all ecosystems: competition, conservation, catalysation and co-creation. Stephen Gatley, co-author of *Comparative Management* (McGraw-Hill, 1995), suggested the following terms in the context of a social-ecology model: *genesis, morphosis, metamorphosis* and *homeostasis*.

With genesis goes survival and the pioneering drive to growth. We compete as Western individuals and depend on our initiative and hard work, building and expanding territorial structures, attributes of the American dream. However, the need to compete is part of a bigger ecology that involves the three other worlds. There is the Northern world of conservation or morphosis in which it is not so much the individual identity that is important as the evolution into an entity. At this stage the ecosystem 'morphoses' (acquires form) into an integrated system.

N

	System CONSERVATION MORPHOSIS	
Structure COMPETETION *GENESIS*		Process CATALYSATION *METAMORPHOSIS*
	HOMEOSTASIS CO-CREATION Value	

W ... E (to the left of the middle row is **W**, to the right is **E**)

S

Resources are no longer used up at the same rate as before but are conserved and fed back into the collective system. This is the Northern world, represented by societies such as the Scandinavians which subsume individuality in favour of the collective good. The Eastern world is that of destabilization where organisms and ecosystems metamorphose and create completely new forms through such processes as catalytic and hypercatalytic cycles. In cultural terms, the Eastern world has a propensity for such flexible processes that destabilize and creatively transform previously held structures and systems. Finally, there is the Southern world of homeostasis in which the ecosystem enters into a partnership with other organisms and ecosystems and creates what Toulmin refers to as 'ethical significance', or what we have referred to as 'value'. Now let us present the overall conclusions of this book, starting with philosophy and ending with business.

From Philosophy to Business

If you are to position yourself and your organization at the centre of the four worlds, you will have to encompass . . .

. . . firstly, from a Philosophical perspective

- In the *pragmatic* world
  1 Focus on competition as your strategy
  2 Create a market-centred enterprise
  3 Learn experimentally through action-learning groups
  4 Become an action-centred leader of your people
- In the *rational* world
  1 Adopt a consolidating role and conserve your resources
  2 Create a networked company

    3   Learn conceptually and create a learning organization

    4   Become an ethical leader of your people

- In the *holistic* world

    1   Set catalytic processes in place to transform your organization

    2   Create a product-innovative company

    3   Learn intuitively and develop a knowledge-creating organization

    4   Become a spiritual leader of your people

- In the *humanistic* world

    1   Work through your vision and participate in co-creating a society

    2   Create a service-based organization

    3   Learn passionately and create a value-laden organization

    4   Become a visionary leader

Each of these four business philosophies is manifested environmentally, knowledge-wise, work-wise and business-wise.

. . . secondly, from an Environmental perspective

In the physical environment

- Adopt a strongly *empirical*, sense-directed perspective

    1   Manage your organization as a machine that needs to function efficiently

    2   Use the empirical method (i.e. first experiment, then draw conclusions and thereafter test again through further experimentation)

- Adopt a *functional*, thought-focused perspective

    1   Manage your organization methodically and objectively as an entity separate from you

    2   Aim for optimum prediction and control and build a stable organization

- Adopt a *holistic*, intuition-based perspective

    1   Manage your organization as a process in flow

    2   Leverage uncertainty as a strategic force rather than aiming for stability

- Adopt a *humanistic*, feeling-orientated perspective

    1   Manage your organization as a value-creating enterprise

    2   Build your organization within the community

In the ecological environment

- Create a pioneering organization: *genesis*

    1   You are highly competitive, expanding your territorial control over the market

    2   You carry the spirit of entrepreneurship and use resources freely for profit

- Build a consolidating organization: *morphosis*

    1   You begin to conserve and consolidate your gains

    2   You develop and implement systems for specialized niches in the market

- Develop a renewing organization: *metamorphosis*

    1   You maintain a highly fluid organization that creates changes in itself and the environment

2 You work through symbiotic processes of mutual benefit
- Establish a mature organization: *homeostasis*
    1 You manage you organization as a self-regulating macroscopic entity in unbroken contact with the rest of society
    2 You nurture and manage the web of relationships that bind your organization to the world outside

In the psychological environment
- In your *youthful* world
    1 Your task is to develop your dream, giving it greater definition and finding ways of living it out
    2 You must have a sense of adventure in whatever you do
- In your *adult* world
    1 Your settling-down phase is your main vehicle for realizing your youthful ambitions and goals
    2 Your overall task is to settle for a few key choices, to create a structure around them and to invest in the components of the structure
- In your *mid-life* world
    1 You now begin to get more engaged with yourself, reducing your involvement in outer-directed struggles
    2 You question every aspect of your life and that of your organization and start attending to the pattern of interrelatedness among things
- In your *mature* world
    1 After having faced the triumphs and disappointments that come with the earlier phases, you now develop a new integrity
    2 You are now ready to leave behind a legacy for future generations

In the cultural environment, as a symbolic analyst
- In the world of *experimentation*
    1 You fuse self and system and internalize knowledge through self-in-action
    2 Your learning arises through the free exchange of knowledge amongst free spirits
    3 You function as a scientist and combine action with reflection
    4 You ground yourself in pragmatic-based experimentation and orient your organization towards the learning company
- In the world of *abstraction*
    1 You create the requisite organizational stratification necessary for learning to take place
    2 You begin to accommodate progressively more complex information through the stratified orders
    3 You function by matching your mental models with those of the organization
    4 You take these depersonalized structures and functions beyond personalized attitudes and behaviours

- In the world of *systems thinking*
  1 You begin to create a framework for seeing interrelationships rather than things
  2 You leverage patterns of change rather than static snapshots of your organization
  3 You view causality in multidimensional and circular terms, rather than in unidimensional, linear ones
  4 As a systems thinker, you embrace a personal mastery, the development of mental models, the evolving of shared values and the exercise of team learning
- In the world of *collaboration*
  1 As a member of a learning community, you must guide and co-ordinate learning efforts to discover strategic value
  2 You align yourself with those technological developments that promote learning and social integration
  3 You value and promote skill development that prepares people for increasing their responsibilities in the workplace
  4 You use 'informated work' as a means of communication through which social systems develop

. . . thirdly, from a Knowledge perspective

In the knowledge-creating mode
- The world of *agreement*
  1 You use the Western world to solve problems by defining their identity
  2 You assume the existence of a singular truth
  3 You draw upon your powers of sensing and experimenting
  4 The knowledge that you create in this mode is content-based knowledge, dealing with the immediate nature of what exists
- The world of *formula*
  1 You use models and formulae to create a logical consistency
  2 You are focused on abstracting out details that will be of specific use
  3 You draw upon your powers of reason and thinking
  4 The knowledge you create in this mode is concept-based knowledge
- The world of *unbounded systems*
  1 You work through contradictions and paradoxes rather than uniformities
  2 You invite divergence in place of traditional convergence
  3 You draw upon your powers of intuition
  4 The knowledge you create in this mode is context-rich knowledge
- The world of *value*
  1 Your work is driven by creating value for the community
  2 You create a communally based family structure
  3 You base all your actions in value and participate in shared feeling
  4 The knowledge you create in this mode is consent-based knowledge

In the knowledge-creating organization
- The world of *internalization*
  1 You are engaged in the creation of a learning enterprise (marked by a horizontal exchange of goods and services) in which knowledges is internalized
  2 You learn by doing
  3 You draw upon best practice
  4 You convert jargon into user-friendly language
- The world of *combination*
  1 You begin the process of putting together the learning organization through which knowledge is progressively combined to evolve into newer forms
  2 You manage ever-greater complexity
  3 You turn ephemeral ideas into focused concepts
  4 You convert raw data into codified information
- The world of *externalization*
  1 You transform a business system with interdependent functions and emergent processes into a learning organism, through which knowledge is externalized
  2 You draw upon powerful metaphors
  3 You turn them into useful analogies
  4 You convert these into products or organizational concepts
- The world of *socialization*
  1 You turn your business into a learning community
  2 You build up such learning communities of practise
  3 You share value in order to add value
  4 You build mutual trust and a sense of common ownership

Your evolving strategy
- The world of *competitive strategy*
  1 You position your organization so that its capabilities provide the best defence against competition
  2 You focus on leadership through strategies such as cost and overhead control, minimizing, for example, research and development and after-sales service expenditures, etc.
  3 You differentiate your products and services to insulate your company against competition and increase your profit margins
  4 You engage in nichemanship by serving a narrow market segment rather than a broader one
- The world of *strategic intent*
  1 You focus on your core competencies, rather than on specific skills and techniques
  2 You create a group of people who become corporate resources loyal to the organization's core competencies

3   To become competent, you synthesize a variety of skills, technologies and knowledge streams

4   You compete not only to protect your organization's position within existing markets but to succeed in new markets

- The world of *strategic dynamics*

1   You become a master of seeing whole patterns where others see only unconnected events and forces to which to react

2   You do this by complex learning which involves questioning and continually adjusting your unconscious mental models

3   You are able to tackle predictable closed change, statistically predictable contained change, and unknowable open-ended change

4   You are able to compete in a climate of change and uncertainty by successfully managing your organization in a far-from-equilibrium mode

- The world of *communal strategy*

1   You become rooted in collective entrepreneurship which is based primarily on trust

2   You become a member of a benevolent community, contributing your skills and insights to the collective pool of your nation's assets

3   You manage a high-value enterprise in which profits derive not from scale and volume but from continuous discovery of new linkages between solutions and needs

4   Your co-creative strategy involves working through new organizational webs by diffusing power based on the capacity to add value to these webs

. . . fourthly, from a Work perspective

Individually speaking

- The job-related world of *skill*

1   Your job brings into focus a specific area that relates to the use of specific skills and techniques

2   To do your job properly, you must perceive the organization in terms of its component parts and the required functions and tasks

3   You use your analytical skills and become a good trouble-shooter

4   You upgrade your skills regularly through specific training programmes

- The role-specific world of *knowledge*

1   You play a broadly based role in the organization that links your hitherto narrowly based job to others'

2   From a skill-based specialist, you evolve to a knowledge-based generalist, capable of multitask functions and networking with many departments

3   You conceptualize problems and use models and theories to solve them

4   You engage in developing methodologies for knowledge creation

- The calling-based world of the *self*

1   You and your organization are now part of an unbroken whole

2   What you do transforms the organization and the organization in turn transforms you

3 You no longer look for answers and solutions to problems but seek to ask the right question
4 Your work becomes a deeply subjective matter and you allow your self to unfold out of your work
- The vocation-based world of *community*
  1 Your work is grounded in the shared value that links your organization to the community and the world outside
  2 Your vocation at your place of work gives you a rootedness in the culture and the society you are in
  3 You no longer perceive problems as existing in themselves; they are a part of interdependencies and you are consciously aware of all the consequences of your actions
  4 Your aim is to create an organizational culture which is based on shared values and a common vision

Organizationally speaking
- The job-related world of *structures*
  1 The structural world is highly differential with clearly laid-out structures making trouble-shooting easy
  2 Structures are based on convergent logic; for every problem, there is only one solution
  3 At their best, structural organizations are highly efficient and youthful
  4 At their worst, structural organizations become heavily top-down with problems of communication
- The role-oriented world of *systems*
  1 The systematic organization conserves resources through linkages and is consequently information-intensive
  2 Systems depend on a common code to prevent deviance from the norm, thereby maintaining a high level of homogeneity
  3 At their best, systematic organizations are highly ethical workplaces
  4 At their worst, systematic organizations turn excessively bureaucratic and impersonal
- The calling-based world of *processes*
  1 Processes provide the underlying principle to structures and systems through a flowing wholeness
  2 Processes serve to simultaneously harmonize and destabilize the organization by undoing the rigid divisions within
  3 At their best, process-based, organizations are dynamic and highly innovative
  4 At their worst they are whimsical and autocratic
- The vocation-oriented world of *value*
  1 Value in an organization provides the ground and the purpose, the *raison d'être*, for everything that is done
  2 Value builds and preserves the organizational culture through consensus

   3   At their best value-based organizations are visionary workplaces, charac-
       terized by a powerful contribution to society

   4   At their worst, they become highly impractical and static

. . . fifthly, and finally, from a Business perspective

- The *competitive* world of Psion Computers
  1 Standing independently on its own two feet
  2 Carrying forward its relentlessly pioneering impulse
  3 Strongly internalized commitment to commercial as well as to technical growth and development
  4 Due moderation by its intellectual capacity to combine knowledge into unique product offerings
- The *conservationist* world of Oticon Hearing Care
  1 Highly developed multitask job profile where all employees are expected to expand their work area beyond their job descriptions
  2 Evolution from a product-based company to a solution-based company aimed at maximizing customer satisfaction
  3 Oticon is dependent on an interactive web of specialists, users, retailers and manufacturers
  4 Commercial success through an atmosphere of openness, trust and access to all information
- The *catalytic* world of Ahuja Home Designs
  1 Based on intuitive knowledge of customer expectations and needs
  2 Virtual company dependent on a series of complex relationships with craftspeople and designers
  3 Lean production through innovative use of human effort and relationship management
  4 Relatedness and lack of formalized structures rather than autonomy and organizational structure as the main characteristic
- The *co-creative* world of Cashbuild
  1 Where profit is a vote of confidence that society gives to the organization
  2 Where people feel themselves to be mutually inclusive
  3 Where the more people are, the more they are able to share and to give
  4 Where a climate is created to make people more productive

Conclusion

Managing in four worlds, then, involves a transformation of yourself as a manager, your organization as an institution, and even of the community in which
you are a part, so that each becomes more worldly wise. In the process, your

philosophical orientation, the environment upon which you draw, the knowledge that you create, the work that you do, and the business you are in will continually undergo genesis, morphosis, metamorphosis and homeostasis. In other words you were born, as a manager and indeed as a person, not only to compete and conserve, but also to catalyse and to co-create. In this book we hope we have enabled you to take some steps along the way to becoming not only a hunter and a herder, but also a gardener and a steward. As such you will have made your own, at least to some extent, the worlds of Psion and Oticon, of Ahuja and Cashbuild. Whether starting out as American or African, Thai or Taiwanese, Dutch or Danish, Maori or Mexican, you will have become somewhat all these things. In case this seems like a tall order, we thankfully acknowledge that Rome was not built in a day, and that our life's journey lasts a lifetime. Hunters do not become stewards, nor do herders become gardeners, overnight. We therefore have time and space on our side. In the epilogue that follows this chapter, taking on from where the prologue left off, we return to the USA, the management laboratory of the world. For if the four worlds cannot be rediscovered in that powerful corner of the globe – so that the 'new world' American dream of perpetual genesis is fused with the 'old world' native Indian vision of prevailing homeostasis – what hope do the rest of us around the global businessphere have?

Finally, a belated word of apology to you the reader. As African and Indian, that is the two of us as authors, even though we are influenced by our European and American leanings, we are bound often to by pass some of your particular worlds. Specifically, our orientations towards humanism and holism may on occasion get in the way of your own rationalism and pragmatism. In one sense, we can but be sorry, though in another this is perhaps an opportunity for us to cast off our 'white man's burden', namely our colonial Anglo-Saxon heritages. We can only hope that in casting off what has been 'morphosed' upon us, and in the process rediscovering our African or Asian genesis, we have created the kind of metamorphosis that might be of help to you. Specifically then, through the unity-in-variety created by the four worlds, we hope to have brought about a new form of homeostasis between business and community, manager and organization, youth and age, the local and the global. In fact we have already begun writing the sequel to this volume, entitled *Community and Enterprise – the Creation of a New Learning Ecology*. While in this instance our intention is to work more concertedly towards a rational and pragmatic end – duly helped by close colleagues in regional police forces, in the City of London, and in multinational enterprises – we need your responses as managers too, to help us along our worldly way. Finally, as we are continually engaged in transforming our own masters programme at City University Business School, to make it more authentically four-worldly, we need your responses as both academics and also practitioners, to catalyse our development. So thank you in anticipation, should you choose to bring your worlds in.

Epilogue: Habits of the Heart

West Meets East

As we come to the end of the book, we return to the prologue where Ronnie Lessem argued how three worlds – Western, Northern and Southern – had shaped the American reality, and lamented the absence of the East. Towards the end of the prologue, he referred to the 'Western blindspot' that fails to perceive the East. A blindspot is an inability to see something that is so near you, that it could almost be a part of you. Most of the time, it is a part of you. If the West doesn't 'see' the East, it is because the East is, in some strange way, its *alter ego* or its shadow.

After spending two years researching for this book and the notion of the four worlds, Ronnie and I (Sudhanshu Palsule) feel strongly that the four worlds are made up of two pairs of opposing yet similar worlds. In other words, North and South on the one hand, and East and West on the other are, paradoxically enough, bound together as opposites. In the ten years that I have lived and worked in Europe, I have never felt European. Yet every time I have lived in or visited the USA I have felt distinctly American. On the surface, there is nothing in my 'Easternness' that can be said to be even remotely similar to 'Americanness', and yet I have always felt a strange, deep connection. Admittedly, from a cultural point of view, I do have a very strong Western orientation and in fact I thought for a long time that this was the reason for my American affinity. I also used to dismiss this connection as proof of the American melting pot syndrome which invites anyone to become American. American identity being essentially an immigrant identity, I fitted in – I believed – as well as anybody else. But, in time, I started doubting the melting pot syndrome, and wondered if there might be a deeper mechanism that I had missed.

In 1994, I spent a long sabbatical in Ojai, Califormia, with my wife and my elder daughter. The more people I met and talked to, the greater was my conviction that West and East were related. I remembered what Robert Pirsig had written in *Lila: An Inquiry into Morals* (Bantam Press, 1991), that the native Indians were the 'originators' of American culture, the laconic, understated, 'plains talk'. None of the Victorian elocution, the American dialect as originated from the Indian was 'straight, head-on, declarative . . . without stylistic ornamentation of any kind, but with a poetic force . . .'. Pirsig states that the so-called frontier values did not come from the Europeans but from the native people of America. So did the value of freedom. 'Of all the contributions America has made to the history of the world,' writes Pirsig, 'the idea of freedom from a social hierarchy has been the greatest.' Pirsig is even more radical when he says further, 'The idea that all men are created equal is a gift to the world from the American Indian.' I couldn't help wondering, what freedom did the native Americans really mean?

One day on a visit to Berkeley, I stood overlooking the Pacific Ocean and understood what it meant to travel so far Westward that it took you East. Those who had stood here in the sixties, probably at the same spot had done just that. But it was not just in California, although the spirit of the East was strongest here; I felt it must come from something deeper, something whose roots went back a long way into a characteristic of the American way of life. Maybe Pirsig was right. Maybe the native American was the unrecognized link between West and East. Maybe, they became the victims of the white Americans because they reflected the 'other side' of the whites. Although yin and yang are one, they also make the worst enemies. It just seems to be a natural, psychological fact: I find myself threatened by another who reminds me of a part of myself that I don't want to acknowledge.

Towards the end of our stay we travelled to the Grand Canyon and spent a night in a pine cottage with our writer friend Jeff Biggers. He gave me a copy of a book by Bellah et al., called *Habits of the Heart: Individualism and Commitment in American Life* (University of California Press, 1985), which described, Tocqueville's expression for the mix of traits essential to American national character. I began reading it on the plane back to Europe and I think I understood what I had missed before.

The Two Faces of American Individualism

Bellah et al. talk of the two kinds of American individualism, 'utilitarian individualism' and 'expressive individualism'. Benjamin Franklin, long regarded as the quintessential American, clearly belonged to the former category. Aphorisms in *Richard's Almanack* such as 'Early to bed and early to rise' or 'God helps those who help themselves' became the commonsense, populist versions of

Adam Smith's and Samuel Smiles' pragmatic philosophy. From generation to generation, the American message was passed down: that individuals can get rich and succeed through their own initiative. But, even in those days, Franklin's individualism had its critics, the most notable being Alexis de Tocqueville, a Frenchman who visited the US in the 1830s. In *Democracy in America*, he wrote that Franklin's brand of individualism only expressed an old notion: egoism. 'As democratic individualism grows,' he wrote, 'there are more and more people who . . . owe no man anything and hardly expect anything from anybody. They form the habit of thinking of themselves in isolation and imagine that their whole destiny is in their hands.'

To be 'shut up in the solitude of his own heart' was what Tocqueville saw of utilitarian individualism. He had great misgivings about the emerging American industrial system and he feared the rise of a new form of aristocracy that would make owners and managers into 'petty despots' and reduce workers to 'mechanically organized, dependent operatives, incompatible with the spirit of democratic citizenship'. Between the Civil War and World War I, pioneering American individualism transformed American life and created the prototype of a society that continues to exist today. Transport, communications, manufacturing capability and the initiative of private citizens generated vast amounts of wealth and a new economic society. New forms of bureacracy and a new social organization emerged out of this functional individualism, and became increasingly all-pervasive. Soon, the business corporation was born, capable of control over vast resources, huge numbers of employees and great distances. The railroad industry changed people's lives as did the newly founded steel, oil, banking, finance and insurance corporations. Life was divided into functional parts: home and workplace, work and leisure, white collar and blue collar, public and private. This model was in keeping with the bureaucratic industrial corporations which organized society as a great business enterprise. Within the corporation, there emerged a new figure, called the professional manager, who epitomized the competetive industrial order and profitability. The essence of the manager's task was the organization of human and non-human resources that the company had access to in order to improve its position in the marketplace. 'His role is to persuade, inspire, manipulate, cajole, and intimidate those he manages so that his organization measures up to criteria of effectiveness shaped ultimately by the market but specifically by the . . . owners.' Social status became a matter of working for 'economic effectiveness'. Even today, work continues to be the defining element in the self-identity of Americans.

But, as Bellah et al. say, the real problem is 'not so much the presence or absence of a "work ethic" as the meaning of work and the ways it links, or fails to link, individuals to one another'. In terms of our four-world model, this failure to link one individual with another is the absence of the Eastern and an active Southern world.

Functional individualism, and the work ethic that goes with it, has provided America with its unique identity. What it hasn't and cannot provide is meaning and coherence. In a final section entitled 'Social Ecology', Bellah et al. make a poignant plea for a reversal of the trend. 'For over a hundred years,' they write, 'a large part of the American people, the middle class, has imagined that the virtual meaning of life lies in the acquisition of ever-increasing status, income, and authority, from which genuine freedom is supposed to come. Our achievements have been enormous. They permit us the aspiration to become a genuinely humane society in a genuinely decent world, and provide many of the means to attain that aspiration. Yet we seem to be hovering on the very brink of disaster . . . What has gone wrong?'

Redefining a Social Ecology

In terms of our model, mainstream America is distinctly Western with a tilt towards the North. The big industries that have come to be identified with American business all have a strong, structural and competitive characteristic as befits the first stage in the four worlds of ecology. It also has a distinct Southern element from the Hispanics, the Latin Americans and the Africans. However, this Southernness has not really been translated into an explicit business or organizational form, and that remains America's biggest challenge. Africa has never entered mainstream, white ways of management and business. It is as if the eclectic side of America is restricted to music and sport. I was convinced that the reason for this was that America had never acknowledged its Eastern *alter ego*. Tocqueville's criticism in the 1830s was aimed at the lack of an active, Southern component in the emergent America. This went hand-in-hand with conditions of slavery and the consequent minimalization of American Southernness. What he probably did not see was the connection between East and South. What America lacked in Tocqueville's perspective was a 'moral ecology', a term used by Bellah et al. of 'Habits'. They define it as 'the web of moral understandings and commitments that tie people together in community'. In other words, the Southern world of community and value.

Expressive Individualism

The *Tao Te Ching*, which we referred to in chapter 3, has a line that says: 'Know a man's strength, but keep the woman's care'. In the Eastern world, life is a synchronicity of opposites. When you are faced with a problem that you cannot solve, says the East, stop 'trying to' solve it, and the problem will solve itself. The real problem is not the problem you are trying to solve but your mind-set. Like breathing in and breathing out, opposites complement one another and create wholeness. What America needs at this stage is not more Westernness ('We must become more competitive') but its shadow, the East. Curiously enough, the East will pave the way for the eventual Southward journey.

I began this epilogue by describing my affinity for America and I shall return to that point here. What makes me feel that I could be American? Where does my Easternness become my Westernness? The answer to these questions is that both the East and the West are essentially characterized by a search for the freedom of the self. While the West's search has been directed outwardly, the East has always looked inwards. While the former seeks it in the form of an identity, the latter seeks exactly the opposite, to subsume it and become a non-entity. The West works on the basis of action, the East prefers non-action. While the structured Western self perceives the organization from the outside to the inside, the Eastern processial self perceives it from the inside out. While the structured self fragments the organization in order to control it, the processial self integrates it, in order to let go of it. While the structured self disassociates itself from the organization in order to be objective, the processial self immerses itself so totally in the organization that it is indistinguishable from it. While the time frame in a structural organization is linear and short term, making for structural efficiency, the time frame in a processial view is circular and long term. It is continually developing and its rhythmic patterns to provide the context for a free flow of processes. The more structured an organization becomes, the greater is the need for processes. The more one goes Westwards, the more Eastward one ends up.

What I find in America is the quality of freedom in which the individual may declare his or her authenticity. The ancient Greek Sophists spoke of 'arete' or virtue, the quality of being true to yourself. My own Easternness had taught me that there was nothing greater than my 'self', which enveloped the universe. The Eastern view of the world is profoundly holographic: each part of the world or each individual self enfolds the whole world in itself. This is what I had seen in America, a boundless, energetic and expressive freedom. But this aspect of freedom had never become part of the manistream, the utilitarian individualism. But underneath the utilitarian exterior, it is there. It is the other half of the story concealed most of the time but nevertheless endemic to the American soil. To truly understand its nature, you have to rediscover the 'American East' and for that you have to turn the pages back once again to people like Emerson and Thoreau – who called themselves the 'Boston Brahmins' – but most importantly, to Walt Whitman.

Song of my 'self'

Walt Whitman (1819–1892) was born in Long Island of poor parents who were Quakers. Largely self-educated, he became a printer and journalist and published his first volume of poetry, *Leaves of Grass* at the age of 36. It begins with a poem he later called 'Song of Myself', with the first line 'I celebrate myself'.

The 'self' for Whitman is simultaneously imminent and transcendent, immediately Western and Eastern. When he wrote.

Afoot and light-hearted I take to the open road,
Healthy, free the world before me,
The long brown path before me, leading wherever I choose

Whitman becomes the quintessential frontier man who was travelling worlds unknown to the genteel, Victorian poets of Europe. But the frontier for him was both physical and spiritual. He identified himself simultaneously with the New World of America and the 'Old World of India. In *Passage to India*, he writes:

Passage indeed O soul to primal thought,
Not lands and seas alone, thy own clear freshness,
The young maturity of brood and bloom,
To realms of budding bibles.

O soul, repressless, I with thee and thou with me,
Thy circumnavigation of the world begin,
Of man, the voyage of his mind's return,
To reason's early paradise,
Back, back to wisdom's birth, to innocent intuitions,
Again with fair creation.

Of the United States he writes in the preface to *Leaves of Grass*:

The Americans of all nations of any time upon the earth have probably the fullest poetic nature. The United States themselves are essentially the greatest poem . . . Here is not merely a nation but a teeming nation of nations . . . The American bard shall be marked for generosity and affection and for encouraging competitors . . . They shall be the cosmos . . . without monopoly or secrecy . . . glad to pass any thing to any one . . . The American bard shall delineate no class of persons . . .

Whitman had none of the materialism that sorrounded the utilitarians and yet he was as individualistic, if not more so, than them. In his self, he discovered the principle that links individual to universal, 'Atman' to 'Brahman', genesis to metamorphosis. The writings of Thoreau reflected the same West–East connection of expressive individualism. He wrote: 'There is an orientalism in the most restless pioneer, and the farthest West is but the farthest East.' When Thomas Paine said 'My mind is my church' or when Thomas Jefferson said 'I am sect myself', they too were expressing a deep sense of individualism that was completely different from the egoism that Tocqueville had criticized. It is through this link with the East that these men were able to draw in the South in the form of community values and a feeling for the land and society. In considering the continued existence of slavery, Jefferson wrote: 'Indeed I tremble for my country when I reflect that God is just; that his justice cannot sleep forever.' The individualism of the 'other' America was and is based on the notion that at the core of every person is a fundamental spiritual harmony that links him or her not only to every other person but to the cosmos as a whole.

Lessons for Business

Most American organizations and businesses even today are based exclusively on utilitarian individualism. An example of this individualism in practical terms is the assumption that for one to win, somebody else must lose. So it follows that maximizing one's profits must depend on the minimization of another's'. Therefore, the relationship between, say, supplier and manufacturer is necessarily adversarial; what is good for one must be bad for the other. So is the relationship between private business and government. As Harold Linstone and Ian Mitroff, whom we introduced in chapter 5, say, 'We're competing today with countries that make quality goods because they have forged close alliances between their employees, managers, governments, and shareholders.' They reckon that the slack that held afloat the US economy in terms of unsaturated domestic markets has been lost. The advantages that the US enjoyed were 'temporary advantages' and these have now been passed on to others.

The only way for America to go is to reach into its own depths and draw upon the strength of its cultural diversity. Its authentic moment will be when it embraces the pioneer spirit once again and breaks old ways of thinking and doing. There are few other countries in the world where the four worlds have the potential of emerging with such resonance as in America. Instead, American organizations continue to flog one world, while attempting to adopt some of the more surface-level concepts of a second one, namely the Northern world. If sales drop, the tendency is to 'improve sales'; if others players threaten to edge older American ones out of the market, the immediate reaction is to 'become more competitive'. As a result, the new ideas and concepts that emerge from the management laboratory of the world are never grounded sufficiently enough in the four worlds and, more particularly, never in the East. Notions such as 'business engineering' remain short-term fads because ultimately they are based on the traditional Western notions of competition and survival and lack any developmental dimension.

Conclusion

Last year, I was driving in the Ojai mountains in Southern California where the wilderness lay pristine and unexploited. I needed directions so I pulled over at the sight of the first person I had seen for miles. I was in a beautiful little township consisting, from what I saw, of a few houses, a couple of stores and sorrounded by some of the oldest mountains in the world. I took the instructions and remarked on the beauty of the place. 'There are some houses coming up on the other side,' she said through the half-open window, a big smile on her face. 'Great place to bring up kids; go grab it.' I couldn't help being struck by this quality of American freshness, the spontaneous expression of a New World citizen for whom the pioneering spirit had never ended. A mountainside, houses being built, houses being sold, new people coming, some others leaving, the American dream builds and rebuilds itself. In this New World, all are welcome, for it belongs to all human beings. 'Give me your poor . . . ,' the cry of pure, expressive individualism.

What has happened to that pioneering spirit on the macroscopic level? Where is that freshness, that expressive individualism, the 'Easternness' of the native American you see so often in individuals but so seldom manifested in social or organizational terms? I think of my friend Carolyn Haynes who grew up in a Chicago ghetto. Refusing to be cowed by her circumstances, she pioneered herself out of there to a scholarship at the University of Chicago and, like a true individual, made her way to a job as a computer professional in San Francisco. The same expressive individualism made her quit that job a couple of years ago and take up work in a community organization that provides professional care and counselling services for immigrant and minority groups in the Bay area. I am sure that there are many other Carolyns, like her whose individualism has been the backbone of modern American culture. But where is it? Why doesn't corporate and political America tap into its generic, innate strength which is right in its own backyard, so close that it can't see it?

Some years ago, Al Gore asked a question in his book *Earth in Balance*, '. . . for a dysfunctional society, where do you go for a cure?' The cure is right there, in the Eastern and Southern worlds that mainstream America has never seen. Albert Einstein once remarked that the mind that wants to solve a problem cannot be the mind that created the problem. If the dysfunctionality of corporate, political and social America is the result of excessive utilitarian individualism, then more of the same will not solve the problem but only exacerbate it. The trick is to look within and to dance with the Eastern shadow and together move Southwards. The American dream in which every individual wants to be a star depends on another dream which has been forgotten: that of living in a society that would really be worth living in.

Index